A BRIEF OF
WILLS AND MARRIAGES IN
MONTGOMERY AND
FINCASTLE COUNTIES,
VIRGINIA, 1733-1831

Compiled by
ANNE LOWRY WORRELL

Originally published: Hillsville, Virginia, 1932
Reprinted by Genealogical Publishing Co., Inc.
1001 N. Calvert St., Baltimore, Md. 21202
1976, 1979, 1984, 1996

To

COLONEL WILLIAM PRESTON CHAPTER
Daughters of the American Revolution

Appreciation is expressed to Mr. T. S. Word, Clerk of the Court of Montgomery, R. S. Willard, D. C., and to Miss Myrtle C. Vest, for their unfailing courtesy shown me while compiling the within records.

Preface

MONTGOMERY COUNTY has the distinction of being one of the oldest counties of western Virginia. It was a part of the vast territory of Augusta, and, for a short period, formed a portion of the short lived county of Fincastle, which was subdivided into the counties of Montgomery, Washington and Kentucky.

Upon its formation in 1776, Montgomery contained 12,000 square miles, and extended as far west as the Ohio River. From this great territory sixty other counties have been entirely, or partially, formed—twenty-six in western Virginia; twenty-five in the state of West Virginia, and nine in Kentucky.

In Braddock's Campaign, the Revolutionary, the Mexican, and the Civil Wars, the county furnished her quota of soldiers, they being always zealous patriots. They were sturdy pioneers, loyal to home and country, and their descendants are to be found in every State in the Union.

On January 20, 1775, the Freemen of Fincastle, including inhabitants of all Montgomery County, assembled at the Lead Mines, and made a declaration, which was the precursor of the Declaration of Independence made by Congress, July 4, 1776. This declaration, frought with the spirit of Freedom, was the first made in America.

Many of these patriots took part in the battle of Point Pleasant; Major Joseph Cloyd was Major of Montgomery County Militia, of which William Preston was Colonel. Three Companies of horsemen, raised by Cloyds, marched to aid in suppressing the Tories in Surry County, N. C., and defeated the British at Shallow Ford. Montgomery also boasts of the band of men, 1000 strong, who assembled and marched across the mountains to turn the tide of battle at Kings Mountain in South Carolina .

To claim descent from these staunch "over the Mountain Men," is a great heritage, and the compiling of the accompanying records has been a privilege.

COMMITTEE ON FINCASTLE RESOLUTIONS, JANUARY 20, 1775

Campbell, Arthur Maj.	McGavock, James Capt.
Campbell, William Capt.	Montgomery, John Capt.
Christian, William Col.	Russell, William Capt.
Crockett, Walter Capt.	Preston, William Col.
Cummings, Charles Rev.	Trigg, Stephen Capt.
Edmundson, William Lieut.	Shelby, Evan Capt.
Inglis, William Maj.	Smith, Daniel Capt.
Madison, Thomas Capt.	Campbell, David, Clerk

The marriage records have been gathered from every possible source, first, the few ministers' returns that were recorded in a register; second, the original bonds ;then the original ministers' returns, and lastly from old lists, filed with the ministers' returns, but usually unsigned. The abbreviations used have been the simplest: Min. for minister; dau. for daughter; sur. for surety, etc. I have only named the surety as the parent when I was assured by the fact being stated in the bond. However, in most instances the bondsman was either the parent of bride or groom. The form used is the plainest: First, the groom; next, the bride; and lastly surety, or minister, and date.

Marriage Records of Montgomery and Fincastle Counties 1773-1831

Abbott, Joseph, and Winna Allen, dau. John Allen Thos. Marshall, sur—Oct. 15, 1795.

Abney, John K. and Tames Robinson. Surety David Robinson (a brother)—Apr. 4, 1803. (See John and Gertrude Robinson Wills)

Abney, William and Mary Rose. Sur. Israel and Gabriel Rose—Aug. 6, 1805.

Adams, William, and Margaret McCorkle. Mar. by Edward Morgan—Aug. 9, 1793.

Addair, James, Sr. and Letitia Page. Thos. Simpkins, surely—Sept. 2, 1810.

Adkins, Josiah, and Rachel McCoy. Mar. by Alexander Ross—Aug. 28, 1797.

Adkins, Parker and Mary Leford, Mar. by Alexander Ross—Jan. 3, 1792.

Adkins, Redman, and Ann McDonald, Mar. by Richard Buckingham—Mar. 25, 1823.

Adkins, Reubens, and Agnes Price. Mar. by Alexander Ross—Dec. 2, 1805.

Adkins, Shadreck, and Christiana Adkins. Mar. by Alexander Ross—Feb. 11, 1797.

Adkins, Sehod and Sarah Lucas, dau. Chas. Lucas, surety—Oct. 18, 1793.

Adkins (See Atkins)

Agnue William B. and Elizabeth Carter, dau. John Carter, sur.—June 7, 1826.

Akers, Aston, and Rhoda Tomson (Lawson?). Mar. by Richard Whitt—Feb. 9, 1785.

Akers, Bird, and Elizabeth Saunders, dau. Robert Saunders, sur.—Nov. 3, 1816.

Akers, Blackburn, and Susanna Skaggs. J. Pouppecofer, surety—Nov. 20, 1786.

Akers, Blackburn, and Elinor Howard. Cyrus Howard, surety—Apr. 17, 1797.

Akers, Charles (son of Joseph) and Rhoda Scaggs, dau. Martha Scaggs. Jacob Akers and William Scaggs, surety—Aug. 10, 1830.

Akers, ClayBurn, and Elizabeth Thompson. John Thompson, surety—Apr. 17, 1789.

Akers, Davis (son of Blackburn) and Claracy Saunders. Robert Saunders, surety—Apr. 18, 1821.

Akers, Drury (son of Thomas) and Mary Gordon, dau. Sara Gordon—Oct. 2, 1833.

Akers, Edward F. and Levina Gearheart. Hiram Gearheart, surety—Nov. 3, 1823.

Akers, Gideon, and Polly Emmons. John Page, surety— ...., 1825.

Akers, Greenbury, and Polly Cooper, dau. Thos. Cooper, Jr. sur—Oct. 12, 1814.

Akers, Howard, and Susannah Garman. Mar. by Richard Buckingham—Apr. 12, 1831.

Akers, Jacob, and Ruth Howard. Boling Rodgers, surety—Dec. 21, 1796.

Akers, Jacob, and Catey Rupe, dau. Henry Rupe, surety—June 27, 1815.

Akers, James and Peggy Altizer, dau. John Altizer surety. Mar. by Peter Howard—Sept. 8, 1819.

Akers, James, and Eliza Thompson. Austin Akers, surety—Nov. 26, 1821.

Akers, Jonathan, and Hannah Howard, dau. Rev.

William Howard. Jeremiah Pate, and Blackburn Akers, surety—Mar. 25, 1795.

Akers, Joseph, and Sevira Chaffin. Mar. by Jonathan Hall—June 8, 1815.

Akers, Moses, and Catherine Altizer, dau. John Altizer, surety—Dec. 24, 1828.

Akers, Randolph, and Nancy Altizer, dau. John Altizer. Mar. by Jonathan Hall—Feb. 10, 1831.

Akers, Thomas, and Sophia Aldridge. Francis Huff, surety—Feb. 11, 1823.

Akers, William, and Nancy Sowers. Jacob Sowers, surety—July 2, 1811.

Albert, Jacob, and Elizabeth Williams, dau. Geo. Wliliams, surety—Oct. 1, 1789.

Albert, James ,and Agnes Glen. John Glen, surety—May 18, 1810.

Alderman, Jacob (of Grayson Co.) and Lucy Bott, dau. Chas. Bott, sur. Mar. by Elisha Beller—Apr. 25, 1822.

Aldrich, James, and Rachel Treadway. Rachel Treadway, sur.—June 4, 1787.

Aldrich, James, and Rachel Treadway. Mar. by Dan'l Lockett. (same as above?)—Feb..... 1785.

Alford, John, and Elinor Hogg, dau. James Hogg. Mar. by E. Morgan—Oct. 22, 1789.

Allbright, Gasper, and Fanny Ally, dau. Thomas Alley, surety—Dec. 9, 1826.

Allen, Thomas, and Polly Brown. William Brown surety—Sept. 3, 1797.

Alley, Carey, and Mary Short. Mar. by Richard Whitt—Feb. 9, 1785.

Alley, James, and Susannah Kelsey. Mar. by Jonathan Hall—July 9, 1812.

Alley, Nicholas, and Mary Dennis. Hercules Ogle, surety—June 4, 1794.

Alley, Robert, and Anne McPherson. Robert Eley, surety—Feb. 14, 1793.

Alley, Thomas, and Rachel Smallwood. Hugh Meridith, surety—Dec. 13, 1816.

Alsberry, Charles, and Jane McElany. Thos. Hatton, surety—May 4, 1791.

Altizer, Jonas, and Sally Ratcliffe. Nathaniel Ratcliffe, surety—Aug. 28, 1819.

Anderson, George, and Polly Burton. Jacob Peck, surety—Mar. 3, 1802.

Anderson, James, and Caroline Douglas. Hamilton Wade, her gurandian, surety. Mar. by Richard Buckingham—Jan. 10, 1822.

Anderson, James, and Nancy Anderson ("no kin") Mar. by J. G. Cecil—Dec. 14, 1826.

Anderson, John, and Catherine Kiplinger. Jacob Anderson and John Kiplinger, surety—Feb. 15, 1813.

Anderson, John, and Elizabeth Miller, dau. James Miller. Christopher Peck, surety. Mar. by J. G. Cecil—Sept. 22, 1825.

—Anderson, William, and Malissa Cosby, Mar. by J. G. Cecil—Jan. 1, 1828.

Anderson, William, and Hetty Carper, dau. John Carper, sur.—Jan. 26, 1829.

Argubright, Joseph, and Peggy Overpeck. John Argubright, sur.—Sept. 8, 1806.

Argubright, William, and Susannah Snyder. Abraham Snyder, surety—Oct. 6, 1812.

Ashley, Thomas, and Priscilla Brown. William Brown, surety—Mar. 20, 1797.

Ashley, Thomas, and Ruth R...... Isaac Booth, surety—Aug. 21, 1797.

Asque, Michael, and Parmelia Weddle. Philip Asque, sur.—Apr. 24, 1824.

Atkins, Elijah, and Nancy Hunter, dau. Robert Hunter. Milliton Atkins, surety—Feb. 28, 1790.

Atkins, Hezekiah, and Mary Levon (Lemon?) Sam'l Cecil, surety—Oct. 2, 1784.

Atkins, Moses, and Mary Hunter, dau. Robert Hunter. Sarah Atkins, surety—Dec. 23, 1794.

Atkins, William and Magdalin Bowen, dau. John Bowen, Hezekiah Atkins, surety—July 25, 1806.

Aul, John, and Lucy Duncan. Elias Owen, surety—Mar. 6, 1792.

Aul, John, and Jensy Duncan. John Wright, surety—Mar. 6, 1792.

Aul, John, and Ann Auch, dau. Elias Auch. William Aul, surety—........, 1799.

Aul, William, and Joanna Owen, dau. Elias Owen. Jas. Robinson, sur.—Oct. 6, 1794.

Aul, Robert, and Margaret Hale, dau. Aggy Hale. Jacob Price, sur.—Apr. 10, 1812.

Aul, William, and Rosannn Owen. Mar. by Alexander Ross—Oct. 23, 1794.

—B—

Blackenstoe, Fliegar, and Jane Edes. John Clifton, surety. Mar. by Richard Buckingham—May 2, 1820.

Bagby, Charles (son of Henry) and Nancy Cox, dau. John Cox, surety—July 27, 1786.

Bailey, Henry, and Elizabeth Peters, dau. John Peters, surety—Aug. 4, 1801.

Bailey, James, and Margaret Stinson, dau. Robt. Stinson, surety—Sept. 1, 1789.

Baisden, John S. and Rhoda Branham, dau. David Branham, surety—Oct. 4, 1795.

Baker, Charles, and Mary Alford, dau. Thomas Alford, sur. Mar. by Richard Whitt—Feb. 10, 1786.

Baker, Douglas, and Mary Hoge. James Hoge, sur. Mar. by Jonathan Hall—May 14, 1812.

Baker, Joseph, and Sukey Hayse, dau. Chas. Hayse. Mar. by Richard Whitt—Aug. 6, 1786.

Baker, Josiah, and Mary Walker, dau. Jas. Walker. Mar. by Edw. Morgan—Sept. 2, 1794.

Ballard, Lewis, and Polly Mennich. John Borden surety—Sept. 10, 1821.

Ballard, Thomas, and Betsy Davis. Jeremiah Davis, surety—Apr. 1, 1811.

Ballenger, John, and Jane Whaffee—Sept. 6, 1803.

Bane, Edmund, and Susannah Brown, dau. George Brown, surety—Sept. 6, 1796.

Bane (Bayne) Henry (son of John), and Susanna Slusher. John Bayne, sur.—Sept. 12, 1804.

Bane, James, Jr., and Polly Henderson, dau. John Henderson, surety—Dec. 25, 1801.

Bangor, Joseph, and Elizabeth Rollins. Mar. by Richard Whitt—Oct. 8, 1786.

Banks, Cassell (son of Thomas, and was born 1790) and Mary Watkins, Ebenezar Watkins, surety—Aug. 26, 1811.

Banks, Thomas, and Elizabeth Howard, dau. Peter Howard. Joseph Howard, surety—Jan. 19, 1825.

Barger, Charles, and Polly Carper, dau. Frederick Carper. Jas. Stewart, surety—Mar. 24, 1828.

Barger, David S. and Polly Carper. Mar. by J. G. Cecil, Jan. 26, 1826.

Barger, Elias, and Nancy Carper. Mar. by J. C. Cecil, Dec. 9, 1824.

Barger, Frederick, and Sally Keister, dau. Peter Keister, surety—Dec. 2, 1815.

Bargar, Isaac (orphan) and Elizabeth Surface, dau. John Surface: Bird Grills, guardian of Isaac, sur—June 12, 1828.

Barger, Jacob S. and Phebe Trollinger. Mar. by J. G. Cecil—Mar. 27, 1825.

Barger, John, and Viney Newly, dau. Jeremiah Newly. Jno. Popper, sur.—eb. 18, 1824.

Barger, John, and Mary Preston, dau. John Preston. John Barger, sur.—Feb. 4, 1822.

Barger, Philip, and Polly Shrader, dau. Adam Shrader, surety—Apr. 17, 1805.

Barger, Philip, and Polly Keister, dau. Peter Keister, surety—Dec. 22, 1819.

Barger, ..., and Elizabeth Rolling. Mar. by R. Whitt (see Jos. Bangor, by same Min.)—Oct. 2, 1786.

Barlaw, Joseph, and Peggy Peck, dau. James Peck, sur. Mar. by E. Morgan—Feb. 25, 1799.

Barnard, William, and Nancy Mattox, dau. William Mattox, surety—Dec. 22, 1817.

Barnett, Charles, and Mary Ann Mitchell. Thos. P. Mitchell, surety—July 8, 1825.

Barnett, James, and Polly Stapleton. George Stapleton, surety—Apr. 2, 1799.

Barnett, James, and Elinor Thomas. Charles Thomas, surety—Nov. 10, 1815.

Barnett, Joseph (son of John) and Elizabeth Harrison, dau. Thomas Harrison, surety—Nov. 22, 1808.

Barnett, Joseph, and Rachel Barnett. Lindsey Crow, surety—July 15, 1812.

Barnett, Josiah, and Jemima Dickerson. Mar. by Peter Howard—Feb. 25, 1824.

Barnett, Nathan, and Margaret Bennett, dau. James Bennett, surety—Jan. 13, 1796.

Barnett, Robert, and Nancy Willis, dau. David Willis. Chas. Willis, sur.—Apr. 22, 1822.

Barnett, Reuben, and Elizabeth Jackson. Isaac Jackson, surety—Apr. 5, 1808.

Barnett, Thomas, and Sally Willis, dau. David Willis. Chas. Willis, sur.—Jan. 21, 1823.

Barnitz, William, and Elizabeth Trivillo. Price Trovillo, surety—Sept. 30, 1823.

Barringer, Adam, and Susannah Hogan—Mar. 26, 1800.

Barringer, Adam, and Hannah Loman. Eldred Rawlins, surety—June 27, 1815.

Barringer, John and Jane Towney. Philip Barringer, surety—July 20, 1792.

Barringer, John, and Jane Lowery. Mar. return (same as above?)—July 28, 1792.

Bates, Elisha, and Priscilla Paterick, dau. Hugh Paterick, surety—Sept. 1, 1789.

Bates, Gilbert, and Rachel Covey—Jan. 17, 1796.

Bates ,Joseph, and Zubey Chase. Obediah Chase, surety—Feb. 9, 1801.

Batteril, John, and Elizabeth Maun (Marr, Mann?) Mar. by R. Whitt—Feb. 2, 1791.

Baugh, Henry, and Margaret Phillips—Mar. 20, 1786.

Mausman, Philip, and Annet Stratton. Wm. Lukin surety—Feb. 17, 1821.

Bayer, Christian, and Patsy Price. Philip Bayer, surety—Jan. 18, 1802.

Beale, John, and Rhoda Trigg, dau. Abram Trigg, surety—Apr. 4, 1805.

Bean, Henry, and Margaret Cruter, dau. Jacob Cruter, surety—Nov. 26, 1786.

Bean, Howard (son of James) and Lettice Huckman—May 7, 1805.
Bean, Walter, and Nancy Roberts. Thoe Roberts, surety—June 29, 1802.
Bean, William, and Ann Smith, dau. Jacob Smith, surety—Aug. 24, 1801.
Betrd, William, and Balinda Burton, dau. Chas. Burton. Wm. Wolf, sur.—Feb. 15, 1830.
Beath, William W. and Mary McMullin. William McMullin, surety—Dec. 25, 1793.
Beavers, Alexander (son of Alex., Sr.(and Sarah Rice. Mar. by Isaac Rentfro—Dec. 17, 1792.
Beavers, James, and Susannah Charlton. Moses Beavers, surety—Aug. 20, 1820.
Beavers, Moses, and Margaret Coffee, dau. James Coffee, surety—Jan. 1, 1794.
Beavers, Thomas, and Susannah Hall. Moses Beavers and Asa Hall, surety (parents of bride and groom)—Mar. 14, 1814.
Beck, Paul, and Nancy Ogle, dau. Hercules Ogle, surety—Sept. 3, 1793.
Beckets, James, and Margaret Peden, dau. John Peden, surety—Sept. 8, 1794.
Beckett, Daniel, and Lydia Wade, dau. Thomas Wade, surety—July 24, 1816.
Beckett, John, and Rhoda Phares. Henry Routrough, surety—Aug. 3, 1824.
Beckett, Thomas, and Nancy McFadden—Mar. 1, 1808.
Beckett, William (son of John) and Lucy Lepeur, Blackburn Akers, sur.—Apr. 20, 1827.
Becknel, James, and Nancy King, dau. Wm. King. Wm. Becknel, surety—Jan. 30, 1828.
Becklehimer, John and Catherine B. Redpath, dau. James Redpath, sur.—March 23, 1822.
Beeson, Isaac, and Esther Morrow—Mar. 29, 1797.
Bell, George, and Sarah Shaw, dau. Samuel Show, sur. Mar. by R. Whitt—Nov. 3, 1786.
Bell, Jeremiah, and Elizabeth Hall. Robt. Bell, and Asa Hall, parents of bride and groow, surety—Aug. 7, 1807.
Bell, John, and Lucy Pate, dau. Catherine and Thomas Pate, surety—Oct. 16, 1786.
Bell, John, and Polly Vineyard. Robt. Bell, and Geo. Vineyard (parents)—Oct. 7, 1818.
Bell, Robert, and Sarah Vineyard, dau. George Vineyard, surety—Oct. . . . , 1820.
Bell, Robert, and Elizabeth VanOver, dau. Henry VanOver, sur.—April 13, 1803.
Bell, William, and Nancy Vineyard. Robert Bell and George Vineyard, surety—Oct. 18, 1820.
Benjamin, Henry, and Mary Wylie, dau. John Wylie, surety—May 1, 1786.
Benjamin, Jacob, and Mary Winter, dau. Moses Winter, surety—Sept. 2, 1794.
Bennett, David M. and Prudence Gardner, dau. John Grdner, dec. William Gardner, surety—Mar. 9, 1823.
Bennett, Jeremiah, and Mary Johnston, dau. Amos Johnston, surety—Sept. 14, 1791.
Bennett, Robert, and Fanny Adkins. Mar. by Alexander Ross—May 8, 1797.
Berry, Isaac, Jr., and Nancy Kelly. William Kelly, surety—Nov. 16, 1808.
Bettshire, John, and Sarah Holsey, a widow—Sept. 3, 1789.
Biggs, Andrew and Susannah Godby. Mar. by Richard Buckingham—Mar. 15, 1830.
Biggs, James, and Elizabeth Price. Michael Price, surety—Apr. 21, 1812.
Biggs, Moses, and Elizabeth Surface, dau. Geo. Surface, surety—Jan. 5, 1818.

Bingaman, Adam, and Polly Guthrie—June 29, 1802.
Bish, David, and Nancy Cain, dau. James Cain, surety. Mar. by J. G. Cecil—Jan. 15, 1828.
Bish, Samuel, and Maria Gordon, dau. Giles Gordon. Peter Gish, surety—Jan. 25, 1830.
Bishop, George, and Nancy Booth, dau. Stephen Booth, surety—June 28, 1790.
Bishop, Henry, and Fanny Simpkins, dau. Daniel Simpkins, surety—Sept. 1, 1789.
Bishop, Henry, and Nancy Crusenberry, dau. Frederick Crusenberry: Henry Bishop, Sr., surety—Mar. 7, 1820.
Bishop, Jacob, and Katherine Elkins. Henry Bishop, surety—Oct. 2, 1792.
Bishop, Jacob, and Catherine Williams. Mar. by Richard Whitt—May 8, 1793.
Bishop, John, and Maria Wilson, dau. Sam'l Wilson. Mar. by Peter Howard—Jan. 7, 1817.
Bishop, Joseph, and Hannah Booth, dau. Isaac Booth, surety—Nov. 8, 1826.
Black, Andrew (son of John) and Susannah Ross, dau. John Ross, surety—Dec. 19, 1804.
Black, John, and Mary Breeden. John Breeden, surety—Jan. 4, 1807.
Black, John, and Matilda Martin, dau. Catherine Martin. D. Charlton, sur.—Apr. 3, 1827.
Black, William, and Jane McBath. John Black, surety—Mar. 27, 1793.
Black, William, and Grizzay Ross. Robert Ross, surety—Feb. 1, 1822.
Blackster, John, and Minny Linder. Mar. by Richard Whitt—Nov. 8, 1783.
Blackston, John, and Nancy Linder. Mar. by Richard Whitt—Nov. . . . , 1793.
Blair, James, and Sally Barnett, dau. John Barnett, surety—Nov. 1, 1796.
Blair, Waller D. and Ellin E. Edmundson, dau. Henry Edmundson, sur.—Oct. 11, 1823.
Blake, James, and Nancy Adkins. Mar. by Isaac Rentfro—Dec. 20, 1797.
Blankenship, Arthur, and Mary Munsey. Mar. by James Craig—Sept. 6, 1794.
Bond, George, and Betsy Sowder. Joseph Sowder, surety—Oct. 6, 1807.
Bones, James, and Delphia Hines—June . ., 1799.
Bones, Joseph, and Nancy Ross—Jan. 1, 1811.
Booth, Daniel and Rachel Graham. John Altizer, surety—June 27, 1827.
Booth, Elisha (son of Geo. and Milly) and Rebecca Lorton, dau. Israel Lorton, surety—Mar. 14, 1791.
Booth, George, and Lucy Reed, dau. Peter Reed. Abijah Booth, sur.—Mar. 13, 1816.
Booth, George (son of Geo. and Mahala) and Sarah Howard, daua. William Howard, surety—Dec. 23, 1789.
Booth, Isaac, and Polly Conner, dau. Jonathan Conner, surety—Mar. 1, 1825.
Booth, Jamison, and Elizabeth Hunter. Mar. by Richard Buckinghom—Mar. 4, 1830.
Booth, Robert, and Adah Booth, dau. Isaac Booth, surety—Nov. . ., 1816.
Booth, Ripley, and Clarissa Akers, dau. Jonathan Akers, surety—Dec. 2, 1823.
Booth, Stephen, and Polly Booth—Jan. 1, 1799.
Booth, William, and Lucinda Trail, dau. Chas. Trail, surety—Oct. 27, 1827.
Borden, John, and Jane Taylor. John Dunlop, surety—June 16, 1809.
Borders, Thomas, and Catherine Sallers, dau. Sam'l Sallers, sur.—Sept. 8, 1788.

Boster, Daniel, and Mary Lake. William Warner, surety—Jan. 7, 1817.

Boucher, Ezekiel, and Jemima Terry, dau. William Terry, surety—June 30, 1796.

Boucher, Ezekiel, and Mary Wilson—May 27, 1797.

Boucher, James, and Abby Lewis. Ezekiel Boucher, surety—May 10, 1797.

Bowen, Hugh, and Elizabeth Owen. John Bowen, and Elias Owen, sur.—June 18, 1805.

Bowen, James, and Catherine Bosters, dau. Jonathan Bosters, surety—Jan. 7, 1815.

Bowen, John, and Rachel Mills—Aug. 3, 1803.

Bowers, Jacob, and Jane Wickham, dau. Nathaniel Wickham, Sr., surety—Aug. 17, 1824.

Bowles, Matthew C. and Mary Howell, dau. Mary Howell, widow, surety—Apri. 1, 1806.

Bowles, Peter, and Nancy Hale, dau. Agnes Hale, surety—Sept. 29, 1826.

Bowles, Reuben, and Elizabeth Worley, dau. Daniel Worley, surety—Oct. 28, 1817.

Bowman, Charles, and Mary Shelor. Thos. Goodson, surety—Apr. 6, 1796.

Bowman, Elisha, and Rebeckah Lorton. Israel Lorton, surety—Mar. 14, 1791.

Bowman, Jacob, and Susannah Price. Mar. by Richard Buckingham—June 28, 1821.

Bowman, John, and Polly Cromer. Lewis Amiss, surety—May 2, 1820.

Bowyer, Thomas, and Nancy Craig. James Craig, surety—May 26, 1814.

Boyd, Andrew, and Jemima Ingram, dau. Wm. Ingram, dec. Mar. by E. Morgan—Jan. 12 ,1818.

Brabson, Robert, and Peggy Raeburn, dau. Joseph Raeburn, surety—Apr. 9, 1804.

Brabston, William, and Mary Runnion. Mar. by Richard Whitt—Aug. 5, 1788.

Bradford, Enoch, and Eve Crowy—Oct. 27, 1818.

Bramfield, Macajah, and Eleanor Hartwell. John Hartwell, surety—Nov. 4, 1793.

Brammer, Sam'l (mother Mary) and Polly Scaggs. Joseph Scaggs, sur.—Oct. 21, 1813.

Brammer, William, and Balinda Lancaster, dau. Lewis Lancaster, sur.—May 4, 1829.

Branham, John, and Martha Finch, dau. Nathaniel Finch, dec.—Jan. 20, 1794.

Branham, Turner (son of David) and Mary Nick, dau. Zack Nick, surety—Mar. 16, 1795.

Bratton, Thomas, and Nancy Chrisman. Abraham Chrisman, surety. Mar. by Isaac Rentfro—Aug. 23, 1797.

Brawley, John, and Martha Hoge. Mar. by Dan'l Lockett—Feb. 8, 1793.

Brawley, John, and Patty Lester. Mar. by Richard Whitt—Feb. 8, 1793.

Brazel, Benjamin, and Rachel Dickens, dau. John Dickens, surety—Mar. 29, 1786.

Briden, Andrew, and Dorothy McNeely, dau. William McNeely, surety—Feb. 5, 1793.

Britt, William, and Dolly Davis, dau. John Davis, surety—Mar. 15, 1795.

Britton, Isaac, and Sabina Hance, dau. Peter Hance. Jno. Wade, sur.—Dec. 22, 1827.

Broie, Jacob, and Sally Echols, dau. Henry Echols, surety—July 26, 1823.

Brookman, David, and Polly Slusher. John Slusher, surety—Oct. 31, 1809.

Brookman, John (son of Valentine) and Rebecca Peck, dau. Jacob Peck. Robert Weeks, surety—Oct. 3, 1822.

Brookman, Samuel, and Mahala Phillips. Mar. by Richard Buckingham—Sept. 24, 1830.

Brown, Abraham, and Polly Fergus. Francis Fergus, surety—Feb. 4, 1820.

Brown, Abram, and Margaret Goins, dau. David Goins. Mar. by J. Wallace—Dec. 22, 1829.

Brown, Daney, and Kezia Grant, dau. John Garnt, surety—Nov. 2, 1799.

Brown, David, and Anna Craig, dau. Benj. Craig. Mar. by Isaac Rentfro—Aug. 6, 1795.

Brown, George, Jr., and Mary Raeburn, dau. James Raeburn, surety—July 28, 1804.

Brown, James, and Catherine Foster, dau. Thomas Foster, surety—Jan. 11, 1790.

Brown, Jacob, and Rebeckah Smallwood, dau. Hugh and Rachel Smallwood—Dec. 12, 1814.

Brown, Joseph, and Nancy Lowry. Jacob Clore, surety—Mar. 19, 1824.

Brown, L . . . ., and Jane Davidson. Mar. by Simin Cockrell—Mar. 1, 1782.

Brown, Michael, and Catherine Black. John Black, surety—June 13, 1803.

Brown, Nimrod, and Sally Lucas. Capt. John Lucas, surety—Jan. 21, 1800.

Brown, Silvenus, and Ruth Johnston, dau. Moses Johnston, surety—Oct. 8, 1794.

Brown, William, and Elizabeth Wright, dau. Humphrey Wright, surety—Oct. 30, 1822.

Bruce, Garland, and Polly Helvey—Apr. 3, 1798.

Bruister, Thomas, and Martha Sarah Davis, Comfort Bruister, surety—June 3, 1788.

Brummett, William, and Catherine Willson. Mar. by Isaac Rentfro—Jan. 2, 1793.

Bryan, James, and Vicey Roberts, Chas. Roberts surety—Jan. 7, 1805.

Bryan, James, and Elizabeth Wilson, widow—Mar. 23, 1804.

Bryan, James, and Mary Taylor, dau. Isaac Taylor, surety—Apr. 10, 1794.

Bryan, John, and Nancy Bowcher. Jomes Bowcher, surety—Dec. 29, 1818.

Bryan, William, and Mary Roberts. Charles Roberts ,surety—Feb. 16, 1799.

Bryant, Ambrose, and Frances Dickerson, dau. Moses Dickenson, surety—May 23, 1796.

Bryant, Elijah, and Lucinda Pedigo, widow of Churchill Pedigoe, and dau. Nathan Crockram, surety—Mar. 28, 1828.

Bryant, Jesse, and Lyda Landon, dau. Joseph Landon, surety—Oct. 7, 1795.

Buck, Daniel (son of Michael) and Sally Hale, dau. Jacob Hale, surety—Apr. 12, 1828.

Buck, Michael, and Catherine Firl (?) Mar. by Ruchard Buckingham—Aug. 4, 1825.

Buford, Henry, and Jane Quirk—Oct. 17, 1805.

Bull, John, and Julia Dunnington, dau. Lawson Dunnington, surety—Jan. 8, 1817.

Bullard, William, and Hannah Smith. Russell Smith, surety—May 2, 1827.

Bumgardner, Philip, and Betsy Chester—Sept. 6, 1804.

Burgess, Garland, and Levina Louisa Brumfield, dau. James and Mary B.—Jan. 8, 1787.

Burk, Henry F. and Fanny Harriss, Henry Rutrough, surety—Nov. 24, 1830.

Burk, James, and Betsy Cooper. John Cooper, sur., Mar. by P. Howard—Dec. 17, 1814.

Burk, John and Effie Boaine—Sept. 3, 1797.

Burk, John, and Margaret Davidson. Mar. by Dan'l Lockett—Apr. 27, 1787.

Burk, John, and Mary Cloud. Mar. by Richard Whitt—Aug. 11, 1786.

Burk, Jonathan, and Sally Cooper. John Cooper, surety—Nov. 6, 1805.

Burk, Joseph, and Jane Raeburn, dau. James Raeburn, surety—Dec. 17, 1794.

Burk, Marshall, and Elizabeth Caldwell. Seth Caldwell, surety—Aug. 31, 1797.

Burk, Samuel, and Ann Sovain, dau. Abraham Sovain, dec. Jesse Pepper, sur.—Dec. 30, 1812.

Burk, William, and Margaret Williams, John Williams, surety—Oct. 2, 1792.

Burnett, Josiah ,and Jemima Dickerson, dau. Moses Dickerson, sur.—Feb. 23, 1824.

Burnett, Stephen, and Nancy King, dau. John King, surety—Oct. 1, 1827.

Burrus, Micajah (son of Wm.) and Rachel McCoy. Mar. by Edw. Morgan—Oct. 13, 1795.

Burton, Benjamin, and Peggy Snavill. John Snavill, surety—Apr. 11, 1807.

Burton, Elisha, and Lydia Stoneman. Wm. Stoneman, sur. Mar. by Alex Ross—May 20, 1800.

Burton, James, and Nancy Marshall. Mar. by Alexander Ross—Feb. 9, 1795.

Burton, John, and Sarah Webb, dau. William Webb, surety—Dec. 12, 1795.

Burton, Joseph, and Peggy Peck. Mar. by Edw. Morgan—Jan. 15, 1799.

Burton, William, and Hannah Lykins—Dec. 15, 1797.

Bushong, George, and Martha Hall—Apr. 19, 1788.

Buson, Isaac, and Esther Merrin—Mar. 20, 1797.

Bustard, Charles, and Sarah Jones, dau. Joseph Jones, surety—Mar. 4, 1788.

Byers, Isaac, and Mary Kennaday. Daniel Kennaday, surety—Feb. 9, 1799.

Byrne, David, and Elizabeth Draper. Andrew Muirhead, surety—Sept. 3, 1811.

Byrne, Soloman, and E...... Ross. Mar. by Isaac Rentfro—Sept. 22, 1797.

—C—

Caddall, Samuel, and Nancy Cecil. Salles Cecil, surety. Mar. by R. Whitt—June .., 1792.

Camm, William, and Rachel Moir A .Lewis, surety—Feb. 7, 1787.

Cain, John, and Catherine Bush. Mar. by J. G. Cecil—Jan. 24, 1826.

Caldwell, James, and Susannah Charlton. John Grills, surety—May 31, 1798.

Caldwell, John, and Nancy White. Chas. Messick, surety—Mar. 27, 1797.

Caldwell, John, and Betsy Akers. Austen Akers, surety—Jan. 8, 1802.

Caldwell, Roland, and Elizabeth Argabright. Mar. by Rev. McIntire—Feb. 25, 1836.

Caldwell, William, and Mary Claeburne. Mar. by Edw. Morgan—Jan. 7, 1799.

Cale, William and Nancy Stratton. Mar. by Sam'l Mitchell—July 15, 1815.

Calfee, Benjamin, and Margaret Dier. Chas. Dier (a brother) surety—Sept. 28, 1785.

Calfee, John, and Elinoe Morgan. Mar. by Edw. Whitt—Oct. 17, 1785.

Calfee, John, and Sophia Howard. Ezekiel Howard, surety—Apr. 16, 1818.

Calfee, John, Jr., and Peggy Howard. Ezekiel Howard, surety—Aug. 15, 1818.

Calfee, Samuel, and Abigal Holbert. Thos. Adkins, surety—June 29, 1819.

Calvel, John, and Mary White. Mar. by Alexander Ross—Apr. 27, 1797.

Calvert, Alexander, and Catey Holly. Peter Holly and Benj. Ragan, sur.—Oct. 30, 1822.

Campbell, Arthur, and Margaret Campbell. John Campbell, surety—May 10, 1773.

Campbell, Archibald, and Sally Gibson. Mar. by Jonathan Hall—Apr. 12, 1815.

Campbell, Edward, and Rhoda Trigg, dau. Daniel Trigg. Jno. Wade, surety—Feb. 25, 1812.

Campbell, Sam'l G. and Elizabeth Goaings, dau. David Goaings—Nov. 30, 1829.

Campbell, William, and Jeanne Dean, dau. Adam Dean. Stephen Sanders, sur.—Mar. 5, 1782.

Canean, Benjamin, and Rebecca Runnan. Edw. Canean, surety—Apr. 7, 1798.

Cannaday, John, and Delila Shipp. Mar. by Edw. Morgan—July 22, 1800.

Cannaday, Pleasant (of Franklin Co.) (the son of James) and Elizabeth Young, dau. Joshua Young, surety—Dec. 23, 1822.

Cannard, James, and Mary Patrick. Mar. by Richard Whitt—May 8, 1793.

Canterberry, Joseph (son of Joel) and Nancy Bowen. James Bowen, sur.—Nov. 4, 1823.

Canterberry, William, and Betsy Ann Lawson, dau. Wm. Lawson. Thos. Mallet, sur. Mar. by Edw. Morgan—Aug. 3, 1789.

Carder, William, and Rosanna Brumfield, dau. Humphrey Brumfield, sur.—Aug. 13, 1794.

Carder, William, and Rebecca Runyan, dau. Richard Runyan, surety—Sept. 27, 1825.

Cardin, Robert, and Jenny Howry. Daniel Howry, surety—Apr. 7, 1808.

Carl, Uriah, and Hannah Breadwater. Jas. Smith, surety—Dec. 1, 1790.

Carlton, Henry, and Susannah Leffler. John Leffler, surety—Aug. 18, 1803.

Carmikle, John, and Margaret Elkins. Francis Gardner, surety—May 28, 1800.

Carnell, Peter, and Henrietta Wineteer. Mar. by Richard Buckingham—May 10, 1830.

Carper, John, and Sally King. Mar. by J. G. Cecil—............., 1807.

Carper, William (son of John) and Judith Thompson, dau. John Thompson: Jas. Hoge, Jr., surety—Mar. 4, 1807.

Carper, William, and Anna Kiplinger, dau. John Kiplinger, surety—July 5, 1817.

Carr, John, and Margaret Crow. Mar. by Edw. Morgan—............., 1788.

Carrell, Joseph, and Polly Booth, dau. Abijah Booth, surety—Nov. 11, 1811.

Carson, Thomas, and Patsy Allison (an orphan). Byrd Grills, surety—Feb. 16, 1816.

Carson, William, and Jane Rutledge. James Rutledge, surety—Oct. 2, 1821.

Carson, William, and Rosanna Allison. Jos. Evans, surety—Oct. 18, 1826.

Carter, Enos, and Ann Snodgrass. John Snodgrass, surety—Sept. 26, 1818.

Carter, Henry, and Malinda Agnew, dau. Agnes Agnew. Sam'l Agnew, surety—Aug. 22, 1826.

Carter, Robert, and Jean Crockett. Mar. by R. Whitt—May 8, 1792.

Cassaday, John, and Mary Hogan. Massinger Lewis, surety—May 13, 1796.

Cassaday, Thomas, and Mary Carder. Mar. by Edw. Morgan—Jan. 19, 1797.

Cassell, Nicholas, and Elizabeth Carder, widow. M. Lindsey, surety—Apr. 21, 1787.

Castle, Edward, and Malinda Martin, dau. Catherine Martin, surety—Apr. 26, 1824.

Castle, Michael, and Catherine Dabler. Jacob Dabler, surety—Nov. 27, 1786.

Cawthan, Lawson, and Sarah Mitchell. S. Davidson, surety—Dec. 10, 1806.

Cecil, Jamey, and Peggy Wiser. Sam'l Mitchell, surety—Dec. 5, 1787.

Cecil, John, Jr., and Rebecca Cecil. Thomas Cecil, surety—Mar. 11, 1810.

Cecil, Philip, and Polly Wygle. Sebastian Wygle, surety—May 19, 1806.

Cecil, Samuel, and Mary Ingram. Kackeriah Cecil, surety—Oct. 24, 1792.

Cecil, William, and Anna Wygle. Thos. Cecil, and Sebastian Wygle, sur.—Sept. 17, 1808.

Cecil, William, (son of Zacheriah) and Elizabeth Guthrie, dau. Richard Guthrie, surety—Aug. 9, 1809.

Cecil, Zacheriah W., and Julia Howe, dau. Dan'l Howe, surety—Oct. 2, 1814.

Certain, Joel, and Nancy Burton, dau. John Burton. J. Brumfield, sur.—July 2, 1787.

Certain, Joel, and Amy Mair. Step-dau. Murdock McKenzie, surety—May 3, 1788.

Chaffin, Gordon, and Elizabeth Berry. Isaac Berry, surety—July 17, 1798.

Chaffin, John and Sally Reed. Peter Reed, surety—Mar. 7, 1826.

Chaffin, John, and Rebecca Cornutt, William Cornutt, surety—July 23, 1798.

Chambers, Moses, and Jane Mavis, dau. Hugh Mavis, surety—Apr. 1, 1794.

Champ, Christopher, and Mary Williams. Henry Williams, surety—June 20, 1802.

Champ, George, and Jane Elkins, dau. Thomas Elkins. Jas. Preston, sur.—Aug. 21, 1798.

Chapman, George, and Patience Clay. John Chapman, surety—May 3, 1789.

Chapman, John, and Dicey Napper. Christian Snidow, surety—.........., 1791.

Chapman, John, and Nancy Deyerle. Peter Deyerle, surety—Nov. 12, 1827.

Chapman, Richard, and Susannah Connely, widow. Alex Ross, surety—May 5, 1790.

Chapman, William, and Anne Painter. Mar. by Jno. Geo. Schrider—.........., 1782.

Chapman, William, and Mary Harrison—June 18, 1787.

Chapman, William, and Elizabeth Burgess, dau. Edw. Burgess. Garland Burgess, surety—July 27, 1787.

Charlton, Francis, and Susannah Acers. James Charlton, surety—Feb. 3, 1792.

Charlton, James, Sr. and Hannah Seigler. Nathaniel Lawrence, surety—Feb. 16, 1821.

Charlton, John S. and Catherine B. G. Pollard: Joseph Pollard, surety—July 21, 1821.

Charlton, John S. and Catherine F. Currin. William Currin, surety—Feb. 15, 1813.

Charlton, John, and Nancy Carter. Israel Lorton, surety—Jan. 8, 1787.

Charlton, John R. and Betsy R. Simpkins, dau. James Simpkins, surety—Jan. 4, 1830.

Charlton, John W. and Armaminter Akers. Mar. by Richard Buckingham—June 30, 1830.

Charlton, William, and Mary Ann Taylor. James Charlton, surety—.........., 1815.

Charlton, William B. and Malinda Ingles. John Ingles, Jr., surety—Dec. 19, 1826.

Chase, Obediah, and .... Pate. Jacob Pate, surety—Jan. 3, 1801.

Childress, Andrew (son of Stephen) and Catherine Hix, dau. John Hix, surety—Nov. 18, 1806.

Childress, Boling, and Nancy Lykins. Marcus Lykins, surety—Mar. 5, 1805.

Childress, William, and Elizabeth Dobbins, dau. Thomas Dobbins, sur.—Mar. 11, 1822.

Christian, Andrew, and Sarah Smith. Mar. by John G. Shrider—.........., 1782.

Christian, John, and Eliza Dawson, dau. Thomas Dawson, surety—Sept. 29, 1830.

Clap, David, and Betsy Graves, dau. Boston Graves, surety—April 22, 1793.

Clark, Henry, and Deborah Banks, dau. John Banks. Jas. Banks, surety—Apr. 1, 1817.

Clark, and Jane Ferguson, dau. Sam'l Ferguson. Robt. Stinson, sur.—Jan. 26, 1788.

Clarke, William, and Jane Ferguson, dau. John Ferguson, surety—July 2, 1787.

Clay, Ezekiel, and Rebecca Williams. Mar. by E. Whitt—.........., 1785.

Clay, James, and Nancy Clay. William Clay, surety, Apr. 5, 1785.

Clay, Meridith, and Agnes Evins. Thomas Evins, surety—Jan. 3, 1804.

Clay, Samuel (son of Sam'l, Sr.) and Mary Sperry. Sam'l Clay, Sr., surety—Nov. 19, 1804.

Clay, William, and Rebecca Cecil. J. Cecil, surety—Apr. 1, 1800.

Claybern, Jonah, and Elizabeth McKenzie. Isaac McKenzie, surety—Nov. 18, 1801.

Clear, Israel, and Betsy Robertson. Mar. by Edw. Morgan—.........., 1795.

Clemens, Edward, and Catherine Johnston, dau. David Johnston—Sept. 1786.

Clevenger, George, and Betty Low. Lewis Clevenger, surety—June 28, 1794.

Clevenson, Levi, and Nancy Elswick, dau. John Elswick, surety—Oct. 21, 1794.

Clifton, John, and Polly Lewis—Apr. 3, 1799.

Clifton, Robert, and Nancy Pratt. Mar. by Edw. Morgan—May 29, 1823.

Cline, John, and Mary Lucas. William Lucas, surety —June 5, 1798.

Clore, Greye, and Rebecca Simpkins. James Simpkins, surety—Nov. 5, 1805.

Clore, Jacob, and Polly Simpkins. James Simpkins, surety—Dec. 28, 1815.

Clowers, Daniel, and Peggy Greff. Mar. by H. Howery—Feb. 22, 1830.

Cloyd, Ezekiel (son of John) and Rebecca Williamson. Henry Thomson, sur.—Sept. 17, 1785.

Cloyd, Joseph (of Rockbridge Co.) and Polly Cloyd, dau. Joseph Cloyd, (of Montgomery Co.) surety—Aug. 21, 1810.

Cloyd, Levi, and Abby Hite—Jan. 3, 1785.

Coats, Charles, and Mary Harrison, dau. John Harrison. Kinsey Coats, sur.—July 2, 1787.

Coats, John, and Lizzie Bough. John Hounchell, surety—Dec. 4, 1787.

Coffee, James, and Sally Collins. Hezekiel Collins, surety—Mar. 9, 1808.

Coffee, John, and Peggy Howard. Ezekiel Howard, surety—Aug. 15, 1818.

Coffman, John, and Nancy Bradley. Thomas Bradley, surety—Jan. 4, 1800.

Cofer, (Copher) John, and Nancy Elkins. Joseph Copher, surety—Feb. 5, 1799.

Cofer, (Copher) Joseph, and Mary Plank, dau. John Plank. Robt. Christian, surety. Mar. by Richard Whitt—July 10, 1793.

Cofer, Joseph, and Margaret Dobbins, dau. Abner Dobbins, surety—Mar. 2, 1827.

Cole, Bird, and Sarah Uunderwood, dau. Jesse Underwood. Thos. Craig, sur.—Oct. 21, 1818.

Cole, John (son of Joseph) and Isabella Wood. John Wood, surety—Jan. 30, 1810.

Cole, Richard, and Sarah Howell. Robt. Bedwell, surety—Apr. 6, 1790.

Cole, Samuel, and Sarah Thrush, Valentine Thrush, surety—Sept. 4, 1792.

Cole, William, and Nancy Stratton, dau. John Stratton. J. B. Goodrich, sur.—July 11, 1815.

Collins, Benjamin, and Kitty Stephens, Mar. by Hezekiah Best—Oct. 28, 1828.

Collins, Jacob, and Letty Shepherd, dau. Abram Shepherd. Stephen Shepherd, surety—June 20, 1825.

Collins, John, and Betsy Johnston, dau. William Johnston, surety—Aug| 12, 1793.

Collins, Randall, and Catey Burton, dau. Joseph Burton. Jacob Burton, sur.—Dec. 8, 1828.

Collins, Richard, and Eveline Lee. Leih Duncan, surety—Feb. 6, 1821.

Collins, Samuel, and Rachel Price. Daniel Collins, surety—July 25, 1801.

Collins, Samuel (son of David) and Permelia Gaines, dau. John Gaines, sur.—Mar. 8, 1813.

Collins, Thomas, and Elizabeth Booth, dau. Abner Booth, surety—May 23, 1829.

Collins, William and Polly Ferrow. Charles Ferrow, surety—Oct. 7, 1820.

Collins, Zecheriah, and Mary Ann McDaniel. Edw. McDaniel, surety—Oct. 27, 1830.

Colhip, Henry, and Catherine Phillippe. Peter Colhip, surety—Feb. 18, 1787.

Combs, Henry, and Rachel Clements, dau. Benj. Clements. Mason Combs, surety. Mar. by Edw. Morgan—Sept. 21, 1788.

Combs, Thomas, and Catherine Stratton, dau. John Stratton. Joseph Campbell, surety—Oct. 21, 1826.

Comparet, John Baptist, and Harriet Jenelle. Wm. Wade, surety—Dec. 6, 1820.

Compton, Joseph, and Elizabeth Alley, dau. Thomas Alley. A Trigg, sur.—Dec. 25, 1787.

Compton, William, and Mary Hall. Asa Hall, surety—Jan. 7, 1822.

Compton, William, and Elizabeth Garlick. Mar. by Richard Whitt—.........., 1788.

Connard, James, and Mary Patrick—........, .., 1791.

Connelly, John, and Mary Munsey. Jeremiah Colwin, surety—Oct. 18, 1803.

Connely, John, and Delilah Ship. Francis Munsey, surety—July 18, 1808.

Connely, Solomon, and Mary Brown. Thomas Brown, surety—Sept. 6, 1826.

Connely, Wesley, and Elizabeth Anderson. John Scott, surety—Sept. 6, 1825.

Conner, Jacob, and Barberry Ferrow. Allen Simpson, surety—Dec. 6, 1803.

Conner, Jonathan, and Betsy Poff, dau. Peter Poff, Jonathan Conner, Sr., surety—June 7, 1822.

Corner, Jonathan and Sarah Reed. Cornelius Reed, surety—Aug. 7, 1798.

Conner, William and Catherine Poff. Peter Poff, surety—May 7, 1811.

Conner, William, and Polly Poff. Mar. by Peter Howard—June 9, 1822.

Conner, William, and Lucinda Cole. Mar. by M. Howry—May 14, 1831.

Conner, Zardock, and Janr Smith. Wm. B. Smith, surety—Aug. 6, 1808.

Cook, Samuel, and Peggy Kipps, John ...., surety—Mar. 8, 1813.

Cook, William, and Mary Simpson. Jacob Louder, surety—Feb. 12, 1800.

Cook, William (son of Thomas) and Rhoda King, dau. William King, surety—June 13, 1807.

Cooper, Cable, and Mary Langley, dau. William Langley. Thos. Adams, sur.—Mar. 22, 1786.

Cooper, George, and Ruth Scaggs. Joseph Scaggs, surety—Dec. 22, 1817.

Cooper, Jacob and Rebecca Barnett. Thomas Barnett ,surety—Dec. 18, 1809.

Cooper, John and Catherine Thrash. Valentine Thrash, surety—Dec. 30, 1797.

Cooper, John, and Polly Thompson. Samuel Thompson, surety—Oct. 2, 1821.

Cooper, Joshua, and Catey Cooper. Richard Whitt, surety—June 9, 1788.

Cooper, Washington, (son of Catey Willson) and Mary Huff. Sam'l Huff, surety—Sept. 18, 1806.

Copeley, John, and Martha Millier. John Hartwell, surety—July 6, 1793.

Copeley, Joshua, and Elizabeth Lawrence. John Lawrence, surety—Apr. 11, 1804.

Copeley, Joshua, (son of Thomas) and Margaret Johnston, dau. John Johnston, surety—Oct. 23, 1804.

Copeley, Thomas, and Rhoda Prater. Abram Ross, sur. Mar. by Alex. Ross—July 23, 1792.

Copeley, Thomas, and Sarah Norris, dau. Ann Lester, wife of Henry Lester: James Heavin, surety—Aug. 7, 1786.

Cornett, Bird, and Polly Romines—May 2, 1814.

Cornett (Cornutt) James, and Elizabeth Dowell. Abram Trigg, surety—Oct. 22, 1792.

Cornett, James, and Keriah Farmer. Mar. by J. G. Cecil—Mar. 16, 1830.

Cornett (John) and Nancy Farmer. William Carnutt, surety—July 21, 1790.

Cornett, William (son of William, dec.) and Molly Farmer. Barnett Farmer, surety—July 28, 1810.

Corp (?) Richard, and Dolly Loeman. Sam'l Munsey, surety—Mar. 31, 1788.

Corty, Henry, and Deborah Davis, dau. John Davis, surety—July 7, 1794.

Costello, Matthew, and Margaret Ross. Mar. by Isaac Rentfro—Aug. 7, 1794.

Costello, Robert, and Elizabeth Compton. Mar. by Dan'l Lockett—.........., 1797.

Couch, Solomon, and Nancy Reedy. Mar. by Richard Whitt—June 18, 1787.

Covey, Daniel, and Rebecca Pate. Mar. by J. G. Cecil—Jan. 31, 1826.

Covey, James, and Sally Kelsey, dau. Thomas Kelsey. Sam'l Covey, sur.—Oct. 4, 1810.

Covey, John (son of Sam'l) and Sarah Cook, dau. John Cook, surety—Feb. 4, 1806.

Covey, Samuel, and Rosanne Barrenger. Abram Barrenger, surety—Jan. 13, 1803.

Covey, William, and Susannah Godbey, dau. William Godbey, surety—Dec. 11, 1810.

Cowan, Andrew, (of Rockbridge Co.) and Elizabeth Montgomery, dau. Joseph Montgomery, surety—Oct. 29, 1784.

Cox, Ambrose, and Sarah Reed, dau. George, and Anna Reed. T. Goodson, sur.—Sept. 5, 1790.

Cox, Carter, Jr., and Neomi Gilham. Ross Cox, and Ezekiel Gilham, sur.—Sept. 13, 1830.

Cox, Jacob, and Franky Geoby. John McGee, surety—Apr. 4, 1797.

Cox, John, and Margaret Carr. Thos. Bigby, sur. Mar. by R. Whitt—Jan. 3, 1786.

Cox, Ross (son of Carter) and Anne Wade, dau. John Wade, surety—Dec. 8, 1810.

Craig, Daniel, and Mary McNeeley. Mar. by R. Whitt—Mar. 27, 1804.

Craig, David, and Polly Mcneely—Mar. 27, 1804.

Craig, George, (son of Benjamin) and Sally Cole,

dau. Joseph Cole: Benjamin Craig, surety—Jan. 3, 1804.

Craig, William, and Catherine Kroftt, dau. Henry Kroftt, surety—Mar. 8, 1830.

Crandall, Allen, and Cynthia Thompson, dau. Archibald Thompson, dec.—Oct. 11, 1824.

Crandall, Ezeriah, and Sarah Smallwood, dau. William, and Rachel Smallwood, surety—Dec. 29, 1809.

Crandall, Nathaniel and Rebekah Simpkins, dau. Robert. June 20, 1793.

Crandall, Reed, and Polly Stephens. Mar. by Jonathan Hall—Oct. 11, 1811.

Crandall, Reed, and Polly Cole, dau. Eleazer Cole. Nathaniel Crandall, surety—Dec. 13, 1816.

Crandall, Thomas, and Mary L. Peterman, dau. Daniel Peterman, surety—May 30, 1827.

Crawford, Edwin, Rev. and Jane McDonald. George McDonald, surety—June 24, 1795.

Crawford, James, and Eliza Deyerle. Thomas Deyerle, surety—Nov. 11, 1828.

Crawford, John, and Elizabeth Mary Hutcheson. Robt. Hutcheson, surety—Sept. 8, 1801.

Crayfude, John, and Elizabeth Wray. (Mar. register)—Sept. 16, 1801.

Crews, John and Sally James. Henry Crews, and Daniel James, surety—Dec. 20, 1797.

Chrisman, Abram, and Margaret Yearout. Jacob Yearout, surety—Nov. 19, 1821.

Chrisman, Jonathan, and Jane Watterson. David Stephens, surety—July 17, 1796.

Cristal, William, and Nelly Brown. David Love, surety—Mar. 11, 1788.

Crockett, Asher, and Sarah Blankenship. Peter Blankenship, surety—Sept. 8, 1800.

Crockett, Filmore, and Elizabeth Dennis. Mar. by Isaac Rentfro—Nov. 1, 1796.

Crockett, Robert, and Sarah Harrison. Thomas Harrison, surety—July 25, 1813.

Crockett, Robert and Elmira Craig, dau. James Craig. Stuart Crockett, surety—May 19, 1829.

Crockett, Samuel, and Margaret Reyburn; James Reyburn, surety—Nov. 6, 1798.

Crockett, Samuel, and Elizabeth Taylor. John Taylor, surety—Aug. 13, 1799.

Crockett, Waller, and Mary Rose, (widow) dau. John Black, surety—Feb. 15, 1819.

Cromer, Abraham, and Hannah Harless. David Harless, surety—.........., 1807.

Cromer, Jacob, and Verena Swanson. Mar. by Richard Buckingham—May 15, 1828.

Cromer, Jonas, and Polly Bowman. Mar. by J. G. Cecil—May 1, 1823.

Cromer, Samuel, and Juliet Bowman. Mar. by J. G. Cecil—Apr. 19, 1827.

Cronk, Joseph, and Elizabeth Bingham, dau. John Bingham. Henry Cronk, surety—Apr. 7, 1823.

Cronk, William, and Betsy Epperley, dau. Christian Epperley. Henry Cronk, surety—Jan. 3, 1820.

Crouch, David, and Polly Bullis. John Bullis, surety—Oct. 15, 1798.

Crouch, James, and Betty Smith. David Crouch, surety—Jan. 28, 1792.

Crouch, James, and Martha Evans. Thomas Evans, surety—Feb. 11, 1802.

Crouch, John, and Rhoda Cecil B....... Cecil, surety—Sept. 24, 1796.

Crouch, Moses, and Elizabeth Hack. Philip Hack, surety—Apr. 3, 1807.

Crouch, Solomon, (son of David) and Nancy Reidy, dau. Shadrack Reidy, surety—Aug. 11, 1787.

Crow, Lindsey, and Sally Barnett. Joseph Warkup, surety—July .., 1809.

Crowy, Adam, and Elizabeth G. Smith. Abraham Smith, surety—Sept. 20, 1817.

Crowy, Andrew, and Sarah Smith, dau. David Smith, surety—Sept. 6, 1817.

Croxten, William, and Polly Peden, dau. James Peden, surety—Oct. 27, 1812.

Croy, Jacob, and Catherine Sour. Martin Surfus, surety—Oct. 31, 1811.

Croy, Peter, and Susannah Bayenger. Peter Bayenger, and Jacob Croy, surety—Mar. 26, 1807.

Crum, Jacob, and Catherine Oldham. Marriage Register—June 16, 1788.

Crum, Jacob, and Betsy Seapall. George Seapall, surety—Aug. 24, 1798.

Crum, John, and Catherine Oldhance. Mathias Oldhance, surety—Oct. 27, 1787.

Crum, Matthew, and Mary Williams, dau. Thomas Williams. J. Dilly, sur.—Dec. 14, 1797.

Crump, Walker, and Susan Akers. Claiburn Akers, surety—Oct. 19, 1813.

Cubbage, George, and Sally Cooper, dau. James Cooper, surety—Oct. 1, 1795.

Cummings, Joseph, and Nancy Camp, dau. James Camp, surety—Sept. 27, 1808.

Cummings, William C. and Maria Patton, dau. Henry Patton. Arnold Patton, surety—Aug. 24, 1829.

Cunningham, Thomas, and Elizabeth Newman. Mar. by Richard Buckingham—July 6, 1828.

Curnute, James, and Elizabeth Douett. Mar. by Richard Whitt—.........., 1792.

Currin, William, and Rhoda Charlton. James Charlton, surety—June 26, 1804.

Curry, Robert, and Susannah Runner. Mar. by Richard Whitt—.......... .., 1792.

—D—

Dabney, John, and Lydia Jones—Mar. 23, 1801.

Damewood, John and Catherine Huffman. James Rowe, surety—June 7, 1798.

Darter (Carter?) Peter, and Elizabeth Moore, dau. Frederick Moore, sur.—June 5, 1787.

Daugherty (see Dougherty)

Davidson, Andrew, and Rebecca Bush. John Davidson, surety—Aug. 25, 1788.

Davidson, Ananias, and Mrs. Anne Feely. James Ingram, surety—Nov. 10, 1825.

Davidson, George, and Jenny Pepper—July 17, 1804.

Davidson, Joseph, and Matilda Patton, dau. Henry Patton. Sam'l Patton, surety—June 16, 1789.

Davidson, William, and Elizabeth Charlton, dau. John and Elizabeth Charlton. Isaac Glass, surety—Apr. 17, 1785.

Davidson, William, and Mary Stevenson. Mar. by Simon Cockrell—Mar. 1, 1782.

Davis, Hiram (son of James,) and Nancy Bateman, dau. Jesse Bateman, sur.—Oct. 23, 1817.

Davis, Isaac, and Sally Guthry. David Love, surety—July 15, 1796.

Davis, John, and Sally Thompson. Wm. Rutledge, and Hugh Gibson, sur.—Mar. 20, 1822.

Davis, Joseph, and Margaret Hays, dau. Joseph Hays, Jesse Evans, sur.—Dec. 4, 1783.

Davis, Joseph, and Lovess Helvey. Peter Riffe, surety—Feb. 13, 1796.

Davis, Joshua, and Sally Moody. Edmund Moody, surety—July 14, 1801.

Davis, Peter, and Ann Surface. Sam'l Shields, surety—Dec. 20, 1819.

Davis, Samuel, and Polly Mitchell. Jordan Mitchell, surety—May 12, 1825.

Davis, Solomon, and Betsy Taylor. Waarick Taylor, surety—Jan. 7, 1797.

Davis, Thomas, and Patsy Jewell. Thomas Jewell, surety—Dec. 29, 1821.

Davis, William, and Hetty Robertson, dau. John Robertson, surety—Aug. 17, 1818.

Davis, William, and Jane Barnett. John Barnett, surety—Apr. 25, 1825.

Davis, Zachariah, and Mary Burgess. B. Davis, surety—Jan. 2, 1790.

Davis, Zacheriah, (son of James), and Elizabeth King. James King, surety—June 20, 1810.

Day, Henry, and Fanny Alsope. John Stobuck, surety—Aug. 16, 1790.

Day, James, and Rebecca Waggonner. John Pruett, surety—Apr. 4, 1786.

Day, Travis, (son of Joshua), and Patience Cooper, orphan: William Wade, guardian, surety—Sept. 1, 1827.

Day, William ,and Elizabeth Waggoner. Mar. by Richard Whitt—. . . . ., 1781.

Dawes, Thomas, and Mildred Willson: William Dawes, surety—June 5, 1792.

Dean, George, and Anna Askins, dau. Thomas Askins, surety—Feb. 16, 1828.

Dean, George, and Polly Fisher: Peter Helvey, surety—May 4, 1813.

Deed (Dud?), Peter, and Naomi Myers, dau. Sam'l Myers. Jas. John, sur.—Nov. 13, 1830.

Devers, John, and Catherine Ingram, dau. Aaron Ingram, surety—Mar. 4, 1830.

Dewese (spelled Dewease, Dewees), Jesse, and Mary Lowder, dau. Jacob Lowder. Abram Gerheart, surety—Nov. 1, 1796.

Dewease, John, and Charlotte Rose, dau. Gabriel Rose, surety—Nov. 25, 1826.

Dewese, Peter, and Esther Poff. Peter Poff, surety—Mar. 15, 1815.

Dewese, Thomas, and Mildred Willson. Mar. by Edw. Morgan—June 7, 1792.

Deyerle, Ab. and Sally Smith—Nov. 18, 1804.

Deyerle, Charles, and Elizabeth Leffler. John Leffler, surety—Dec. 12, 1803.

Deyerle, Crockett, and Polly Taylor: John Taylor (guardian), surety—Dec. 27, 1824.

Deyerle, John, and Jenny Crockett: Hugh Crockett, surety—Dec. 12, 1797.

Diamond, Jesse, and Judith Hall. Joseph Bengiffon, surety—July 3, 1802.

Dickerson, Andrew, and Mahala Dodd, dau. John Dodd, surety—Oct. 28, 1829.

Dickerson, (Dickinson?), Griffith (son of Obediah), and Mary Huff, dau. Mary Huff: Sam'l Kirk, surety. Mar. by Robert Jones—Apr. 17, 1793.

Dickerson, James, and Permelia Reed, dau. Andrew Reed. Griffith Dickerson, surety—Sept. 7, 1825.

Dickerson, John, and Elizabeth Waitman. Hugh McNeal, surety—Mar. 9, 1830.

Dickerson, Leonard, and M. . . . . Rentfro: Jonathan Isom, surety—June 20, 1787.

Dickerson, Leonard, and Susannah Hylton, dau. Archelius Hylton, sur.—Mar. 15, 1826.

Dills, Peter, and Polly Wysor (Wisor), dau. Henry Wysor, surety—May 21, 1799.

Dinkle, John, and Sarah Fisher, dau. William Fisher. Adam Fisher, sur.—Mar. 23, 1825.

Diskins, Harvey, and Nancy P. Howe, dau. Daniel Howe. Wm. Howe, surety—May 6, 1828.

Ditty, Abraham, (son of John), and Jensy Fergus. Francis Fergus, sur.—Dec. 4, 1811.

Doak, Alexander, and Margaret Hannah. Samuel Doak, surety—Aug. 9, 1786.

Doak, David, and Rachel Gibb: Mar by Richard

Whitt—Apr. 5, 1787.

Doan, David, and Rachel Gibb: (mar.. register. Same as above?)—Apr. 5, 1787.

Doan, Joseph, and Eliza Carper. Sam'l Shields, sur. Mar. by J. G. Cecil—June 12, 1826.

Dobbins, Abner, and Mary Kirk. Mar. by Alexander Ross—Mar. 21, 1795.

Dobbins, Dangerfield, and Eve Barger. Mar. by Isaac Rentfro—Nov. 3, 1795.

Dobbins, Isom ,and Katurah Wineteer, dau. John Wineteer, surety—June 7, 1826.

Dobbins, John, and Druscilla Winters John Winters, surety—Aug. 28, 1821.

Dobbins, John, and Polly Wilson, dau. Benjamin Wilson. Jas. Lester, sur.—July 4, 1823.

Dobbins, John, and Batsy West. Isaac West, Sr., surety—Dec. 4, 1811.

Dobbins, Martin, and Nancy Elliot, dau. Curtis Elliot. Abner Dobbins, surety—Aug. 24, 1818.

Dobbins, Thomas, and Mary Huff, widow. Nathan Ratcliff, surety—Sept. 20, 1787.

Dodd, William, and Elizabeth Tice. Manassah Tice, surety—Nov. 1, 1822.

Dolton, (Dalton), Adam, and Catherine Stephey, dau. John Stephey, sur.—Mar. 6, 1787.

Donnaly, John, and Elizabeth Haines, widow. Geo. Humphreys, surety—May 2, 1788.

Dougherty (Daugherty), John and Nancy Moody. Edmund Moody, surety—Nov. 3, 1800.

Dougherty, John, and Elizabeth Donneho—Aug. 7, 1804.

Dougherty, Joseph (son of William), and Susan Sanger: Joseph Sanger, surety—Mar. 8, 1808.

Dougherty, William, and Patsy Woodrick, widow. Noah Hawkins, surety—Nov. 20, 1811.

Dougherty, William, and Lucinda Collins. Hezekiah Collins, surety—Nov. 4, 1819. .

Douglass, George and Catherine Harris. Isom Harris, surety—Dec. 10, 1784.

Douglass, Jacob, and Nancy Burk. William Pepper, surety—Oct. 4, 1798.

Douglass, Jacob, and Catherine Simpson: William Simpson, surety—July 19, 1828.

Douthat, Jacob, and Maria Woolwine: Robt. Douthat and John Woolwine, surety—Aug. 2, 1827.

Doyle, Henry, and Betsy Silver. Aaron Silver, surety—Apr. 16. 1821.

Drake, George, and Nnacy Rollins. Mar. by Isaac Rentfro—June 7, 1798.

Drake, James, and Christina Adkins. David Adkins, surety—Oct. 24, 1793.

Drake, James, and Nancy Adkins. Joshua Adkins, surety—Dec. 6, 1797.

Drake, John, and Martha Lester, dau. Abner Lester. J. Elswick, security. Mar. by Isaac Rentfro—Feb. 12, 1793.

Draper, Abraham, and Rosanna McMullin. Sam'l Shanklin, surety—Oct| 6, 1807.

Draper, John (son fo John, Sr., and Jane), and Jane Crockett. George Draper, surety—Feb. 2, 1785.

Draper, Thomas, Jr., and Rachel Hawkins, dau. Noah Hawkins. Jos. Wilson, surety — Sept. 18, 1810.

.surety—Oct. 4, 1791.

Drury, Spurlock, and Olive Clur. Georgee Spurlock, surety—Oct. 4, 1791.

Duckwiler, Isaac, and Salmah Deyerle, dau. A. Deyerle. Thos. Mitchell, surety—Sept. 5, 1820.

Dugan, Hugh and Sarah Disch, widow. Henry Wiser, usrety—Mar. 20, 1788.

Dulaney, James, and Nelly Cannaham, James Cannaham, surety—Nov. 4, 1795.

Dulaney, Richard (son of William), and Maram Reed. Griffith Reed, sur.—Oct. 29, 1829.

Duncan, Blanch, and Nancy Reed. John Duncan, surety—Apr. 4, 1797.

Duncan, Blanch, and Mary Morricle, dau. William Morricle. Blanch Duncan, Sr., surety — Mar. 26, 1828.

Duncan, George, and Elizabeth Morricle. William Morricle, surety—Jan. 18, 1826.

Duncan, Henry, and Levina Akers: Solomon Akers, surety—Jan. 14, 1799.

Duncan, Henry, and Elizabeth Weddle, dau. David and Pegga Weddle. Blanch Dncan, surety—Oct. 24, 1820.

Duncan, John, and Ann Reed, dau. Peter Reed. Blanch Duncan, surety—Sept. 3, 1822.

Duncan, Peter, and Violet Cox, dau. Ross Cox. Blanch Duncan, surety—Mar. 2, 1830.

Duncan, Robert, and Elizabeth Lions. John Graybill, surety—Nov. 21, 1809.

Duncan, Seth, and Polly Kirby. Francis Gardner surety—Feb. 21, 1798.

Duncan, William, and Mary Kirk: Joseph Kirk, surety—Oct. 3, 1786.

Dunlop, James, and Mary Howell. Wm. Raeburn, surety—Feb. 21, 1801.

Dunn, Joseph, and Christina Waggoner: David Waggoner, surety—July 17, 1797.

Durman, William, and Unas Reed. Cornelius Reed surety—May 14, 1810.

—E—

Ealis (Ellis?), Isaac, and Catherine Lucts, widow. of Chas. Lucas. Milliton Atkins, surety—Aug. 17, 1787.

Earheart, Abraham, and Sarah Shufflebarger, dau. John Shufflebarger. Wm. Snavely, surety—Sept. 27, 1824.

Earheart, George, and Nancy Taylor, dau. William Taylor—Mar. 28, 1825.

Earl, Hugh, and Hannah Broadwater. Mar. by Richard Whitt—May 8, 1791.

Early, Abner, and Rebecca Crockett. Hugh Crockett, surety—Dec. 29, 1817.

Early, Jeremiah, and Nancy Cecil. Philip Cecil, surety. Mar. by Edw. Morgan—........., 1818.

East, Anderson R., and Mary A. Goaings, dau. David Goaings. James Williams, surety—Oct .31, 1829.

Eastes, John, and Mary Mitchell, dau. Henry and Jean Mitchell, John Calfee, surety—July 7, 1785.

Eaton, Crozier, (son of David), and Keziah Cecil, dau. John Cecil. Jas. Stafford, surety—Mar. 18, 1822.

Eaton, George, and Ann Jane Wright. Alexander Wirght. surety—June 28, 1828.

Ebling (see Epling)

Eclus, Michael, and Elizabeth Robinson, dau. John Robinson, surety—Sept. 28, 1824.

Edie, Joseph, and Elizabeth R. White. Isaac Hudson, surety—June 14, 1826.

Edings, Thomas, and Sterling. Mar. by M. Howry—Oct. 19, 1830.

Edmundson, Henry, and Peggy King, dau. Robert King. Jas. P. Preston, sur.—Dec. 3, 1799.

Edwards, Joseph, and Elizabeth Howell, dau. Benjamin Howell, surety—July 23, 1827.

Elam, Walter (son of William), and Nancy Rughs, dau. Susannah Hughs, widow—Dec. 15, 1795.

Elem, William, and Susannah Rugins. John Patton, surety—July 20, 1792.

Elkins, Elijah. and Jerushe Booth, dau. Stephen and Nancy Booth—Nov. 28, 1789.

Elkins, John, and Elizabeth Farmer. Thompson Farmer, surety—Apr. 5. 1824.

Elkins, Richard, and Nancy McGuire. Richard Elkins, Sr., surety—Dec. 2, 1787.

Elley, Robert, and Amy McPherson. Mar. by Alexander Ross—........., 1792.

Eller, Henry, and Katherine Kittering—June 22, 1787.

Ellis, John. and Betty Calwell. Thos. Fadison, surety—Apr. 6, 1796.

Elliot, Curtis, and Polly Pate (widow of Jeremiah Pate, who was son of Jacob Pate)—Nov. 11, 1819.

Elliot, James, and Frances Greyson. Mar. by Alexander Ross—........., 1796.

Elliot, Martin, and Polly Heaviner. John Trollinger, surety—Sept. 1, 1818.

Elliot, · Robert Capt. and Elizabeth Childress, dau. Stephen Childress. Hugh Crockett, surety—June 17. 1793.

Elswick, Abraham, and Molly Farmer. Thompson Farmer, surety—Mar. 14, 1815.

Elswick, Stephen, and Jerriday Nester. Frederick Shelor, surety—June 2, 1795.

Emmons, John, and Hannah Peterson, dau. Matthias Peterson, surety—Oct. 4, 1791.

England, Jacob, and Rebecca Ann Sumner. Thos. Goodson, surety. Mar. by Robt. Jones—Mar. 1, 1791.

English. Stephen, and Rebecca Chrisman. Mar. by Richard Whitt—........., 1781.

Epling, Daniel, and Hannah Rebel. Christopher Rebel, surety—Feb. 25, 1800 .

Epling, John, and Lattice Parson—Nov. 3, 1801.

Epling, Paul, and Lucy Kerr—Oct. 6, 1801.

Epling. P..........., and Elizabeth Harless, dau. Ferdinand Harris, surety—July 7, 1801.

Epling, Paul, and Margaret Wysong, dau. Joseph Wysong. Jas. Dowdy, sur.—July 20, 1830.

Epperley, Daniel, (son of Jacob), and Elizabeth Lawrence, dau. John Lawrence, Sr., surety—Oct. 6, 1828.

Epperley, George, and Sally Sowers. Henry Sowers, and Jacob Epperley. surety—Dec. 4, 1814.

Epperley, Jacob, and Polly Howry. Michael Howry, surety—Dec. 2, 1817.

Epperley, Jacob, and Elizabeth Wade. John Wade, surety—Jan. 7, 1820.

Epperley, Jacob, and Eliza Pfleger, dau. Abram Pfleger, surety—Sept. 24, 1824.

Epperley, John, and Nancy Bishop. dau. Jacob Bishop, surety—Jan. 1, 1822.

Epperley, John, and Nancy Phares, dau. Amariah Phares. Jacob Epperley, surety. Mar. by Peter Howard—Mar. 3, 1814.

Epperley, William, and Ally Wade. John Wade, surety—Jan. 7, 1820.

Ervin, William, and Freelove Booth. Isaac Booth, surety—Feb. 4, 1806.

Ervin, William, and Peggy Robertson. James Robertson, surety—Feb. 1, 1797.

Evans, Drewry, (son of Thomas), and Theodocia Jacobs, dau. Riley Jacobs; Richard Runyon, surety—July 24, 1809. .

Evans, John, and Sarah Haines. Richard Haines, surety—Aug. 22, 1795.

Evans, John and Mary Rutledge. Geo. Rutledge, sur. Mar. by J. Burgess—Oct. 11, 1812.

Evans, Thomas, Jr., and Anne Crow. Jas. Hogge, surety—Sept. 15, 1789.

Evans, William, and Betsy Saunders. Jas. Newell, surety—Jan. 4, 1788.

Ewing, Alexander, and Euphemy Purnel. Benjamin Cox—Sept. 6, 1786.

—F—

Failey, John, and Jane Harmon, dau. John Harmon, surety—Jan. 7, 1797.

Fannin, Joseph, and Barbara Davis. Peter Barclay, surety—Apr. 8, 1790.

Farley, Ezekiel, and Judy Marcum. Thomas Farley, and John Marcum, sur.—Feb. 4, 1804.

Farley, Thomas, and Patsy Lester, dau. Henry Lester, Richard Pugh, sur.—Mar. 20, 1789.

Farmer, Abram, and Fanny Marris. Henry Morris, surety—Sept. 3, 1805.

Farmer, Barnett, and Elizabeth Elkins. Thos. Farmer, surety. Mar. by Richard Whitt—May 6, 1785.

Farmer, Barnett, and Neomi Cornutt. Mar. by J. G. Cecil—May 15, 1830.

Farmer, Christian, and Polly Golden. Mar. by J. G. Cecil—May 2, 1826.

Farmer, Elijah (son of Branett), and Mary Runnion, dau. Richard Runion, surety—Mar. 6, 1819.

Farmer, James, and Anne Runnion. Richard Runnion, surety—Nov. 30, 1818.

Farmer, Samuel Jeremiah, and Betsy Redpath. Mar. by Jonathan Hall—Mar. 17, 1812.

Farmer, Thompson, and Patty Godby. Mar. by Edw. Morgan—May 8, 1793.

Farmer, Thompson, and Pauline Hedge, dau. William Hedge, surety—May 12, 1828.

Farmer, William, and Patsy Bell, dau. Robert Bell, surety. Mar. by Jonathan Hall—Nov. 13, 1812.

Farmer, William, and Patsey Melton, dau. Jesse and Judith Melton. Mar. by Sam'l McNutt—Apr. 18, 1820.

Feeley, James R., and Ann Ingram. James Ingram, surety—Apr. 7, 1823.

Fergus, James (son of Francis), and Rachel Mears. Alexander Mears, sur.—Jan. 10, 1807.

Fergus, John, and Nancy Guthrie. Richard Guthrie, surety—Aug. 10, 1815.

Ferguson, George W. and Neomi West. Sam'l Smith, surety—Sept. 12, 1815.

Ferguson, John, and Margaret McKennce. William Wynn, surety—Sept. 1, 1789.

Ferguson, Kinder, and Mary Robins. Mar. by Edw. Morgan—June 1, 1792.

Ferguson, Thomas, and Rachel Munsey. John Cofer, surety—July 2, 1790.

Ferrill, John ,and Sarah Simmons. Charles Simmons, surety—Sept. 30, 1807.

Ferrill, John, and Catey Tabor: Archibald Tabor, surety—Mar. 13, 1815.

Fieldon, George, and Sarah Davis. John Black, surety—June 1, 1780.

Finch, John, and Nancy Bishop, dau. Henry Bishop, surety. Mar. by J. B. Cecil—Mar. 17, 1823.

Fisher, James, and Elizabeth Helvie, dau. Peter Helvie, surety—Feb. 26, 1794.

Fizer, George, and Eve Harless. G. H. Fizer, surety —Apr. 8, 1803.

Fizer, Peter, and Nancy Owens, dau. John Owens. Thos. C. Trigg, sur.—Mar. 14, 1825.

Flanagan, William, and Peggy Wall. John Davis, and Wm. Gardner, surety: Mar. by James Watts—July 18, 1822.

Fleger, David, and Nancy Slusher—June 5, 1828.

Fletcher, Aaron, and Elizabeth Davis. Mar. by Alexander Ross—Nov. 8, 1797.

Fletcher, William, and Mary Milom. John McElvins, surety—Jan. 29, 1791.

Flick, Michael, and Nancy Barnett. Jas. Law, surety—Feb. 19, 1822.

Fogle, Philip, and Elizabeth Fillinger. Peter Etter, surety—May 16, 1811.

Fogelman, George, and Sally Hooger. Mar. by Alexander Ross—Dec. 10, 1798.

Forler, Forest, and Mary Munsey. Nathaniel Munsey, surety—Mar. 7, 1786.

Forler, William, and Elizabeth Thomson. John Thomson, surety—Sept. 1, 1789.

Forman, Samuel, and Mary Mullins. Mar. by Richard Buckingham—Apr. 14, 1824.

Foster, James, and Elizabeth Hoge, dau. John Hoge, surety—Oct. 5, 1801.

Foster, Joseph (son of Robert), and Nancy Moss, widow—Jan. 7, 1797.

Foster, William, and Elizbaeth Thompson, dau. William Thompson: John Thompson, surety—Sept. 11, 1789.

Fowler, Clay, and Letty Cartar (By Publication)—May 10, 1798.

Francis, Miles, and Jane Hall, dau. David Hall, surety—Apr. 3, 1827.

Francis, Peter, and Sally Toler (Taler?) Chas. Taylor, surety—Nov. 7, 1817.

Franklin, John, and Nancy Oliver, dau. Thomas Oliver: Wm. Surface, surety. Mar. by Geo. Adams—Feb. 2, 1829.

Franklin, William, and Ann Cumming. Joseph Cumming, surety—Jan. 9, 1809.

French, David, and Polly Dingess, dau. William Dingess, surety—June 8, 1787.

French, Isaac, and Elizabeth Stowers, dau. William Stowers, Matthias French, surety. Mar. by Alex. Ross—June 5, 1791.

French, James, and Anne Chapman, dau. John Chapman. Geo. Chapman, surety—Oct. 18, 1787.

French, James, and Susannah Hughes. Reuben Hugher, surety—Oct. 18, 1789.

French, John, and Biddle (Betty?) Clay, dau. Michel Calay. James French, sur.—Jan. 16, 1787.

Friel, Manassas, and Elizabeth Montgomery, dau. John Montgomery; Sam'l Montgomery, surety—Aug. 20, 1788.

Fry, George, Jr. (son of Nancy Fry, widow), and Mary Ann Johnson—Jan. 21, 1799.

Fry, John, and Anne Johnston, widow. Milliton Adkins, surety—Nov. 3, 1787.

Fry, Peter, and Agnes Stanley. Joseph Stanley, surety—Feb. 4, 1805.

Fugate, John, and Elinor Morgan, dau. Ezekiel Morgan. Evan Morgan, sur.—Nov. 8, 1785.

Fuller, James, and Diamie Akers, dau. Austen Akers, Norhup Fuller, sur.—June. ., 1813.

Fuller, John, and Mary Wright. Obediah Wright, surety—Feb. 16, 1801.

Fuller, Robert, and Margaret Thompson: George Thompson, and Northup Fuller, surety — Jan. 11, 1813.

Fungate, William, and Mary Beckett, dau. Richard Beckett, surety—June 27, 1799.

Furrow, Abram, and Mary Jewell. Chas. Ferrow, father of Abram, surety—Aug. 17, 1826.

Furrow, Charles, Jr., and Nancy Howard. David Howard, surety—Apr. 26, 1826.

Furrow, James, and Polly Peterman, dau. Michael Peterman, surety—Sept. 22, 1813.

Ferrow, John, and Mary Simpkins. Mark Thompson, surety—May 7, 1797.

Furrow, Mathias, and Barbara Weaver. John Ferrow, surety—Apr. 7, 1812.

G

Gannaway, John, and Kezia Barringer, dau. Adam Barrniger, surety—Nov. 3, 1809.

Gardner, Alexander, and Nancy Shanklin, dau. Capt. Samuel Shanklin, deceased. Samuel Shanklin, surety—Nov. 10, 1821.

Gardner, James, and Ann Gardner. John Gardner, surety. Mar. by Samuel McNutt—Mar. 5, 1817.

Gardner, James, and Elizabeth Zeiglar. Seth Duncan, surety—Sept. 12, 1807.

Gardner, John, and Betsy Page, dau. John Page, surety. Mar. by Jonathan Hall—Jan. 20, 1813.

Gardner, Robert, and Juliet Smith. Thomas Smith, surety—Apr. 2, 1814.

Gardner, Robert, and July Peterson. Mar. by Jonathan Hall—May 3, 1814.

Gardner, Robert, and Sarah Glen. John Glen, surety—Apr. 13, 1819.

Gardner, Robert, and Ellin T. Wright, dau. Humphrey Wright. Henry Stephens, sur.—Dec. 11, 1822.

Garlick, John, and Sally Parse, dau. Richard Parse, surety—June 11, 1797.

Garlick, Samuel, and Elizabeth Hall. Mar. by Jacob McEnally—Aug. 23, 1831.

Garmand, John, and Catherine Garmand, dau. Adam Garmand, surety—May 12, 1825.

Garman, Peter, and Magdalin Brunk, dau. Jacob Brunk, surety—Nov. 1, 1830.

Garman, Peter, and Elizabeth Peterman. Adam Garman, and Michael Peterman, surety--Feb. 7, 1826.

Garnes, Joseph, and Peggy Mennick. Jacob Mennick, surety—Jan. 4, 1810.

Garvin, Isaac, and Sally Morton. Mar. by Peter Howard, Mar. 7, 1825.

Gauf, Joel (son of John), and Elizabeth Owens, dau. Barnett Owens, sur.—Feb. 23, 1827.

Gentry, Samuel, and Eliza Ann Stoddard, dau. Solomon Stoddard, surety: Mar. by John Bull — Oct. 30, 1817.

George, John, and Catherine Bryans. James Bryans, and Boswell Johnson, surety—Jan. 10, 1797.

George, William, and Jennett Patton, dau. Henry Patton. Sam'l Patton, surety. Mar. by Edward Morgan—Feb. 9, 1793.

Gibson, John, and Elizabeth Kinser. Jacob Kinser, surety—Feb. 11, 1828.

Gibson, Johnston, and Sally Pence: Jacob Pence, surety—May 8, 1815.

Gibson, William, and Lucinda Hatton. Jas. Simpkins, surety—Jan. 14, 1823.

Gilham, Isaac, and Mary Slusher, dau. Christopher Slusher, surety—June 6, 1826.

Gallaspy, William, and Elizabeth Allicor (Allicon?) Mar. register—Apr. 2, 1785.

Gillaspy, William, and Nancy Allison, dau. James Allison, deceased. David McGavock, surety—Aug. 18, 1803.

Gilmore, Samuel, and Catherine, dau. Peter Hornbarger, surety—Oct. 4, 1822.

Glimp, John A., and Franky Mills, widow. Milliton Akers, surety—Nov. 9, 1788.

Godbey, Benamin ,and Nancy Elkins. John Elkins surety—Jan. 29, 1821.

Godbey, Francis, and Rhoda Whitt. Archibald Whitt, surety—Apr. 3, 1806.

Godbey, George, and Nancy Elswick, dau. Jonathan

Elswick, John Godbey, and Wm. Hays, surety—Dec. 16, 1811.

Godbey, John, and Elizabeth Walker. Mar. by Richard Whitt—May 8, 1793.

Godbey, John, and Elizabeth Harless, widow. Abram Trigg, surety—Oct. 24, 1799.

Godbey, John, and Neomi Bane, Adam Wall, surety —Dec. 10, 1785.

Godbey, William, and Nancy Dickenson, dau. Obadiah Dickenson, sur.—June 7, 1798.

Godbey, William, (son of Francis), and Rhoda Miller, dau. Daniel Miller: Daniel Miller, Jr., surety—Oct. 4, 1825.

Goodby, James B. and Rebecca Smith, dau. Henry Smith, surety—Apr. 1, 1817.

Godding, Cornelius, and Margaret Scott, niece of Gabriel Scott. Abram Godding, surety—Aug. 22, 1786.

Good, Abraham, and Nancy Sullins. William Wade, surety—Mar. 27, 1822.

Goodrick, Edmund B., and Elenor Bell. John Bell, surety—June 20, 1829.

Godson, John, and Mary Shelor, dau. William Shelor: Wm. Goodson, sur.—Oct. 20, 1828.

Goodson, Robert, and Dianna Scott. Matthew Scott, surety—Feb. 1, 1819.

Goodson, William, and Abigal Banks. Thomas Banks, surety. Mar. by Peter Howard—Dec. 18, 1823.

Goodwin, Enos, and Elizabeth Early. John Lefler, surety—May 16, 1813.

Goodwin, Enos, and Martha Mitchell. Fabus Mitsurety—May 16, 1813.

chell, surety—May 8, 1830.

Goodykoontz, David, and Ruth Harter. Mar. by M. Howry—Nov. 17, 1830.

Gordon, John, and Mary Davis, dau. George Davis. Patrick Kindres, sur.—Nov. 17, 1787.

Gordon, John, and Mary Taylor. James Charlton, Jr., surety—Nov. 27, 1812.

Gordon, Samuel, and Ann Hance. Wm. Currin, surety—Jan. 23, 1826.

Gore, Thomas, and Priscilla Smith. Mar. by Peter Howard—July 31, 1827.

Graham, James, and Martha Hall, dau. Asa Hall, Sr. Archibald Graham, sur.—Nov. 17, 1823.

Graham, James, and Isabella Smith, dau. Samuel Smith, surety—Dec. 2, 1783.

Graham, Jesse, and Elizabeth Pratt. Mar. by Richard Buckingham—June 8, 1826.

Graham, John, and Bridget Bonds, widow of Henry Bonds. John Craig, surety—July 24, 1786.

Graham, John J., and Cassandra Guthrie, dau. Richard Guthrie, sur.—Oct. 3, 1828.

Graham, Jonathan, and Mary Shealor. Mar. by Robt. Jones—Nov. . . , 1796.

Graham, Lawrence, and Mary Simmons. Mar. by J. Jones—Feb. 6, 1831.

Graham, Lawson adn Riziah Terry. Ezekiel Boucher, surety—June 21, 1797.

Graley, John, and Evy Rineheart. Thos. Goodson, surety—Sept. 8, 1814.

Gray, Daniel, and Peggy Wilson. Joshua Wilson, surety—Mar. 2, 1819.

Gray, James H. and Rhoda Wilson, dau. Peter Wilson, surety—Nov. 6, 1830.

Gray, William and Elizabeth Thrash. John Thrash, surety—Dec. 6, 1825.

Graybill, John, and Rachel Duncan. William Lyon, surety—Aug. 6, 1805.

Grayson, Ambrose (son of William, Dec. and Rachel), and Betsy Wysor. Henry Wysor, surety—Mar. 28, 1807.

Grayson, John, and Sarah Carter. Mar. by Richard Whitt–.........,1792.
Green, William, and Margaret Alley, dau. Thomas Alley, surety–Apr. 28, 1828.
Greenway, Joseph, and Polly Lakeland. George Lakeland(surety–Mar. 7, 1822.
Greer, James, and Catey Underwood: Joseph Underwood, surety–Sept. 24, 1822.
Griffith, Joseph, and Phebe Hudson. Jesse Smithers, surety–Sept. 6, 1792.
Grills, John, and Philadelphia Ingles, dau. Maury Ingles, Bird Smith, sur.–Aug. 18, 1785.
Grills, John, and Peggy Robinson, dau. John Robinson........ Rife, sur.–Aug. 8, 1791.
Grills, John, and Mary English. Mar. by Isaac Rentfro–Aug. 11, 1803.
Grills, John, and Harriet Robinson. John Wade, surety–Mar 21, 1820.
Grimes, Andrew, and Nancy Webb: Stephen Webb, surety–Feb. 1, 1826.
Grimes, Archibald, and Lucinda Hall. Wm. Grimes, and Asa Hall, surety–Oct. 19, 1816.
Grimes, James, and Polly Holliday. Levi Holliday, surety–Mar. by Peter Howard–May 12, 1821.
Grimes, Jonathan, and Mary Shelor. Wm. Terry, surety–May 17, 1796.
Grimes, Samuel, and Polly Reed: Peter Reed, surety–June 6, 1820.
Grimes, William, and Polly Elkins. Henry Bishop, surety–May 17, 1796.
Grisom, Charles, and Nancy Martin. James Whalen, surety–July 6, 1810.
Grisom, William and Polly Robertson. John Robertson, surety–July 22, 1820.
Gros. Jacob, and Catey Taylor. Wouldrey Taylor, surety–Sept. 20, 1802.
Guerrant, John R. and Octavia Gibson. William Gibson, surety–Apr. 15, 1828.
Guinn, Isham, and Mary Canterbury, dau. Samuel Canterbury. P. Romme, surety–Aug. 3, 1787.
Guillion, Barnabas, and Kittering Keath. Matther Lindsey, surety–June 3, 1788.
Gunter, John, and Sarah Godbey, dau. William Godbey, surety–Jan. 7, 1804.
Guthrie, John, and Elizabeth Vanlear, dau. John Vanlear, Sr. John Anderson, surety. Mar. by Sam'l McNutt–Feb. 22, 1817.
Guthrie, John, and Margaret Wysor. David Miller surety–May 30, 1821.
Guthrie, William, and Jane Reyburn, dau. William W. Reyburn, surety–Sept. 27, 1830.

–H–

Haffee, Andrew M. a,nd Catherine Harless. David Harless, surety–June 22, 1803.
Hairs, Joseph, and Neomi Clay. George Pearis, surety. Mar. by R. Whitt–Apr. 9, 1789.
Hairs, Joseph, and Phebe Perdue, dau. William Perdue. Geo. Pearis, sur. Mar. by Jeremiah Masten–June 7, 1791.
Hale, Edward ("Late of Lunenberg Co."), and Martha Perdue, dau. William Perdue. Thos. Addair, surety–Sept. 26, 1786.
Hale, Jobe, and Fanny Love. Adam Wall ¿guardian of Fanny), surety–Aug. 28, 1824.
Hale, Peter (of Farnklin Co.), and Lockey Ingles. Crockett Ingles, sur.–Oct. 4, 1821.
Hale, Thomas, and Agne s Price. Mar. by Richard Whitt–........., 1780.
Hale, William, and Catherine Snidow. John Snidow, surety–Mar. 18, 1811.

Halfpenny, John, and Eliza Prewett. Thomas Raeburn, surety–Mar. 5, 1799.
Hall, Andrew, and Tibitha Covey, dau. Samuel Covey, surety–Feb. 23, 1828.
Hall, Asa, Sr., and Mary VanOver (and wife). Henry VanOver, surety–July 31, 1802.
Hall, Asa, Jr., and Matey Crnadall. Mar. by Jonathan Hall–Feb. 23, 1813.
Hall, Benjamin, (son of David, Sr.), and Margaret McKenzie, dau. of Murdock McKenzie, surety–July 16, 1799.
Hall, Charles, and Elizabeth Iddings. William Iddings, surety–July 3, 1820.
Hall, David, (son of Asa, Sr.), and Elizabeth Pate, dau. Jeremiah Pate, Jr., surety–Apr. 5, 1803.
Hall, Fleming, and Sarah Tice. Nicholas Tice, surety–Oct. 22, 1818.
Hall, Freeburn (son of Jesse), and Catherine Pate. Geo. Pate, surety–Apr. 27, 1807.
Hall, James, and Margaret Wiley. Mar. by J. G. Schrider–.........., 1782.
Hall, Jesse, and Catherine Huff, widow of Sam'l Huff. Jacob Zoll, surety–Dec. 15, 1828.
Hall, Jesse, and Ann Watterson, dau. Thomas Watterson, surety–Jan. 12, 1798.
Hall, John, and Sally Pate. Mar .by Jonathan Hall–Sept. 10, 1811.
Hall, Jonathan, and Margaret Bell. Robert Bell, surety–Dec. 15, 1798.
Hall, William, (son of Asa, Sr.) and Sarah VanOver, dau. Henry VanOver–Aug. 2, 1803.
Hall, William, and Nancy Ledgerwood, dau. James Leogerwood, surety–Jan. 12, 1820.
Hall, William, and Mary Craig, dau. Thomas B. Craig, surety–July 21, 1830.
Hambleman, George, and Ruth Howell. Daniel Howell, surety–Nov 3, 1800.
Hamliton, Abner, and Mary Clendenin. Mar. by Richard Whitt–Oct. .., 1785.
Hamilton, Ferdinand, and Alice Clendenin, dau. Adam Clendenin, sur.–Jan. 11, 1791.
Hamilton, John, and Bettina Newberry, widow. James Polley, surety. Mar. by Edw. Morgan–Sept. 7, 1789.
Hammon (Harmon?), ..., and Catey Myers, Samuel Myers, surety–July ..., 1814.
Hance, James, and Juliet Cecil. Samuel Cecil, surety–Dec. 6, 1814.
Hance, John, and Catherine Hewitt. Bird Grills, surety–Jan. 5, 1829.
Hance, Peter, and Elizabeth Harper. Adam and Robt. Currin, surety–Aug. 2, 1796.
Hancock, William, and Nancy Hylton. Archelus Hylton, surety–June 25, 1825.
Hanes, Christopher, and Polly Patterson. Sayres Smith, surety. Mar. by Henry Holstine, in Botetourt Co., Va.–June 29, 1819.
Hanes, Jacob, and Hannah Martin. Mar. by Richard Buckingham–Sept. 27, 1827.
Haney, Hiram, and Angelina Crandall, dau. Sam'l Crandall. Jas. Overstreet, surety, Mar .by J. G. Cecil–Mar. 5, 1828.
Hank, Jehu, and Malinda Bratton. Hamilton Wade, surety–May 13, 1830.
Harberton, James, and Jane Mavis. Hugh Mavis, surety–Jan. 13, 1797.
Harbour, David, and Mary Spurlock. John Spurlock, surety–Aug. 21, 1787.
Hardy, Thomas, and Nancy Collins, dau. Dan'l Collins, surety–Feb. 15, 1794.
Hardman, John, and Jane Lockhart. Mar. by Edw. Morgan–Nov. 5, 1791.

Hardwick, Younger, and Susannah Kinser. Philip Kinser, surety—July 3, 1728.

Harless, Daniel, and Elizabeth Nash. Mar. by John Geo. Shrider—Dec. 3, 1787.

Harless, David, and Polly Hill. John Hill ,surety—Jan. 7, 1800.

Harless, David, and Betsy Paine. David Lewis, and Ambrose Paine, sur.—Apr. 15, 1807.

Harless, Israel and Mary Brose. Peter Brose, surety—Mar 1, 1830.

Harless, Jacob, and Elizabeth Hornbarger. David and Peter Hornbarger, surety—Mar. 3, 1814.

Harless, John, and Polly Willson, dau. Thomas Willson, surety—Feb. 8, 1796.

Harless, John, (son of Daniel) ,and Elizabeth Harless, dau. Isaac Harless, surety—Sept. 29, 1828.

Harless, Michael, and Jenny Adkins. Mar. by Alexander Rsos—Apr. 3, 1797.

Harless, Peter, and Mary Harless, dau. David Harless, Sr., surety—Sept. 12, 1797.

Harless, Philip, and Milly Stanley. Martin Harless, surety. Mar. by Jeremiah Masten—June 18, 1790.

Hraless, Philip, and Polly Price: Henry D. Price, surety—Feb. 4, 1806.

Harless, Philip, (son of David), and Susannah Ott. Henry Ott, surety—Jan. 14, 1812.

Harless, hilip, and Sally Johnson. John Sheppard, surety—May 26, 1800.

Harless, Samuel, and Elizabeth Price, dau. Henry Price, surety—June 17, 1798.

Harmon, Adam (son of Henry), and Anne Gardner. Henson Gardner, sur.—Dec. 24, 1787.

Harmon, Benjamin, and Martha Hylton. Hiram Hylton, surety—Apr. 22, 1828.

Harmon, Daniel, and Phebe Harmon. Mar. by Simon Cockrell—Feb. 6, 1792.

Harmon, David, and Priscilla Hance. Henry Hance, surety—Feb. 11, 1812.

Harmon, Henry, and Charity Popicoffer, surety—Aug. 15, 1787.

Harmon, Henry, and Mary Canterbury. Mar. by Richard Whitt—June .., 1787.

Harmon, Henry, and Polly Hornbarger. Peter Hornbarger, surety—Apr. 6, 1819.

Harmon, John, and Elizabeth Bird, dau. William and Sarah Burch, (step-dau. of Wms?)—Dec. 16, 1787.

Harmon, John, Jr, and Sarah Low (Law, Love?). John Harmon, Sr., surety—Aug. 8, 1805.

Harmon, John, and Catherine Hall, dau. David Hall, surety—Dec. 16, 1826.

Harmon, Joseph, and Hannah Vickers. Alexander Vickers, surety—Mar. 7, 1826.

Harmon, Peter, and Betsy Mann (Marr?), widow of George Mann (Marr?): John Sharp, surety—Nov. 13, 1797.

Harmon, Paul, and Sarah Miller. Peter Harmon, surety—......... .., 1791.

Harmon, Revel, and Mary Lawrence. Nathaniel Crandall, surety—July 20, 1797.

Harmon, Solomon, and Elizabeth Slusher, Christopher Slusher, surety—Mar. 6, 1810.

Harmon, William, and Anne Hance. Henry Hance, surety—Jan. 12, 1809.

Harold, William, adn Nancy Rutherford. James Newell, surety—Sept. 9, 1773.

Harris, Francis, and Hannah Helms. Mar. by John Bull—July 16, 1819.

Harris, James, and .... Helms. Mar. by John Bell (Bull?)—Sept. 29, 1818.

Harris, John, and Mary Pepper .Howard Weaver, surety—Oct. 22, 1785.

Harris, John, and Mary Willson. Mar. by Isaac Rentfro—Feb. 8, 1796.

Harris, Joseph, and Priscilla Lambert. Jacob England, surety—Jan. 30, 1797.

Harris, Samuel, and Mary Booth, (orphan). Benjamin Harris, surety—Mar. 24, 1828.

Harris, Thomas, and Elizabeth Harris. Sam'l Harris, surety. Mar. by Peter Howard—Mar. 9, 1826.

Harrison, David, and Anna Chase. John Chase, surety—Jan. 11, 1791.

Harrison, John, and Sarah Carter, dau. Henry Carter, surety—Dec. 15, 1795.

Harrison, John, and Mary Crockett. Walter Crockett, surety—Feb. 13, 1816.

Harrison, John, and Eleanor Leslie. William Leslie, surety—......... .., 1818.

Harrison, Thomas, and Jean Childress, dau. Stephen Childress, surety—Aug. 15, 1812.

Hart, Meridith, and Ruth Beckett. John Greybill, surety—Dec. 8, 1810.

Hart, Nathanial, and Susannah Preston. James P. Preston, surety—Aug. 26, 1797.

Harter, Adam, and Peggy Stickleman. Philip Stickleman, surety—Apr. 14, 1817.

Harter, Christian, and Jane White, dau. Richard White, surety—July 24, 1816.

Harter, Christian, and Orpha Wilson. John Wilson, surety—Apr. 8, 1822.

Harter, David, and Sally Boen. John Boen, surety—Apr. 7, 1812.

Hartman, John, and Jane Lockhart. Sam'l Patton, surety—Mar. by Edw. Morgan—Nov. 5, 1791.

Hartsook, John and Peggy Simpson. William Simpson, surety—Mar. 27, 1812.

Hatch, Nathaniel, and Barbary Harmon (Marmon?) Moses Beavers, sur.—Sept. 28, 1816.

Hatfield, Adam, and Mary Williams. George Williams, surety—Dec. 3, 1799.

Hatfield, Andrew, and Mary Marr (Mann?). John Battersall, surety—Oct. 13, 1798.

Hatfield, Isaac, and Mary French. Matthew French, surety—May 13, 1788.

Hatfield, John, and Mary McComas. William McComas, surety—Feb. 26, 1788.

Hatfield, Jonas, and Ann Williams. Edward Williams, surety—Aug. 8, 1801.

Hatfield, William, and Anny Brumfield, dau. James Brumfield, sur. Mar. by Alexander Ross—Apr. 2, 1793.

Hatten, George R. (son of Lucinda Gibson, wife of Wm. Gibson), and Rhoda Kirby, dau. James Kirby, surety—June 3, 1803.

Hatten, George, and Rhoda Kirby. Mar. by Richard Buckingham—Oct. 15, 1829.

Hatten, Jonathan, and Lucy Rutledge, dau. George Rutledge, Gent., surety—May 21, 1806.

Hawley, Andrew, and Sapphira Pearsons. Mar. by Alexander Ross—......... .., 1796.

Hawkins, John, and Margaret Cloyd, dau. Joseph Cloyd. Patrick Shockley, surety. Mar. by Edw. Morgan—Dec. 17, 1789.

Haymaker, Michael, and Mary Douthat. Robert Douthat, surety—Dec. 25, 1825.

Haymaker, Samuel, and Susan Surface. Geo. Surface, surety—Apr. 3, 1829.

Hawley, (Hailey), William, and Sally Gun. Mar. by Jonathan Hall—Feb. 22, 1813.

Hayse, Charles, and Elizabeth Adkins. Joseph Davis, surety—Aug. 5, 1788.

Heaven, Jacob, and Polly Trollinger, dau. John Trollinger, surety—Feb. 5, 1814.
Heavin, John, and Sarah Wall. Edmun Wall, surety—Apr. 9, 1819.
Heaven, Joseph, and Molly McGee. Robert McGee, surety—Oct. 13, 1800.
Heaven, Philip, and Patsy Couch—Feb.—, 1799.
Heavin, Richard, and Sarah Burk, dau. Margaret Burk. Christian Shell, surety—Dec. 17, 1789.
Heaven, William, and Barbara Shell, dau. Jacob Shell. Jno. Wylie, sur.—Mar. 4, 1786.
Hedge, James, and Polly Loomas. Mar. by J. F. Cecil—Mar. 25, 1824
Hedge, William and Lucy Godbey William Godbey, surety—Mar. 4, 1804.
Hellenberg, ... and Barbara Shrider, dau. John Shrider, surety—Mar. 25, 1787.
Helm, George, and Polly Patton. Mar. by Edw. Morgan—Feb. 23, 1797.
Helm, Jacob, and Elizabeth Smith, dau. Humphrey Smith, surety—Sept. 24, 1812.
Helm, John D. and Catherine Barringer. Philip Barringer, surety—Oct. 13, 1798.
Helm, John W. and Susannah Cox, dau. Carter Cox, surety—June 6, 1826.
Helm, John B. and Christina Peterman. George Peterman, surety—Dec. 19, 1829.
Helm, Thomas, and Olivia Smith, dau. Humphrey Smith, surety—Mar. 10, 1812.
Helm, Thomas, and Mary Weddle. Thomas Weddle, surety—Mar. 26, 1818.
Helman, William, and Peggy Burton. Mar. by Alexander Ross—. . . . ., 1793.
Helton, Archibald, and Catherine Weddle. Benjamin Weddle, surety—Nov. 19, 1803.
Helton, George, and Tabitha (?) Green. Jos. Spurlock, sur. Mar. by Robt. Jones—Apr. 7, 1793.
Helton, John, and Nanc yHowell. David Howell, surety—Oct. 4, 1798.
Helton, John a,nd Nancy Howell. David Howell, surety—Sept. 11, 1820.
Helvey, Frederick, and Nancy Cane. Sam'l Hutcheson, surety—Oct. 22, 1798.
Helvey, John, and Rebecca Mitchell Samuel Mitchell, surety—Jan. 3, 1805.
Helvey, Peter, and Peggy Price. Michael Price, surety—Dec. 31, 1804.
Henderliter, Isaac, and Susan Keister, dau. Philip Keister. Geo. Keister, surety—Aug. 25, 1825
Henderliter, Michael, and Sarah Shopshire. Robt. Gardner, surety—Oct. 16, 1826.
Henderson, Abraham, and Rachel Whitt. Mar. by Richard Whitt—. . . . ., 1780.
Henderson, John, and Polly Bean. James Bean, surety—June 2, 1801.
Henderson, Jonas, and Betsy Thomas, dau. Giles Thomas, John Henderson, surety—Apr. 16, 1806.
Hednerson, Joseph, and Jane McGee, dau. Robert McGee, surety—Mar. 4, 1794.
Henderson, William, and Elizabeth Lester. John Lester, surety—Aug. 18, 1833.
Henderson, William, and Nancy Deyerle. David French, surety—Jan. 7, 1800.
Henderson, Zacherah, and Mary Owen, dau. Elias Owen. Jas. Robinson, sur.—Sept. 19, 1795.
Hendricks, Zacheriah (see Henderson, Zacheriah) and Mary Owen. Mar. by Isaac Rentfro—Sept. 25, 1795.
Henry, William, (of Washington Co., N. C.), and Margaret Davis, dau. Samuel Davis, surety—July 22, 1780.

Henry, William, and Jane Stafford. John Stafford, surety—Oct. 24, 1800.
Hiffer, George, and Ruthy Caldwell. Mar. by John Bull—July 2, 1818.
Hill, James A. and Anna Rebecca Deyerle. John Hank, surety—Dec. 7, 1830.
Hildruth, John, and Darcus Shaw, dau. William Shaw. Jas. Shaw, surety—Feb. 9, 1775.
Hiltno, ..., and Elizabeth Hilton, dau. Elijah Hilton. Jos. Spurlock, surety—Jan. 3, 1792.
Hinton, George W. and Elizabeth Smith. David Smith, surety—Nov. 6, 1804.
Hix, John, and Elizabeth Brown. James Addair, surety—Aug. 6, 1789.
Hix, Joseph, and Sarah Lestor (Sentor?). Bird Smith, surety—Sept. 3, 1797.
Hix, Richard, and Susan Thompson. Mar. by Richard Whitt—Nov. . ., 1793.
Hix, Robert ,and Susannah Thompson. Austin Godsey, surety—Nov. 22, 1793.
Hoback, David, and Sophia Conner, dau. Andrew Conner, surety—Pan. 24, 1829.
Hoback, David, and Anne Moore. Mar. by M. Howry—Dec. 10, 1829.
Hofe, Joseph, and Nancy Dilnman, dau. William Robt. Dilnman, surety—Nov. 1, 1796.
Hogan, David, and Polly Barringer. Adam Barringer, surety—Oct. 6, 1813.
Hogan, Harmon, and Peggy Elliot Philip Hogan, and Carter Elliot, sur.—Oct. 19, 1813.
Hogan, Philip, and Elizabeth Payte, dau. Jeremiah, Sr., and Christina Payte. Jacob and Adam Pate, surety—Mar. 31, 1787.
Hoge, Daniel (son of James), and Nancy Stafford, dau. James Stafford, surety—Mar. 25, 1806.
Hoge, James, and Elinor Howe. Daniel Howe, surety—June 5, 1810.
Hoge, John and Jenny Rutledge. George Rutledge, surety—June 12, 1802.
Hoge, Joseph (son of James) and Barbara Brawley, dau. John Brawley, sur.—Nov. 9, 1790.
Hollans, John, and Polly Mauer, dau. John Mauer, surety—Oct. 4, 1814.
Hollans, John and Polly Mower. Geo. Songer, surety—Oct. 18, 1816.
Hollidays, Charles, and Sarah Watkins. Jos. Raeburn, surety—May 2, 1793.
Holliday, Hnery (son of William), and Letty Holliday. Wm. Holliday, surety—Oct .27, 1827.
Holly, James, and Catherine Copher. John Copher, surety—Mar. 19, 1818.
Holley, Joseph, and Mary Harmon, dau. Catherine Harmon. John Copher, sur.—Feb. 8, 1812.
Holmes, James, and Nancy Warden. Mar. by Richard Buckingham—Dec. 10, 1824.
Holmes, John, and Betsy Miller. William Holmes, surety—Mar. 5, 1822.
Holston, Henry, and Mary Webb. George Webb, surety—Apr. 5, 1802.
Holt, Spratley, and Nancy Walters: George Walters, Jr., surety—Jan. 2, 1829.
Honaker, Isaac, and Susannah Penner. John Penner, surety—Mar. 29, 1796.
Hornbarger, Daniel, and Nancy Walters. Peter Hornbarger, and John Walters, surety—Apr. 28, 1824.
Hornbarger, Jacob, and Elizabeth Stapleton. Mar. by J. G. Shrider—. . . . ., 1792.
Hornbarger, Peter, and Elizabeth Smith, dau. Jacob Smith. Jacob Hornbarger, surety—Oct. 26, 1788.
Horntz, Jacob, and Leah John, dau. John John. Timothy Lake, surety—Dec. 14, 1829.

Hosier, Joseph, and Elizabeth Coffin. Chas. Morgan, surety—Feb. 23, 1797.

Hounshell, Adam, and Anna Ott. Henry Ott, surety—Aug. 30, 1815.

Hounshell, Andrew, and Lovelass Lambard. Henry Bean, surety—Sept. 17, 1786.

Hover, Philip, and Sarah Boardman. Mar. by . . . . Morgan—Feb. 10, 1825.

Howard, Cyrus, and Milly Booth, dau. Geo. Booth. Walter Crickett, sur.—Apr. 4, 1787.

Howard, Edward, and Mary Burchett. Mar. by Edw. Morgan—Aug. 29, 1787.

Howard, Ira, and Permelia Lester, dau. John Lester. Peter Howard, sur.—Dec. 3, 1816.

Howard, Isaiah, and Anne Howard. Isaiah Stephens, and Bastian Howard, surety—Mar. 14, 1791.

Howard, Jobe, and Abigail Howard, dau. Peter Howard, surety—Feb. 22, 1817.

Howard, Major, and Sarah Shelor, dau. William Shelor, surety—Nov. 5, 1821.

Howard, Stephen, and Ally Musgrove. John Stephens, surety—Apr 10, 1798.

Howard, William, and Elizabeth Collingsworth. Hiram Howard, surety—May 9, 1826.

Howard, William, and Martha Belcher. John Bird, surety—Sept. 15, 1818.

Howard, William. (See mar. bond William Harold. Almost obl. Might be Howard)

Howe, Daniel, and Nancy Heavin, dau. Ruth Heavin. John Gitts, surety—Aug. 28, 1790.

How, Edward, and Mary Burchett. A. Fannery, surety—(See Edward Howard)—Aug. 29, 1787.

Howell, Benjamin, and Elizabeth Kendall Daniel Howell, surety—Dec. 1, 1801.

Howell, David, and Jean Allen. Mar. by Richard Whitt—Oct. 17, 1785.

Howell, David, and Susanna Hilton. Mar. by Richard Whitt—. . . . ., 1789.

Howell, David, and Nancy Carter. John Carter, surety—May 25, 1820.

Howell, David, Jr., and Charlotte Pratt .Benjamin Howell, surety—Aug. 6, 1822.

Howell, James, and Catherine Russell. Mar. by Jacob Weddle—Nov. 15, 1829.

Howell, John, and Elizabeth Parkerson. Joshua and Dan'l Parkerson, surety—. . . . ., 1805.

Howell, John, and Sarah Rakes, dau. Henry Rakes, Benj. Howell, surety—Mar. 2, 1823.

Howell, John, and Oilett Harter, Henry and Dan'l Harter, surety—Jan. 23, 1822.

Howell, Joseph, and Jane Dunlop. Irving Dunlop, surety—Jan. 22, 1805.

Howell, Joshua, and Christina Mickabell. David Mickabell, surety—Nov. 3, 1800.

Howell, Mark, and Susannah Helton. Martin Weddle, surety—Dec. 22, 1814.

Howell, Thomas, and Sally Stapleton. William Stapleton, surety—Nov. 6, 1802.

Howell, Thomsa, and Delila Wilson. John Wilson, and Dan'l Howell, sur.—Jan. 5, 1820.

Howerton, James, and Malinda Vickers. Joseph Harman, surety—Aug. 25, 1830.

Howerton, John, and Christina Pate. John Howerton, Sr., and Jacob Pate, surety—Sept. 4, 1810.

Howerton, John, and Mariam Grimes, dau. Robin Grimes. Geo. Reed, surety—Mar 1, 1825.

Howerton, Obadiah, and Christina Hogan. John and Thomas Alley, sur.—Feb. 13, 1808.

Howerton, Thomas, and Margaret Williams. John Howerton, surety—July 5, 2803.

Howerton, William, and Susannah Whitt. Mar. by J. G. Cecil—May 27, 1823.

Howery, George, and Peggy Martin. Philip Martin, Sr., surety—Feb. 17, 1810.

Howery, Jacob, and Catey Hess, dau. Henry Hess, surety—July 27, 1814.

Howery, Philip, and Betsy Hest, dau. Henry Hest, surety—Feb. 5, 1812.

Hudson, Allen, (born Sept. 9, 1795), and Rocksey Ballard, dau. Louiss and Martha Ballard, surety—Sept. 23, 1816.

Hudson, Calvin, and Ann Collins, Mar. by Richard Buckingham—June 12, 1827.

Hudson, Reuben, and Martha Pannel. Wm. Moses, surety—July 27, 1826.

Huel, John, and Jane Lore. Michael Lore, surety—June 3, 1803.

Hueston, John, and. . . . . . . Dean, dau. Adam Dean, surety—Sept. 27, 1785.

Huff, Francis, Jr., and Betsy Charlton. Francis Charlton, surety—Sept. 2, 1816.

Huff, Henry (son of Philip), and Rachel Jackson, dau. Robt. Jackson. Alexander Wiley, sur.—June 5, 1811.

Huff, James, and Stacey Litterall. Thomas Litterall, surety—May 8, 1814.

Huff, acob, and Eleanor Millikin, dau. Jesse Millikin, surety—June 11, 1822.

Huff, John, and Elinor Corder. Mar. by Simon Cockerell—Oct. 6, 1782.

Huff, John, and Nancy Cox. Dan'l Peterman, surety—Mar. by P. Howard—July 13, 1818.

Huff, Joseph (see Hofe)

Huff, Samuel, and Anne Wiley, dau. Alexander Wiley, surety—May 2, 1804.

Huff, Samuel, and Peggy Weddle. John Weddle, surety—Feb. 1, 1816.

Huff, Samuel, and Nancy Aldridge, dau. William and Amy Aldridge—Sept. 4, 1813.

Huffman, John, and Chiren Happerch Bell, Robert Bell, surety—Nov. 24, 1818.

Huffman, William, and Lucinda Myers, dau. Peter Myers, surety—Sept. 27, 1830.

Hughs, James, and Polly Bowing. Mar. by Richard Buckingham—Feb. 24, 1826.

Hughes, John, and Rachel Lorton, dau. Thomas Lorton, surety—May 13, 1824.

Humphreys, Joseph, and Mary Lock. Daniel Graybill, surety—Nov. 3, 1805.

Hunsgate, William, and Margaret Hood, Richard Wills, surety—Dec. 5, 1797.

Hunter, Samuel, and Agnes Reyburn, dau. Joseph Reyburn, surety—Oct. 21, 1816.

Hunter, Thomas, and Elizabeth Smith. Mar. by J. G. Shrider—. . . . ., 1782.

Hunter, William, and Maria B. Smith. Mar. by Geo. Adams—July 9, 1829.

Hurford, David, and Martha Taber, dau. John Taber ,surety—Feb. 20, 1829.

Hurst, John, and Patty Menifee. James Menifee, surety—Apr. 5, 1791.

Hurt, John, and Lawsey West .Roland Hurt, and John West, surety—Nov. 30, 1824.

Hurt, William, and Elizabeth Goad, dau. Abram Goad, surety—Feb. 17, 1787.

Hutcheson, Augustus, and Nancy Fisher. Mar. by Richard Buckingham—May 30, 1830.

Hutcheson, Charles, and Jean Allicorn Lawrence Hutcheson, surety—Oct. 1788.

Hutcheson, James, and Martha Cannaday. John Draper, surety—Jan. 16, 1787.

Hutcheson, Samuel, and Isabella Anderson, dau. Joseph Anderson, sur.—July 6, 1804.

Hyde, Cyrus, and Margaret Ingles, dau. John Ingles, surety—Aug. 14, 1829.

Hylton (See Hilton)

Hylton, Archelius, Jr., and Levina Stegall. John Qusenberry, surety—Feb. 27, 1827.

Hylton, Briant, and Nancy Wade, dau. Hamilton Wade, surety—May 12, 1827.

Hylton, Burwell, and Mary Slusher, dau. Christopher Slusher, surety—Mar 4, 1823.

Hylton, Henry (born Dec. 6, 1808) (son of Archelius and Catherine Hylton), and Margaret Hylton. Hiriam H .Hylton, surety—May 7, 1830.

Hymes, Isaac, and Rhoda Fowler. Mar. by Richard Buckingham—Mar. 19, 1824.

–I–

Iddings, Henry, Jr., and Lydia Wilson, dau. Peter Wilson. Henry Wilson, Sr., surety—Sept. 25, 1812.

Iddings, William, and Sally Conner, dau. Jonathan Conner, surety—Oct 18, 1818.

Idle, Henry, and Catey Trump. Samuel Trump, surety—June 26, 1816.

Ingram, Aaron, and Mary Litner. Jonathan Ingram, surety—Nov. 4, 1795.

Ingram, Ebenezar, and Hannah Johnston. Comfort Bruister, surety—May 18, 1787.

Ingram, James, and Rhoda Menifree. Nimrod Menifree, surety—Dec. 17, 1785.

Ingram, John, and Rachel Davis. William Davis, sur. Mar. by E. Morgan—Dec 12, 1789.

Ingram, Nimrod, and Margaret Patton. Sam'l Shields, surety—Dec. 20. 1819.

Ingram, Nimrod, Jr., and Nancy Cecil, dau. Sam'l Cecil, Zacheriah Cecil, surety—Feb. 4, 1820.

Ingram, Samuel, and Elizabeth McDonald. Joseph McDonald, surety. Mar. by Richard Whitt—Dec. 9, 1785.

Ingram, William (son of James), and Mary Currin George Currin, sur—Feb. 18, 1799.

Irick, John, and Mary Holms. Jacob Barringer, surety—Dec. 25, 1806.

Irving, Alexander, and Jane Taylor, dau. Thomas Taylor: John Peatropp, surety—Sept 23, 1799.

Irving, James ,and Mary Oglesby, dau. David Oglesby, surety—Sept 28, 1785.

Irving, James, and Betsy Roberts. Thomas Roberts, surety—Feb. 16, 1802.

–J–

James, John, and Nancy Lockett. John Robinson, sur. Mar. by John Bell—Jan. 2, 1817.

James, William, and Elizabeth Wells, dau. Samuel Wells. Abram Gooding, surety—Apr. 8, 1786.

Jameson, Alexander, and Elizabeth Rose. Esau Rose, surety—Dec. 25, 1792.

Jenkins, John, and Christina Watkins, dau. Ebenezer Watkins, surety. Mar. by Edw. Morgan—Nov 5, 1822.

Jett, James, and Margaret Robinson, dau. William Robinson, Wm. Dill, surety. Mar. by Isaac Rentfro—Jan. 25, 1791.

Jett, Joseph, and Phebe Chrisman, dau. Abraham Chrisman, surety—Sept. 12, 1792.

Jett, Stephen, and Fannt Howerton. William Howerton, surety—Feb. 19, 1784.

Jewell, James, and Priscilla Ferrow, dau. Charles Ferrow, surety—Dec. 22, 1823.

Jewell, John, and Christina Hall, dau. Asa Hall, Sr., surety—May 21, 1823.

Jewell, William, and Mary Hall, dau. Asa Hall, Sr., surety—Jan. 25, 1825.

John Griffith and Liona Hambrick, dau. Joseph Hambrick. Redman Eakin, surety—Feb. 5, 1829.

Johnson (see Johnston)

Johnson, Abraham, and Rebeckah Reyburn, dau. James Reyburn. Boswell Johnson, surety—Sept. 7, 1810.

Johnson, David, and Jane Scaggs. James Johnson, surety—June 3, 1788.

Johnson, Ephrian, and Katey Daugherty. Mar. by Edw. Morgan—Apr. 23, 1792.

Johnson, James, and Rachel Copley, dau. Thomas Copley, surety—Jan. 28, 1786.

Johnson, James, and Betsy Honaker, dau. Abraham Honaker, John McTaylor, surety—Nov. 12, 1821.

Johnson, John, and Rebeckah McNealy. Thomas Barnett, surety—June 28, 1800.

Johnson, Richard, and Martha Cox, dau. John Cox, Wm. Cox, surety—July 29, 1786.

Johnson, Thomas, and Mary Reyburn. Epriam Johnson, surety—May 27, 1793.

Johnson, William, and Hannah Barnett. Isaiah Johnson, surety—July 8, 1798.

Johnston (see Johnson)

Johnston, Andrew, and Jane Henderson, dau. John Henderson, dec., Thomas Henderson, surety—Sept. 7, 1816.

Johnson, Benjamin, and Theadocia Willson, dau. Capt. Sam'l Willson: Capt. John Lucas, surety—Sept. 24, 1794.

Johnston, Boswell, and Patsy Barnett. Isaiah Johnsto,n surety—July 8, 1798.

Johnston, David, and Sarah Miller, widow. John Chapman, surety—Mar. 2, 1803.

Johnston, John and Rebecca Beckett. Josiah Terry, surety. Mar. by Robt. Jones—Dec. 3, 1792.

Johnston, John, and Sarah Blair. David Stephens, surety—Oct. 27, 1810.

Johnston, John, and Elinor Rentfro. Mar. by Richard Whitt—. . . . ., 1793.

Johnston, Reuben, and Sarah Johnston. David Johnston, surety—Jan. 27, 1802.

Johnston, William, and Anne Beckett, dau. Richard and Susannah Beckett. R. Wells, surety. Mar. by Randolph Hall—June 23, 1793

Jones, George, and Martha Christian. William Christian, and John Jones, surety—Feb. 17, 1818.

Jones, Joshua, and Mary Canterbury. Joseph Canterbury, surety—Jan. 16, 1797.

Jones, Moses, and Betsy Murphy. Abraham Deyerle, surety—Jan. 1, 1805.

Jones, Robert, (son of Henry), and Lucy Cox, dau. Carter Cox. John Wilson, surety—Nov. 23, 1811.

Jones, Thomas, and Nancy Quesenberry. Mar. by Randolph Hall—June 7, 1791.

Jones, William, and Jane Rhodes. Henry Rhodes, surety—Mar. 14, 1815.

Jordan, Michael, and Elizabeth Trollinger, dau. John Trollinger, sur.—Sept. 1, 1818.

Journell, Lewis, and Melvina Turner. Thomas Turner, surety—Jan. 23, 1826.

Journell, William, and Margaret Honaker. Mar. by Richard Buckingham—July 19, 1827.

–K–

Kean, Israel, and Betsy Robinson. Edw. Bane, surety—Feb. 13, 1796.

Keen, James, and Elizabeth Carper John Carper, surety—Sept. 7, 1802.

Kronk, Joseph, and Elizabeth Bingamon. Mar. by Peter Howard—Jan. 10, 1822.

Kegley, Lewis, and Barbara Ribble. Jas. Craig, sur. Mar. by Alex. Ross—Apr. 17, 1800.

Keister, Jacob, and Philipine Keister, dau. George Keister. Jas. Newell, surety—Feb. 6, 1787.

Keister, John, and Sally Martin. Philip Keister, and Barbara Martin, surety—Nov. 6, 1814.

Keister, Peter, and Catherine Shell. Mar. by Richard Buckingham—Mar. 9, 1826.

Keith, James, and Peggy Huff. Sam'l Keith, surety—Apr. 17, 1793.

Keith, John, and Mary Rodgers. Jacob Helms, surety—Dac. 27, 1825.

Keitley, James (son of Francis), and Lidia Sovine. Harmon Safford, sur.—May 2, 1809.

Kelsey, Daniel, and . . . . Cole. Ebeneazer Cole, and Thos. Kelsey, sur.—Feb. 7, 1810.

Kelsey, Elipheler, and Elizabeth Covey. Thos. Kelsey and Sam'l Covey, surety—July 24, 1811.

Kelsey, John S. and Rachel Helvey, dau. Frederick Helvey, surety—Nov. 25, 1826.

Kemplin, William, and Elizabeth Garlick, dau. Gasper Garlick. Robt. Stinson, surety—Nov. 2, 1788.

Kent, David, (son of John), and Rachel Barnett. Jacob Kent, and Joseph Barnett, sur. Mar. by R. Buckingham—Nov. 12, 1822.

Kent, Germanicas, and Arabella Amiss, orphan. John Wade, surety—June 6, 1827.

Kent, Hugh M G., and Ann C. Bratton. Thos. Bowyer, surety—July 3, 1822.

Kent, James R. and Mary Cloyd, dau. Gordon Clyod. John Taylor, surety—Mar. 30, 1818.

Kent, John, and Jane Cooper, dau. Jacob Cooper, surety—May 14, 1830.

Kent, Joseph, and Peggy McGavock, dau. James McGavock. Adam Trigg, sur.—Oct. 5, 1787.

Kent, Robert, and Elizabeth Craig. James Craig, surety—Apr. 14, 1819.

Kent, Robert, and Sarah McRonald (McDonald?), dau. Wm. McRonald. Rice Montague, surety—Aug. 7, 1828.

Kerr, John, (son of James), and Margaret Crow, widow. John Cox, sur.—Dec. 2, 1788.

Kesler, John, and Nancy Wall. Mar. by R. Buckingham—Jan. 10, 1828.

Keyton, David, and Mary Watterson, dau. Thomas Watterson, surety—May 14, 1830.

Kiffer, George, and Ruthy Caldwell. Mar. by John Bell—Oct. 7, 1818.

Kimball, John, and Elizabeth Lowry. Philip Smith, surety—Jan. 6, 1796.

Kinder, Jacob, and Elizabeth Stiffey, dau. Michael Stiffey. Duncan Gullison, surety—June 6, 1787.

King, Babel, and Nancy Shopshire. Mar. by Richard Buckingham—Apr. 22, 1827.

King, Charles W. and Anne (Nancy in Min. Return) Napper. Christian Snidow, surety—Feb. 6, 1798.

King, Henry, and Sarah Bartlett, dau. Reuben Bartlett, surety—Sept. 4, 1827.

King, James, nad Peggy Turner, dau. Richard Turner. Jacob Howry, sur. Mar. by John Bell—Oct. 23, 1817.

King, John, and Peggy Anderson. Jacob Anderson, surety—Jan. 6, 1796.

King, John, and Polly Brannon. Daniel Brannon, surety—Jan. 1, 1818.

King, John, Jr., and Sarah Becklehimer. Jacob Becklehimer, surety—Aug. 11, 1815.

King, John, and Nancy Wimmer. Jacob Wimmer, surety—Dec. 11, 1824.

King, John S. and Sally S. Vanleer ,dau. John Vanleer, Sr., Eldred Rawlins, surety. Mar. by Sam'l McNutt—Dec. 27, 1815.

King, John, and Saarh Addims. James Addims, surety—Dec. 4, 1799.

King, Merriday, and Rebekah Hammond. George Hammond, surety—Jan. 7, 1796.

King, William, (of Washington Co.), and Polly Trigg. Daniel Trigg, sur.—May 27, 1799.

King, William, and Frances Beckner. Mar. by Richard Buckingham—July 15, 1828.

King, Zacheriah, and Elizabeth Henderliter, dau. Mcihael Henderliter, surety—Dec. 27, 1824.

Kinser (Kinzer)

Kinser, Chrsitian, and Polly Surface. John Surface, surety—Dec. 26, 1826.

Kinser, George, and Catherine Wampler, dau. George Wampler. Sam'l Irvine, surety—Sept. 28, 1786.

Kinser, George, and Margaret Bane. James Bane, surety—Sept. 4, 1827.

Kinser, Jacob, and Rebecca Bane. George B. Bane, surety—Feb. 2, 1829.

Kinser, John, and Catey Brose, dau. John Brose, surety—June 4, 1814.

Kinser, Michael, and Ann Brose, dau. John Borse, surety—Nov. 13, -823.

Kinser, Philip, and Ann Robertson. John Robertson, surety—Nov. 20, 1816.

Kintzley, Jacob, and Hannah Price, dau. Alexadner Price, surety—Nov. 2, 1829.

Kintzley, John, and Hannah Hess. Henry Hess, surety—Aug. 31, 1829.

Kirby, James, and Rhoda Williams. David Stephens, surety—Mar. 25, 1799.

Kirby, James, and Mary Ann Fisher, dau. Adam Fisher, surety—July 16, 1822.

Kirby, John and Polly Craig. Benjamin Craig, surety—June 4, 1799.

Kirby, John, and Jane Addair. Thomas Addair, surety—July 13, 1795.

Kirby, Stephen, and Margaret Brown, dau. George Brown, surety—Aug. 16, 1828.

Kirby, William, and Lida Kimball. Philip Smith, surety—Jan. . ., 1797.

Kirk, Anthony, and Martha Claxton. Nimrod Kirk, surety. Mar. by Alexander Ross—Feb. 13, 1793.

Kirk, Benjamin, and Hezekiah Webb, dau. Julius Webb. Jos. Kirk, sur.—Jan. 17, 1788.

Kirk, David, and Sarah Callwell. Seth Callwell, surety—Aug. 13, 1796.

Kirk, James, and Mary Hudson, dau. Isaac Hudson, Sr., Isaac Hudson, Jr., sur.—Aug. 5, 1823.

Kirk, Joseph, and Martha Harless, dau. Martin Harless. Benj. Kirk, sur.—Jan. 18, 1788.

Kirk, Nimrod, and Mary Ann Hackett, dau. Thomas Hackett, surety—Sept. 2, 1794.

Kirk, Thomas, and Nancy Webb. Joseph Kirk, surety—Dec. 15, 1787.

Kirk, Thomas, and Susannah Caldwell. Mar. by Isaac Rentfro—May 3, 1798

Kitts, Peter, and Elizabeth Wyrick, dau. Nathaniel Wyrick. Paul Passenger, surety—Aug. 23, 1786.

Kittering, Randolph, and Bethana Aldrich. Leonard Aldrich, surety—July 31, 1821.

Kitterman, George, and Harriet Shelor, dau. George Shelor, surety—Apr. 21, 1827.

Kitterman, Philip, and Sally Sowers. George Sowers, surety. Mar. by Peter Howard—Jan .31, 1821.

Kronk, Jacob, and Polly Sowers. Henry Kronk, and Geo. Sowers, surety—Dec. 28, 1815.

Kyle,, William, and Celina Craig. James Craig, surety. Mar. by J. Bell—Feb. 2, 1817.

—L—

Lacy, James, and Sarah Chapman, dau. Richard Chapman, surety. Mar. by Richard Whitt—Sept. 11, 1786.

Lacy, William, and Hannah Evans. Mar. by Richard Whitt—June 18, 1787.

Laffell, Joshua, and Hannah Bacon. Mar. by Richard Whitt—. . . . ., 1794.

Lake, Daniel, and Elizabeth Garmon, dau. Jacob Garmon. Geo. Lake, sur.—Oct. 30, 1823.

Lamb, Jacob, and Catherine Hance, Milliton Adkins, sur. Mar. by Alex. Ross—Jan. 17, 1792.

Lamb, Jacob, and Sarah Bean. William Pain, surety—Sept. 3, 1800.

Lambert, Jeremiah, and Sarah Alsup, dau. John Alsup. Francis McGuire, surety—Jan. 29, 1788.

Lampee, William, and Catherine Epperley. Jacob Epperley, surety. Mar. by Peter Howard—Feb. 19, 1820.

Lancaster, William, and Margaret Wygal, dau. Sebastian Wygal, sur.—Aug. 27, 1823.

Landon, Samuel, and Anne Clifeall. . . . . . . Clifeall, surety—Feb. 6, 1799.

Landon, Samuel, and Zella Booth. Isaac Booth, surety—Aug. 2, 1815.

Lane, John, and Polly Snavel. Wm. McCoy, surety—Dec. 3, 1805.

Lang, Joseph and Elizabeth Snodgrass. Alexander Snodgrass, sur.—May 11, 1799.

Langdon, ... and Susannah Cifeall. Mar. by Alex Ross—Feb. 20, 1799.

Latimore, Christy, and Martha Glen, dau. John Glen, surety—Sept. 20, 1820.

Latimer, Robert, and Catherine Glen. John Glen, surety—Dec. 5, 1795.

Lawrence, ... and Elziabeth Huff, dau. Samuel Huff, surety—Sept. 5, 1820.

Lawrence, James P., and Sarah Epperley, dau. Jacob Epperley, surety—Sept. 7, 1829.

Lawrence, Nathaniel, and Nancy Gardner, dau. Robert Gardner, surety—May 2, 1811.

Lawrence, Thomas, and Catherine Kesler (Kester?). Jam. Simpkins, sur.—Mar. 21, 1824.

Lawrence, William, and Agnes Smith. Mar. by Richard Buckingham—Apr. 12, 1831.

Lawson, John, and Elizabeth Davidson. William Davidson, surety—Apr. 22, 1797.

Lawson, Robert, and Anne Goad. Abraham Goad, surety—Aug. 1, 1793.

Lawson, Thomas, and Jane Aul. John Aul, surety—July 9, 1805.

Lawson, Travis, and Maysee Simpkins. Thos. Mallett, surety—Jan. 4, 1788.

Lawson, William, and Nancy Baker. Travis Lawson, surety. Mar. by Richard Whitt—Apr. 22, 1797.

Lay, Thomas, and Mary Bevers. Mar. by Richard Buckingham—July 15, 1820.

Leastly, Robert, (see Lesley), and Elizabeth Compton. Mar. rec.—Apr. 5, 1787.

Lee, James, and Sally Kelly. Richard Collins ,surety—Oct. 15, 1827.

Lee, J . . . . . . and Susannah Lee. Edward Lee, surety—Dec 21, 1799.

Lee, Matthew, and Theadocius Pratt. Mar by Richard Buckingham—Dec. 23, 1829.

Lee, Robert, and Polly Lowry. Benjamin Collins, surety—Mar. 25, 1825.

Lee, Thomas, and Mary Beavers, dau. Moses Beavers, surety—July 12, 1820.

Lefaun, John, and Polly Bowen. Mar. by Jacob Pack—July 18, 1797.

Leitz, Leonard, and Juda Ghost, dau. Stopel Ghost, surety—May 14, 1788.

Lemmons, John, and Elizabeth Morgan. Richard Wells, and John Morgan, surety. Mar. by Peter Howard—July 7, 1807.

Lemon, Isaac, (son of Isaac, Sr.) and Sarah Young, dau. Joshua Young, surety—Feb. 12, 1827.

Lemon, Peter, and Lucy Helms, dau. John D. Helms, surety—Nov. 23, 1816.

Leonard, Robert, and Susannah Barnett, dau. William Barnett, surety—Oct. 4, 1830.

Lesley, John, and Martha Cloyd. Samuel Cloyd, surety—Dec. 3, 1789.

Lesley, Robert, and Elizabeth Compton. Samuel Cloyd, surety—May 21, 1787.

Lesley, William, and Elmira Hogan. Mar. by Richard Buckingham—Sept. 3, 1830.

Lesneur, Moseby, and Catherine Goodykoontz. Geo. Goodykoontz, sur.—Feb. 2, 1819.

Lessener, James, and Rebecca Goodykoontz. David Goodykoontz, sur.—Feb. 7, 1826.

Lester, Abner, (son of John and Rachel), and Rachel West, dau. Isaac West. Isaac, West, Jr., surety—Oct. 14, 1806.

Lester, Alexander, and Margaret Eley. Mar. by publication—Dec. 20, 1798.

Lester, Anderson, and Martha Fortune, dau. John Fortune, surety—July 6, 1829.

Lester, Harry, and Mary Morgan. Mar. by Richard Whitt—. . . . ., 1792.

Lester, Henline, and Elinor Simmons. Chas. Simmons, surety—May 31, 1819.

Lester, Hewlins, and Margaret Snyder. Mar. by Peter Howard—Feb. 20, 1823.

Lester, Henry, and Elizabeth Philips, dau. Thomas Philips, sur.—Jan. 12, 1828.

Lester, James, and Mary Elswick, dau. John Elswick, surety with William Lester—June 5, 1792.

Lester, James, and Cloaty Willson, dau. Benjamin Willson. Hiram Willson, surety—May 11, 1815.

Lester, John, and Polly Terry. Jonah Terry, surety —Oct. 5, 1802.

Lester, Pleasant, and Jessie Stafford. Mar. by publication—Sept. 13, 1798.

Lester, Samuel, and Nancy Cox, dau. Ambrose Cox. Thos. Bowyer, surety—Dec. 5, 1818.

Lester, Stephen, and Nancy Howerton. John Howerton, surety—Feb 12, 1810

Lester, William, (son of Abner and Martha), and Rebecca Scaggs, dau. Ruth Bishop, wife of John Bishop. Sam'l Sadler, sur.—Mar. 22, 1786.

Lester, William, and Rachel Scaggs. Mar. by Richard Whitt (see above)—. . . . ., 1786.

Lester, William, and Rebecca Simmons. John Lester, and Chas. Simmons, surety—Jan. 10, 1809.

Levers, William, and Catherine Peck. Mar. by Richard Whitt—Feb. 26, 1794.

Lewis, Charles, and Isabella Trigg, dau. Abram Trigg, surety—June 24, 1800.

Lewis, Charles, and Juliett Trigg. Mar. by Edw. Morgan (see above)—. . . . ., 1800.

Lewis, David, and Matilda Ross. Jesse Edwards, surety—Oct. 8, 1803.

Lewis, James, and Levina Langdon. Jas. Boucher, surety—Aug. 31, 1797.

Lewis, Jacob, and Mary Chrisman, dau. Adam Chrisman. Jonathan Chrisman, surety—Dec. 2, 1794.

Lewis, John, and Mary Preston. John Preston, surety. Mar. by Henry Ogburn—Nov. 7, 1793.

Lewis, Moses, and Charlotte Wright. John Wright, surety—Dec. 9, 1818.

Lewis, Peter Francis, and Sarah Toler. Chas. Taylor, sur. Mar. by Edw. Morgan—Nov. 7, 1817.

Lewis, Peroclus, and Lucinda Barnett. Jacob Kent, surety—Mar. 17, 1823.

Lewis, Samuel, and Frances Anderson Montague. Rice D. Montague, surety—Dec. 6, 1827.

Light, Elijah, and Susannah Wilson, dau. Peter Wilson, surety—Feb. 14, 1820.

Light, Henry, and Lydia Hathaway. David Iddings, surety—Nov. 6, 1792.

Light, Henry, and Nancy Kitchen. Sam'l Langdon, surety—June 6, 1816.

Light, James, and Sally D. Smith. James Smith, Sr., surety—Sept. 28, 1825.

Lilly, Thomas, and Rosanna Meadows. Edmund Lilly, surety—Aug. 22, 1798.

Lindsey, Taylor, and Elizabeth Auldridge, dau. Elizabeth Auldridge. Edmund Sumpter, surety—Apr. 8, 1820.

Lindsey (see Lynsey)

Link, Christian, and Catherine Scibold. John Scibold, surety—Apr. 27, 1818.

Link, David, and Elizabeth Holliday, dau. Levi Holliday, surety—Jan. 12, 1829.

Link, Gasper, and Mary Nozler, dau. Boston Nozler, surety—Sept. 22, 1787.

Link, Jacob, (son of Wliliam), and Jane Weddle, dau. Martin Weddle, sur.—June 6, 1826.

Linkous, Adam, and Nancy Long. Mar. by Richard Buckingham—Sept. 15, 1825.

Linkous, Adam, and Peggy Rader. John Rader, surety—. . . . . , 1816.

Linkous, Alexander, (son of Henry), and Polly Allen. Jas. Biggs, sur.—Mar. 11, 1799.

Linkous, Henry, and Peggy Shell. Mar. by R. Buckingham—Mar. 4, 1823.

Linkous, John, and Hannah Whitt, dau. Archibald Whitt, surety—Oct. 22 ,1827.

Whalen, surety—Dec. 7, 1807.

Litten, William, and Susannah Whalen. Patrick Whalen, surety—Dec. 7, 1807.

Litteral, George, and Elizabeth Logan. William Logan, surety—Aug. 2, 1803.

Litteral, Thomas, and Betsy Bartlett, dau. James Bartlett, surety—Dec. 1, 1807.

Litterall, William, and Mary Terry. Josiah Terry, surety—Apr. 12, 1814.

Litteral, William, and Martha Terry. Mar. by Peter Howard (same as above?)—Apr. . . . . , 1814.

Loan, Luke, and Lydia Bryant. Levi Vail, surety—Aug. 8, 1788.

Lockhart, William, and Jean Waggoner. John Craig, surety—June 15, 1786.

Logan, James, and Lucy Vanlear. John Vanlear, surety—Apr. 28, 1827.

Long, Adam, and Eliza Hoge, dau. John Hoge. Jonathan Brooks, surety—Sept. 16, 1823.

Long, Henry, and Lydia Bishop. Mar. by Richard Whitt—. . . . . , 1785.

Long, John, and Peggy Poff. Robt. Wiley, surety—June 3, 1823.

Long, John, and Dora Linkous, dau. Jacob Linkous, surety—Nov. 13, 1824.

Long, Ormand, and Sarah Reed. George Reed, surety—Nov. 8, 1808.

Long, Philip, and Rhoda Wygle, dau. Sabastian Wygle, surety—Dec. 20, 1820.

Loomis, Abraham, and Polly Elkins, dau. John Elkins, surety—Nov. 15, 1819.

Louthain, George, (son of John and Milly), and Polly Shell, dau. John Shell. Christian Shell, surety—May 31, 1808.

Louthain, John, and Elizabeth Cecil, dau. John Cecil. Wm. Cecil, sur.—Oct. 13, 1795.

Love, David, and Mary Draper, dau. John Draper. F. Preston, surety—July 9, 1784.

Lovern, Moses, and Maria Lunday. Mar. by R. Buckingham—Feb. 7, 1822.

Lower, Andrew, and Eva Pour. Harmon Lower, sur. Mar. by E. Morgan—Sept. 10, 1795.

Lower, Henry, and Christina Writesman. Harmon Lower, surety—Nov. 25, 1785.

Lower, John, and Prudence Grisom. Thos. Warden, surety—Sept. 5, 1805.

Lower, Peter, and Catey Rightman. Andrew Lower, surety—Feb. 9, 1790.

Lower, Peter, and Elizabeth Artrip, dau. Susannah Artrip, surety—Dec. 5, 1795.

Loyd, Levi, and Abby Hall (Hale?). Mar. by Richard Whitt—. . . . . , 1785.

Loyd, William, and Malinda Cummings, dau. Joseph Cummings, sur.—Jan. 8, 1825.

Lucas, Charles, and Esther Barnett. John Barnett, surety—July 9, 1806.

Lucas, Charles, and Nancy Haymaker. Samuel Haymaker, surety—Oct. 2, 1821.

Lucas, Charles, and Elizabeth Akers, dau. Jacob Akers, surety—Nov. 15, 1825.

Lucas, David, and Polly Hale. Parker Lucas, surety. —Nov. 7, 1809.

Lucas, Edward, and Elizabeth Hale. Thomas Hale, surety—Nov. 7, 1801.

Lucas, Esau, and Christine Maddin, dau. Margaret and Michael Maddin, sur. Mar. by Edw. Ross—Apr. 14, 1800.

Lucas, James, and Catherine Davis. Wm. Dougherty, surety—Sept. 3, 1799.

Lucas, Manuel, and Mima Adkins, dau. William Adkins, surety—Dec. 8, 1784.

Lucas, Randal, and Patience Williams. Parker Lucas, surety—Dec. 25, 1790.

Lucas, Samuel, Jr. and Margaret Rayburn. Sam'l Lucas, Sr., surety—Oct. 22, 1825.

Lucas, Thomas, and Hannah Hale. Thomas Hale, surety—Mar. 28, 1801.

Lucas, Thomas, and Mahala Harless, dau. Samuel Harless, surety—Nov. 20, 1828.

Lucas, William, and Elizabeth Price, dau. Michael Price. John Lucas (father of William), surety—Oct. 2, 1782.

Lucas, William, and Sarah Johnston. Parker Lucas, surety—Aug. 3, 1802.

Lucas, William, and Esther McKim Carson. Mar. by R. Buckingham—Mar. 20, 1826.

Lugar, George, and Margaret Echoles. William Kirby, surety—Aug. 19, 1800.

Lukens (see Lykins)

Lukens, Peter, and Susannah Huff, dau. Samuel Huff, surety—Sept. 19, 1799.

Lukens, Samuel, and Lydia Huff, sister of John Huff, surety—Nov. 1, 1816.

Lybrook, Henry, and Hannah Hankey. George Walters, surety—Oct. 4, 1796.

Lybrook, John, and Anne Chapman, dau. George Chapman, surety—Jan. 2, 1787.

Lykins, Jonas, and Lydia Willson, dau. John Willson, surety—Oct. 15, 1796.

Lykins, Mark, and Nancy Smith, dau. Jacob Smith, surety—Dec. 4, 1794.

Lykins, Philip, and Rhoda Light, dau. Henry Light, surety—Sept. 9, 1813.

Lykins, Philip, and Rhoda Wilson. Mar. by Peter Howard. (see above)—Sept. 9, 1813.
Lynsey, Moses, and Letty Breckenridge. John Alcorn, surety—Sept. 27, 1785.

—M—

Mabary, Henry, and Rebecca Berry. Mar. by Edw. Morgan—Apr. 5, 1799.
Maddox, John, and Nancy Watterson, dau. Thos. Watterson, surety—Apr. 20, 1817.
Maddox, Richard, and Sarah Venover. Enoch M. Vanover, surety—Jan. 28, 1823.
Madison, William, and Elizabeth Preston, dau. William Preston. Gabriel Madison of Botetourt Co., surety—Jan. 8, 1799.
Mallet, Noah, and Sarah Jones. Jas. Addair, surety—Nov. 1, 1788.
Mann, George, and Betsy Moyer. Boston Graves, surety—Aug. 25, 1790.
Mann, Henry, and Catherine Noah. Jacob Lamb, surety—Oct. 12, 1795.
Mann, John, and Fanny Williams. John Mann, Sr., surety—Apr. 6, 1791.
Mann, John, and Barbara Williams, dau. Michael Williams, surety—Oct. 23, 1793.
Mann, William, and Elizabeth Williams, dau. Michael Williams, sur.—Aug. 20, 1794.
Mairs, Abram, and Jeremima Oaks. William Morgan, surety—Apr. 8, 1789.
Mairs, Christopher, and Mary Fowler, step-dau. Sam'l Maire, sur.—. . . . ., 1788.
Mairs, Samuel, Jr., and Lydia Thompson. Sam'l Mairs, surety—Oct. 8, 1788.
Mairs, Samuel, and Mary Baker. Mar. by Richard Whitt—. . . . ., 1792.
Mares, Archibald, and Elizabeth McMullin. Wm. Barger, surety—Aug. 15, 1816.
Marcom, Archibald, and Nancy Kelly. Mar. by Alexander Ross—Aug. 25, 1800.
Marcom, Mager, and Rachel Kelly. Mar. by Alex. Ross—Sept. 28, 1800.
Markey, Leonard, and Mary Ribble. Christopher Ribble, surety—Apr. 20, 1800.
Marricle, Jacob, and Hannah Ruetrough. Sam'l Ruetrough, surety—Dec. 27, 1804.
Marrucle, William, and Peggy Weaver, dau. George Weaver. Jacob Marricle, surety—Jan. 31, 1804.
Marshall, David, and Susannah Abbott. Thomas Marshall, surety—Aug. 25, 1795.
Marshall, James, and Rachel Burton. Mar. by Alexander Ross—Apr. 29, 1800.
Marshall, John, and Elizabeth Flannory, dau. Styles Flannory. Thos. Marshall, surety—Mar. 21, 1793.
Marshall, Thomas, and Mary Abbott, dau. Matthew Abbott. Jacob Snido, surety—Sept. 20, 1794.
Martin, Abram, and Sally Martin. Thos. Reynolds, Surety—Dec. 23, 1795.
Martin, Andrew, and Catherine Surface. John Chapman, surety—Dec. 1, 1818.
Martin, Augustine, (son of James), and Elizabeth Peck, dau. Jacob Peck. John Anderson, surety—Mar. 19, 1822.
Martin, Barth H. and Mary Reynolds. William Reynolds, surety—Feb. 22, 1796.
Martin, Bartlett, and Lydia Hall. Thos. Beavers, sur. Mar. by Hezekiah Best—Sept. 8, 1828.
Martin, Christian, and Barbra Snidow, widow Robt. McGee, surety—July 17, 1793.
Martin, David, and Nancy Martin, Philip Martin, surety—Dec. 19, 1811.

Martin, George, and Rheuanna Miller. Philip Martin, surety—Nov. 4, 1806.
Martin, John, and Susannah Waggoner. James Curtus, surety—Nov. 3, 1802.
Martin, Joseph, (a doctor), and Matilda L. Charlton, dau. James Charlton. John Wade, surety—Dec. 8, 1812.
Martin, Philip, Jr., and Phebe Trollinger, dau. Henry Trollinger, dec. Philip Martin, Sr., surety—Sept. 8, 1807.
Martin, Robert, Jr., and Elizabeth Dickerson. Robt. Martin, Sr., sur.—Mar. 31, 1812.
Martin, William, and Betsy Keeplinger. Robert Martin, Sr., and John Keeplinger, surety. Mar. by Jonathan Hall—Mar. 11, 1812.
Masey, James, and Rebecca Goodykoontz. Mar. by John Turner—Mar. 16, 1826.
Masoner, John, and Maisie Runeon. Mar. by Edw. Morgan—July 5, 1789.
Matthews, Anderson, and Amy Heavin. John Heavin, surety—May 1, 1810.
Mavis, Sam'l, and Mary Baker, dau. Joshia Baker. Geo. Strambler, sur.—Dec. 8, 1792.
Maxwell, Joel, and Milly Brogin. James Smith, surety—Apr. 2, 1811.
Maxwell, John, and Patsey Vanlear. John Vanlear, surety—Nov. 4, 1810.
Maxwell, Samuel, and Martha Patton. John and Sampson Patton, sur.—Jan. 30, 1802.
Mayer, Gasper, and Nancy Mason. John Pennar, surety—Oct. 30, 1798.
Mayer (Moyer?) George, nad Elizabeth Barrister, Michael Price, sur.—June 25, 1785.
Mays, George, and Rhoda Peterson. Mar. by Richard Buckingham—May 22, 1824.
Mays, James, and Sarah Webb. Mar. by Alexander Ross—Apr. 22, 1800.
Mays, William, and Fanny Atkins. Moses Atkins, surety—Sept. 17, 1798.
McAleand, Samuel, and Bier Luster. Mar. by Jesse Jones—Mar. 11, 1830.
McAlexander, Alexander, (son of William), and Mary Booth, dau. Alijah Booth, surety—Jan. 16, 1815.
McBath, Robert, and Frances Dunlop, dau. Moses Dunlop, surety—Aug. 29, 1792.
McBeath, William, and Rachel Mcgee, dau. Robert McGee, surety—Jan. 29, 1794.
McCall, Edward J., and Martha E. McCall. Brookin Griffin, surety—Feb. 6, 1833.
McCauley, John, and Cynthia Robinson. John Grill, surety—Nov. 17, 1825.
McCalley, Thomas, and Nancy McCoy. William McCoy, surety—June 7, 1803.
McCaston, David, and Esther Shell, dau. George Shell, surety—Mar. 16, 1789.
McClanahan, David, and Mary Aul, dau. Benjamin Aul, dec. John Aul, sur.—July 28, 1804.
McClanahan, Elijah, and Agatha Lewis, dau. Col. Andrew Lewis. Wm. Taylor, surety. Mar. by Randolph Hall—Sept. 1, 1795.
McCluer, John S. and Ruth Heavin. John Heavin, surety. Mar. by Randolph Hall—Jan. 14, 1813.
McCombs, Emmanuel, and Elizabeth Ribble. Christopher Ribble, sur.—July 17, 1797.
McCombs, Samuel, and Elizabeth Rebel. Mar. by Alexander Ross (same as above?)—July .., 1797.
McComas, McCommas.
McCommas, David, and Cloe Bailey. George Chapman, surety—Jan. 11, 1787.
McCommas, Elisha, and Anne French, dau. Matt-

hew French. J. C. Snidow, sur.—July 3, 1792.

McCommas, Elijah, and Mary French .Mar. by Alex. Ross—Jan. 3, 1792.

McCommas, Jesse, and Judith Nappier. John Certain, sur. Mar. by Richard Whitt—Feb. 17, 1789.

McCommas, John, and Catherine Hatfield, dau. Andrew Hatfield, sur.—Feb. 21, 1786.

McCommas, Moses, and Lucy Napper. David McCommas, and Patrick Napper, sur. Mar. by Alex. Ross—Feb. 5, 1793.

McCommas, Stephen, and Sarah Certain. John Certain, surety—. . . . ., 1787.

McCommas, Thomas, and Mary Aldrich. David . . . ., surety—Feb. 12, 1799.

McCommas, William, and Dicey Chapman. Major McCommas, surety—May 20, 1797.

McoCmmas, William, and Jane McGee, dau. Robt. McGee, surety—Jan. 29, 1794.

McConley, Archibald, and Sarah Slusher. Henry Ribble, surety—Sept. 9, 1828.

McCorkle, James, and Paulina Cartey. John Harrison, surety—Jan. 1, 1812.

McCoy, Ezekield, and Nancy Davis. Jonathan Davis, Sr., surety—Apr. 7, 1798.

McCoy, Richard, (son of William), and Maria Sifford. Jno. Sifford, sur.—Feb. 6, 1827.

McCoy, Samuel, and Margaret Long. William McCoy, surety—Mar. 12, 1793.

McCoy, William, and Susannah Hunter, dau. Robt. Hunter. Abijah Atkins, sur. Mar. by Alex. Ross—Dec. 6, 1800.

McCoy, William, Jr., and Barbara Trollinger. Wm. McCoy, Sr., surety—Nov. 23, 1796.

McDonald, Bryant, and Rebecca Hoofman, dau. Jacob Hoofman, surety-·Aug. 2, 1813.

McDonald, Bryan, and Elizabeth McDonald. Mar. by Richard Buckingham—Aug. 17, 1824.

McDonald, Clemons, and Elizabeth Ross. John Hartsook, surety—Oct. 8, 1822.

McDonald, Edward, and Kezia Stephens. Joseph McDonald, surety—Sept. 9, 1786.

McDonald, Edward, and Susannah Ross. Frederick Holliday, surety—Feb. 23, 1820.

McDonald, Frederick and Sarah Halpain. William Halpain, surety—Feb. 21, 1805.

McDonald, George, and Ruth Owen. Elias Owen, surety—June 22, 1803.

McDonald, Hercules, and Margaret Brown, dau. George Brown. Joshua Brown, surety—Oct. 1, 1816.

McDonald, John, and Mary Williams. Mar. by Simon Cockrell—Oct. . . ., 1785.

McDonald, John, and Sarah Ann Vickers, dau. Phebe Vickers. Jacob Zoll, surety—July 30, 1830.

McDonald, John, and Elizabeth Kennaday, dau. John Kennaday. Jonas McDonald, surety — Aug. 25, 1794.

McDonald, Magness, and Tabitha Morris. Peter Riffe, sur. Mar. by Edw. Morgan—May 19, 1788.

McDonald, Richard, and Polly Ingram, dau. Aaron Ingram, surety—Jan. 15, 1822.

McDonald, Stephen, and Susanna Black, dau. John Black, surety—Sept. 3, 1823.

McDonald, Thomas, and Martha Saunders. Mar. by Edw. Morgan—July 29, 1824.

McDonald, William, and Ursula Hoff. John Preston, surety—Aug. 4, 1788.

McDonald, William, and Nancy Cassidy, dau. John Cassidy, surety—Apr. 1, 1823.

McDonald, William, (son of James), and Nancy McDonald. Jonas McDonald, surety — Sept. 20, 1823.

McDowell, James, and Sarah Preston. William Trigg, surety—Feb. 22, 1792.

McDowell, William (of Greenbrier Co.), and Polly Patton, dau. Henry Patton. Mar. by Edw. Morgan —Jan. 22, 1798.

McGuire, Neeley, and Esther Strutton. Geo. Peery, surety—Dec. 29, 1787.

McHenry, Andrew, and Martha Goodson, dau. Thomas Goodson. Chas. Taylor, surety—July 12, 1794.

McHenry, William, and Jean Staffar. Mar. by Alex. Ross—Oct. 3, 1800.

McKee, William, and Phebe Baker, widow. Mar. by Edw. Morgan—Apr. 11, 1788.

McKenzie, Isaac, and Jean Johnston. Murdock McKenzie, surety—Feb. 1, 1789.

McKenzie, Murdock, and Abigail Marrs—. . . . ., 1781.

McKenzie, Murdock, and Sarah Hurt, widow of John Hurt. Thos. H. Napper, surety—July 20, 1786.

McKinney, Francis, and Mary Hawley, dau. Peter Hawley. William Hawley, surety—Mar. 5, 1814.

McKinney, Joseph, and Elizabeth Copley, dau. Thomas Copley, sur.—Dec. 20, 1791.

McKinney, Lampkin, and Sarah Copley. James Heavins, surety—Aug. 7, 1787.

McLaughlin, James, and Rebecca Strobough. Henry Strobough, surety—May 3, 1804.

McMullin, George and Frances Philips, dau. Thomas Philips. James McMullin, surety. Mar. by Richard Buckingham—Mar. 18, 1825.

McMullin, James, and Jane McDonald, dau. William McDonald. Chas. Grissom, surety—Dec. 12, 1810.

McMullin, John, and Polly Crow. Mar. by R. Buckingham—June 17, 1824.

McNeeley, William, and Susannah Hall, dau. Jesse Hall, surety—Dec. 25, 1811.

McPeek, Ezekiel, and Asena (?) Egnew, dau. Sam'l Egnew. Elijah Hylton, sur.—Sept. 16, 1830.

McPherson, Jacob, and Phebe Sugar (Sengar?). George Sengar, surety—Feb. 8, 1803.

Meadows, James, and Elizabeth Gardner, dau. John and Amy Gardner, sur.—Oct. 11, 1803.

Mears, James, and Ann Shannon. William Mears, surety—Apr. 22, 1782.

Meeks, Anderson, and Rhoda Cook. Mar. by Richard Buckingham—Aug. 16, 1824.

Menifee, Jones, and Nancy Newell. Mar. by Simon Cockrell—Sept. 19, 1785.

Menifee, Nimrod, and Jemima Ingram, dau. Sam'l Ingram. Aaron Ingram, surety—Oct. 12, 1788.

Menifee, William, and Elizabeth Vardeman, dau. John Vardeman. William Vardeman, surety — Dec. 19, 1774.

Meredith, Hugh, and Catherine Bell. Mar. by J. G. Cecil—May 20, 1824.

Meridith, James, and Sally Bell. Mar. by J. G. Cecil—Oct. 10, 1827.

Middleton, Henry Hawkins, and Catherine Harles. Martin Harles, sur.—Feb. 7, 1789.

Mikesell, John, and Anna Reed. Humphrey Reed, surety—Aug. 30, 1813.

Millikin, Jesse, and Polly Scott. Robt. Goodson, surety—Oct. 30, 1827.

Miller, Abram, (son of James), and Mary Raines, dau. William Raines. David Whipple, surety—Aug. 3, 1808.

Miller, Adam, and Catherine Phipps. Jesse Evans surety—June 3, 1788.

Miller, Charles, and Mary Clevinger, dau. George

and Hannah Clevinger. Levi Clevinger, sur. – May 25, 1791.

Miller, Daniel, and Mary Francis, (marries her guardian). Sam'l Crandell, surety–Oct. 1, 1822.

Miller, David, and Mary Muirhead, dau. William Muirhead. Andrew Muirhead, sur. Mar. by J. G. Cecil–Oct. 8, 1727.

Miller, Henry, and Hannah Reynolds. Wm. Reynolds, surety–May 1, 1810.

Miller, Henry, and Susannah Reidinger, Sam'l Reidinger, sur. Mar. by Peter Howard–Feb. 15, 1820.

Miller, Jacob, and Sarah Chapman, dau. John Chapman, surety–Dec. 12, 1794.

Miller, James, and Rebecca Meurhead, dau. Andrew Muerhead. Wm. Meurhead, surety–Aug. 20, 1810.

Miller, James, and Hannah Wygle, dau. Sebastian Wygle. Jas. Wygle, sur.–Mar. 23, 1818.

Miller, James, and Nancy Kirby, Jas. Addair, sur.– Apr. 1, 1816.

Miller, John, and Sarah Carter. Mar. by register– Aug. 30, 1785.

Miller, John, and Mary Poor. John Certain, surety– Oct. 1, 1791.

Miller, John, and Margaret Whitt. Mar. by J. G. Cecil–Jan. 22, 1823.

Miller, Michael, and Tibitha Adkins. James Adkins, surety–June 3, 1795.

Miller, Philip, and Mary Burgess. Peter Blankenship, surety–June 13, 1793.

Miller, Samuel, and Catherine King. George King, surety–Aug. 21, 1830.

Miller, William, and Jeriah Adkins. Milliton Adkins, surety–Feb. 8, 1794.

Miller, William, and Mary Kirby, dau. John Kirby, Jas. Addair, sur.–June 2, 1818.

Minnick, Michael, and Margaret McCristie, dau. Ellin McCristie. Wm. Moses, surety–Jna. 31, 1821.

Mitchell, Alexander, and Elizabeth Woods, dau. Joseph Woods. George Carter, surety–Nov. 9, 1787.

Mitchell, James, and Sally Henderson. John Henderson, surety–July 2, 1799.

Mitchell, Thomas, and Mary Ann Barnett, widow. A. Deyerle, surety–Nov. 18, 1801.

Mitchem, Elijah D. and Elizabeth Smith. Mar. by Simon Cockrell–Nov. 9, 1782.

Mitchem, William, and Catherine Wertz. Mar. by Richard Buckingham–Feb. 1, 1830.

Montgomery, Alexander, and Margaret Nappier. Mar. by Alex. Ross–May 13, 1798.

Montgomery, Joseph, and Elizabeth Draper. John Mnotgomery, sur.–Sept. 30, 1786.

Montgomery, Robert, and Mary Love. James Love, surety–Sept. 10, 1784.

Moody, John, and Nancy Wallerman–Jan. 8, 1800.

Moody, John, and Elizabeth Guthrie. Levy Squires surety–Dec. 24, 1805.

Moore, John, and Mary Elizabeth Ramsey. Joseph Ramsey, surety–Oct. 15, 1786.

Moore, John (son of Joseph) and Sarah Bishop. Henry Bishop, surety–June 27, 1806.

Morgan ,Charles, and Sarah Hoziem. Archibald Tabor, surety–Aug. 20, 1792.

Morgan, Edward, and Susannah Cardner. Jas. Addair, surety–Mar. 3, 1791.

Morgan, Francis, and Nancy Ingram. Richard McDonald, surety–July 19, 1825.

Morgan, John, and Martha Kirby. David Willis, surety–Nov. 3, 1801.

Morgan, Wesley, and Martha Raines. William Raines, surety–Dec. 5, 1820.

Morgan, William, and Sarah Cunningham. John Wylie, surety–Dec. 25, 1788.

Morgan, William and Polly Songer. John Morgan, surety–Aug. 3, 1813.

Morris, Clayburn, and Phebe Hall. Jesse Hall, surety–Oct. 5, 1808.

Morris, Henry, and Polly Bowcher, dau. James Bowcher, surety–Jan. 23, 1804.

Morris, Powell, and Julanna Hix, dau. Mary Bennett. John Frith, sur.–Oct. 20, 1788.

Morris, William, and Nancy Evans. William Evans, surety–Sept. 21, 1796.

Morton, Benjamin, and Polly Willson. Jas. Kirby, surety–. . . . ., 1810.

Morton, Robert, and . . . . Brammer. Mar. by Michael Howry–. . . . ., 1829.

Moss, ..., and Fanny Adkins. Mar. by Publication–Sept. 20, 1798.

Mountz, David, and Margaret Clive. Peter Clive, and Jas. Addair, sur.–Apr. 5, 1809.

Muirhead, Andrew, Jr., and Martha Caddall (Crandall?). Sam'l Crandall, surety–Oct. 6, 1822.

Muirhead, Andrew, (son of William, of Wythe Co.) and Nancy Godby, dau. Francis Godby. George Godby, surety–May 12, 1825.

Muirhead, George, and Sarah Miller. Daniel Miller, surety–Sept. 1, 1812.

Muirhead, James (son of Andrew), and Mary Miller, dau. Daniel Miller. John Miller, sur.–Mar. 22, 1813.

Muirhead, Joseph, and Elizabeth Miller. Daniel Miller, and Eli Muirhead, surety–Aug. 20, 1807.

Mullins, James, and Margaret Walker. Joseph Baker, surety–Sept. 7, 1799.

Mullin, William, and Elizabeth Dillon. James Dillon, surety–June 16, 1794.

Mullin, William, and Nancy Wright, dau. John Wright, surety–Aug. 18, 1817.

Murray, Lawrence, and Elizabeth Smith. Mar. by Simon Cockrell–Nov. 9, 1782.

Murphy, George, and Nancy Thompson. Christopher Taylor, surety–Feb. 25, 1802.

Murphy, James, and Hannah Elder. John Adams, surety–Nov. 28, 1786.

Munsey, David, and Nancy Nicewonger, dau. Jacob Nicewonger. John Munsey, sur.–Sept. 12, 1793.

Munsey, Isaiah, and Hettie Guthrie, dau. Richard Guthrie. Wm. Guthrie, surety–Aug. 17, 1830.

Munsey, John, and Eliza Guthrie. Richard Guthria. Jno. Guthrie, sur.–Sept. 29, 1830.

Munsey, John, and Neomi Munsey. John Crow, sur–Mar. by E. Morgan–May 29, 1787.

Munsey, John (son of Luke), and Agatha Elliot, dau. Robt. Elliot. John Moore, sur.–Dec. 21, 1816.

Munsey, Jeremiah, and Elizabeth Sykes. Richard Guthrie, surety–May 2, 1799.

Munsey, Luke, and Olivia Wilson, dau. Peter Wilson, surety–July 18, 1826.

Munsey, Nathanial, and Betsy Vickers. Elias Vickers, surety–June 23, 1814.

Munsey, Samuel, and Anne Workman. Richard Corp, surety–June 16, 1788.

Munsey, Taniss, and Rhoda Simpkins. William Simpkins, surety–Nov. 12, 1804.

Mustard, James, and Sarah Munsey. Jeremiah Munsey, surety–Aug. 4, 1791.

Myers, David, and Ann Oatawalt. Mar. by Richard Buckingham–Dec. 11, 1821.

Myers, John, and Magdalin Rebel. Christopher Rebel, surety–Sept. 15, 1797.

Myers, John, and Dorcas Halbert. Thos. Akers, surety–Oct. 18, 1819.

Mynatt, George, and Mary Smith. Thomas Smith, surety—July 30, 1787.

—N—

Napper, Nappier
Nappier, Donald, and Rachel Gly. Mar. register — Jan.15, 1787.
Nappier, Edward, and Rachel Ely. Milliton Atkinson, surety—Dec. 28, 1786.
Nappier, Patrick, Jr. (son of Patrick, Sr.) and Fanny Brumfield. Garland Burgess, surety—June 9, 1788.
Napper, Renne, and Jean Eley. Mar. by Richard Whitt—Jan. .., 1787.
Nece, Valentine, and Peggy Fizer, dau. Peter Fizer, surety—Nov. 15, 1823.
Neel, Elias, and Nancy Patton, dau. Henry Patton. Thos. Patton, surety—Nov. 16, 1822.
Neil, Charles, and Elizabeth Dingus. William Dingus, sur. Mar. by Edw. Morgan—Jan. 14, 1793.
Neiswonger, David, and Judith Farley. Mar. by Alex. Ross—Apr. 24, 1800.
Nester, Jacob, and Catherine Goad, dau. Abram Goad, surety—June 2, 1789.
Nester, Jonathan, and Polly Eskue. Mar. by Richard Buckingham—Sept. 24, 1810.
Newell, James, Jr., and Susannah Trigg. Abram Trigg, surety—Oct. 8, 1807.
Newell, John, and Jane Bell ,dau. George Bell. Sam'l Thompson, surety—Oct. 1, 1777.
Newman, James, and Jane Madlin. J. Madlin, surety—Dec. 3, 1825.
Newmad, Walter, and Elizabeth Later. .... Evens, surety—Nov. 27, 1786.
Nicely, John, and Sarah Rineheart. Mar. by R. Buckingham—Sept. 10, 1823.
Nicholas, Samuel, and Margaret Moffett. Mar. by Simon Cockrell—Jan. 1, 1782.
Nida, David, and Mary Caldwell, dau. Stephen Caldwell, surety—Nov. 13, 1824.
Nida, Jacob, and Unice Caldwell. Henry Caldwell, surety—May 12 ,1825.
Nida, Peter, and Delila Caldwell, dau. Stephen Caldwell, surety—Sept. 25, 1824.
(All the above Nidas married by Richard Buckingham)
Noland, Martin, and Mary Welch. Mar. by J. G. Shrider— ...., 1782.
Norton, Edward, and Martha Hill. Andrew Kincannon, surety—Sept. 1, 1789.
Nozler, Boston, and Rosanna Smith, dau. Jacob Smith. Jas. Bane, sur.—Oct. 5, 1790.
Nozler, Boston, and Sarah Kirk, dau. John Kirk, Elijah Kirk, surety—Jan. 4, 1802.
Nozler, Conrad, and Sarah Pains. William Pains, surety—June 2, 1801.
Nozler, John, and Martha Snavell. John Snavell, surety—July 18, 1795.
Nuton, Richard, and Tabitta Jenkins. Abner Lester, surety—Nov. 17, 1787.

—O—

O'Donald, Fielding and Phebe Elswick, dau. Jonathan Elswick. Isaac O'Donald, sur. Mar. by R. Whitt—May 20, 1793.
O'Donald, Owen, and Darkey Gothrin. Jacob Bishop, surety—Feb. 20, 1796.
Odewalt, Abram, and Mary Pratt. Mar. by R. Buckingham—Aug. 26, 1828.

Odewalt, George, and Joanna Aul. Geo. Odewalt. Sr., surety—Aug. 16, 1813.
Odewalt, Jacob, and Mary Hendricks. Mar. by R. Buckingham—May 1, 1828.
Ogle, John William, and Sarah West, dau. Rosnock and Isaac West. Hercules Ogle, sur. Mar. by Randolph Hall—Oct. 3, 1791.
Olinger, Philip, and Elizabeth Shroder. Adam Schroder, and Jacob Olinger, surety—July 30, 1806.
Ott, Henry, and Polly Bethel, Jonas McDonald, surety—Aug. 22, 1815.
Otey, Jonathan, and Nancy Sowers, dau. Henry Sowers, surety—Aug. 7, 1827.
Otey, Samuel, and Jane Elliot, dau. Robt. Elliott, surety—May 2, 1823.
Outhouse, Peter, and Jeretta Evans. Mar. by Alex. Ross. James Evans, sur.—May 10, 1791.
Overstreet, James, and Sarah Caddell, dau. Sam'l Caddell, sur.—Feb. 10, 1817.
Owen, Daniel, and Mary Shoatman, dau. Michael Shoatman, surety—Oct. 9, 1793.
Owen, John, and Lydia Picklesimer. Jacob Picklesimer, surety—Mar. 14, 1803.
Owens, Robert, and Phebe Robinson. James Robinson, surety. Mar. by Isaac Rentfro—Oct. 7, 1795.

—P—

Page, Archilles, and Betsy Shoopman, dau. Nicholas Shoopman, sur.—Aug. 11, 1807.
Page, David, and Catherine Keith. Wm. Pepper, sur. Mar. by J. Burgess—Dec. 2, 1812.
Page, Robert, (son of John), and Jenny Smith. James Smith, surety—Mar. 16, 1807.
Page, Samuel, and Christina Peterman, dau. Michael Peterman, sur.—Jan. 6, 1816.
Painter, Matthias, and Catherine Harless. Mar. by J. G. Cecil—July 13, 1830.
Pain, David, and Ann Garrison ,dau. John Garrison, sur. Mar. by Alex Ross—Apr. 5, 1791.
Pain (see Yayne)
Pannell, William, and Elizabeth Reece, dau. George Reese, surety—Dec. 25, 1830.
Parkham, Ephrian, and Polly Sperry. Thomas Sperry, surety— ...., 1810.
Parkison, ... (son of Dan'l Parkison) and Sally Miller—Feb. 13, 1808.
Parks, David, and Isabella Vanlier. Jacob Vanlier, surety—Nov. 4, 1800.
Parmer, James, and Mary Reed, dau. George Reed. Geo. Reed, Jr., surety—Feb. 18, 1826.
Pate, (Payte) Adam, and Phebe Collingsworth—Sept. 29, 1807.
Pate, Anthony, and Nancy Shearlock (Shadrick?). John Bell, surety. Mar. by Richard Whitt—Feb. 1, 1787.
Pate, Daniel, (son of Jacob), and Laurs Jacobs. Roland Jacobs, sur.—July 6, 1799.
Pate, Daniel, and Jane Bell. John Bell, Sr., surety—Mar. 26, 1799.
Pate, George, and Sarah Watterson, dau. Agnes Watterson. Jeremiah Pate, and Joseph Watterson, surety—Sept. 5, 1810.
Pate, Henry, and Nancy Pate. Jeremiah and Jacob Pate. surety—Mar. 5, 1805.
Pate, Jeremiah, (son of Jacob), and Polly Howerton. John Howerton, surety—Jan. 6, 1810.
Pate, John, and Elizabeth Thomas— ...., 1781.
Pate, William, and Nancy Compton. Matthew Compton, surety—Sept. 2, 1797.
Pate, William, and Susannah Dobbisn. Jacob Pate,

and Thomas Dobbins, surety—Mar. 1, 1808.
Patrick, William, and Mary Bims (Burs?). Mundy Bims, surety—Sept. 25, 1798.
Patterson, James, and Mary Smith. Wm. Davidson, sur. Mar. by Edw. Morgan—Aug. 23, 1794.
Patterson, William and Agnes Patton. Thos. Godfred, surety—June 10, 1789.
Patterson, William and Rhoda Ingram. Aaron Ingram, surety—Dec. 16, 1815.
Patten, Henry, and Elizabeth Hickman, dau. Lawsend Hickman, sur.—Feb. 11, 1795.
Patton, John, and Barbary Rains. Mar. by Richard Whitt—May 3, 1793.
Patton, Samuel, and Nancy Draper. Mar. by Richard Whitt—. . . . ., 1792 .
Patton, Thomas, and Nelly Cecil. John Patton, sur.—May 15, 1797.
Patton, William, and Anne Fergus, dau. Francis Fergus, surety—July 5, 1815.
Payne, Joseph, and Mary Payne. John Simmons, sur. Mar. by Alex. Ross—June 23, 1796.
Pearis, George, and Betsy Howe, dau. Dan'l Howe, surety—Apr. 9, 1808.
Pearce (See Pierce)
Pearce, Thomas, and Susannah Thomson, dau. John Thomson. Mar. by Peter Howard—May 24, 1819.
Pearce, William, and Jane Smith. Sam'l Pearce, and Philip Smith, surety—Oct. 29, 1811.
Peatress, John, and Sally Sue Eller. Robt. Smithers, surety—June 14, 1797.
Peck, George, and Catey Wiser. Jacob Wiser, surety—Feb. 20, 1792.
Peck, George, and Barbary Sekletter. Henry Wiser, surety—Jan. 10, 1803.
Peck, John, and Elizabeth Snidow. Christopher Snidow, surety—Feb. 23, 1801.
Peck, Jacob and Eva Wiser, dau. Adam Wiser. David Love, sureyt—Jan. 5, 1796.
Peden, Benjamin, and Margaret Reed. Cornelius Reed, surety—Feb. 6, 1798.
Peden, Francis, and Zilphia Lawrence. John Lawrence, surety—Apr. 28, 1803.
Peery, James, (son of Thomas and Sarah), and Margaret Martin. Sam'l Martin, surety—Apr. 25, 1786.
Peery, John, and Deborah Kidd, dau. W. Kidd. John Perry, "the song man", sur.—Dec. 15, 1786.
Peery, John, and Catey Parkerson. David Parkerson, surety—Dec. 17, 1804.
Peary, John, and Elizabeth Chrisman, dau. Abraham Chrisman, surety—June 30, 1788.
Peary, Thomas, and Eli₇abeth Chrisman, dau. Abram Chrisman, surety—Jan. 31, 1796.
Pefley, Jacob, and Mary Myers, dau. Peter Myers, surety—Aug. 27, 1827.
Pendleton, John, nad Katey Flinn. Matthew Smith, surety—Aug. 8, 1805.
Penny, Horace, and Nancy Snavell. John Snavell, surety—Oct. 29, 1810.
Pepper, George P., and Ellen Henderson, dau. Jonas Henderson, surety—May 29, 1830.
Pepper, John, and Polly Robertson, dau. James and Margaret Robertson, surety—Nov. 9, 1807.
Pepper, John, Jr., and Nancy Martin. Reed Wright, surety—Aug. 29, 1817.
Pepper, Joseph, and Jenny Raeburn, dau. Joseph Raeburn, sur.—Nov. 4, 1800.
Pepper, Samuel, and Nancy Heavins, dau. William Heavins. John Heavnis, surety—July 31, 1821.
Pepper, William, and Jane Raeburn. James Pepper, surety—Oct. 10, 1791.
Pepper, William and Sally Pepper, dau. Samuel Pepper. John Pepper, surety—Jan. 5, 1804.

Perdue, Josiah, and Mary Sarah Belcher. Isom Belcher, surety—June 30, 1788.
Perdue, Jesse, and Neomi Potts. Mar. by Richard Whitt—Feb. 26, 1794.
Perdue, Zachreiah, and Mary Connely. Peter Blankenship, surety—June 5, 1792.
Perrin, Solomaon, and Sally Bott. Joel Bott, surety—Jan. 4, 1810.
Pershinger, Daniel, and Susanna M. . . . . Mar. by J. G. Shrdier—. . . . ., 1782.
Peters, John, and Sarah Clay. Mar. by Alexander Ross—July 4, 1800.
Peterman, Daniel, (son of Michael), and Susanna Lucas, dau. Capt. John Lucas, surety—Jan. 7, 1807.
Peterman, George A. and Mary Lucas, daus. John Lucas. Jacob Clore, sur.—Apr. 20, 1825.
Peterman, John, and Jane R. Hoge, dau. John Hoge. Wm. Thomas, surety—Jan. 12, 1825.
Peterson, Eli, and Mary Tornes (Tinnes?). John Smith, surety—June 6, 1785.
Peterson, Isaac, and Mary Ann Byrn. Thomas Vain, surety—Jan. 1, 1779.
Peterson, John Solomon, and Honour Burk. Joseph Russell, sur.—July 17, 1790.
Peterson, Morten, and Elizabeth Duffey (mother named Mary). George Walters, sur.—Mar. by Isaac Rentfro—Nov. 3, 1795.
Peterson, William, and Ruth Heavins, (mother named Ruth). Thos. Smtih, surety—Aug. 15, 1791.
Peyton, Garnett, and Agatha S. Madison. Mar. by Randolph Hall—July 8, 1802.
Peyton, John H. and Susanna Smith Madison. Garnett Peyton, surety—July 8, 1802.
Pfleger, David, (son of George), and Nancy Slusher, dau. Christopher Slusher, surety—June 2, 1808.
Pfleger, Isaac, and Sophiah Kitterman, dau. Daniel Kitterman, surety—Dec. 29, 1821.
Pfleiger, Joseph, and Nancy Boon, dau. John Boon, surety—May 1, 1817.
Pharis, John B. and Rachel Rupe. Henry Rupe, sruety—Oct. 20, 1823.
Philips, Hezekiah, and Catherine Lynbrook, dau. Catherine Lynbrook—Sept. 11, 1780.
Philips, Richard, (son of Tobias), and Catherine Goad, dau. James Goad, surety—Jan. 12, 1806.
Goad, dau. James Goad, surety—Jan. 12, 1806.
Philips, Stephen, and Pennis Alsby. Mar. by Jacob Weddle—Nov. 3, 1827.
Philips, Thomas, and Polly Goad. Jacob Nester, surety—Jan. 9, 1798.
Phillipe, Stoppel, and Elizabeth Hiffey. George Vaught, surety—Mar. 6, 1777.
Phillinger, Jacob, and Sally Jones. Mar. by Richard Buckingham—Nov. 19, 1822.
Phlummer, Samuel, and Elizabeth Peck. George Peck, Jr., surety—Feb. 15, 1793.
Pickle, Frederick, and Elizabeth Foutz (Lontz?). Michael and John Poff, surety—. . . . ., 1810.
Picklehimer, David, and Elizabeth Smith, dau. Edeneazer Smith, sur.—June 18, 1794.
Picklehimer, Isaac, and Rosanna Ferguson, dau. Robert Ferguson, sur.—Apr. 1, 1812.
Picklehimer, ... and Sally Rentfro, dau. Isaac Rentfro, surety—Jan. 23, 1793.
Pierson, John, and Genny Cooper, dau. John Cooper. Geo. Cooper, sur.—Feb. 11, 1817.
Pierce (see Pearce)
Pierce, Jonathan, and Polly Soloman. Francis Gardner, surety—Mar. 23, 1805.
Pierce, Samuel, and Mary Page, dau. John Page, surety—Feb. 3, 1801.

Redpath, Alanson, and Rebecca Kelsey, dau. Thomas Kelsey, surety—Oct. 26, 1822.

Pines, William, and Catherine Walker. Jacob Lamb, sur. Mar. by A. Ross—Nov. 6, 1792.

Pinks, Thomas, and Mary Hock (Hack?). Peter Hock (Hack?), surety—Nov. 3, 1803.

Plasters, Conrad, and Hannah Howell, dau. Benj. Howell, sur. Mar. by Robt. Jones—Nov. 17, 1795.

Plasters, Michael, and Delila Weddle. Martin Weddle, surety—Aug. 15, 1820.

Platt, Simon, and Rebecca Link, dau. Henry Link. Mar. by F. Hower, Lutheran—Nov. 20, 1830.

Plumby, John, nad Catherine Kayler. David Iddings, surety—Dec. 23, 1799.

Poage, Robert, and Mary Goodson, dau. Thomas Goodson, surety—Jan. 22, 1773.

Poff, Anthony, (son of Peter), and Sally Wilson, dau. Joshua Wilson, suerty—May 16, 1828.

Poff, Charles, and Rebecca Sowder. Michael Sowder, surety—Dec. 16, 1826.

Poff, George, (son of Charles), and Peggy Wilson. William Wilson, sur.—Feb. 7, 1810.

Poff, George, and Lucy Trail. Henry Trail, surety—Oct. 15, 1825.

Poff, Henry, and Sally Sowers, dau. Jacob Sowers, surety—Mar. 25, 1812.

Poff, John, and Ruth Wilson. Charles Trail, surety—May 23, 1826.

Poff, Michael, and Sally Whitenick. Peter Poff, surety—Mar. 24, 1821.

Poff, Samuel, and Sally Huff, dau. Sam'l Huff, dec., and of Catherine Hall. Peter Huff, and Jesse Hall, sur.—Aug. 31, 1829.

Polley, Thomas, (son of Joseph), and Abagail Munsey, dau. Skidmore Munsey, sur.—Oct. 16, 1785.

Polley, William, (son of Joseph), and Margaret Munsey, dau. Skidmore Munsey. Mar. by Chas. Cummings—Apr. 11, 1787.

Polley (Pauley) William, and Mary Harrison, dau. Thomas Harrison, sur.—Nov. 27, 1818.

Pailes, Jacob, and Christine Francis. David Price, surety—Feb. 6, 1783.

Potts, Joseph, and Nancy Crockett. Hugh Crockett, surety—Feb. 8, 1799.

Powers, Jonas, and Lucy Sperry, dau. Sam'l Sperry. Reuben Powers, sur.—Feb. 11, 1791.

Pratt, Josiah, and Eve Hatton. Date and minister gone—very old—1780-85.

Preston, John, and Peggy B. Preston. Thomas S. Preston, surety—Oct. 5, 1802.

Preston, Walter, and Letitia Robinson. David Robinson, surety—Mar. 3, 1809.

Priddy, Burk, and Catherine Zentmeyer. Daniel Zentmeyer, surety—Jan. 8, 1822.

Pridy, John, and Catherine ...., Mar. by J. G. Shrider—........, 1782.

Price, Adam, and Nancy Collins, dau. Hezekiah Collins, surety—Sept. 11, 1826.

Price, Alexander, Jr., and Elizabeth Keister. Michael Price, and Peter Keister, surety — June 12, 1809.

Price, Augustine, and Mary Trump, dau. Sam'l Trump, surety—Aug. 2, 1825.

Price, Christian, and Nancy Grissom, dau. Robert Grissom, surety—May 3, 1794.

Prcie, Christian, and Sannah Kipps. Henry D. Price and Michale Kipps, surety—Oct. 23, 1819.

Price, David, Jr., and Polly Martin. Christian Martin, surety—Dec. 23, 1805.

Price, David, and Polly Schell. Henry D. Price, surety—Feb. 2, 1812.

Price, Henry, and olly Surface, dau. George Surface. Henry D. Price, surety—June 4, 1814.

Price, Henry, Jr., and Anne Grissom, dau. Robert Grissom. Michael Price, surety—Dec. 2, 1791.

Price, Hiram, and Catherine Surface. George Surfase, surety—Feb. 3, 1824.

Price, Isaac, and Catherine Cromer. Mar. by Richard Buckingham—Feb. 2, 1826.

Price, Jacob, and Hannah Harloss. Philip Harloss, surety—Sept. 10, 1794.

Price, Joseph, and Delilah Scott, dau. Matthew Scott, dec. Chas. Devin ,surety—May 12, 1821.

Price, Lewis, and Margaret Hairless (Harless). Michael Price, and Philip Hairless, sur.—July 6, 1794.

Price ,William, and Margaret Hayes. Mar. register —Jan. 8, 1787.

Price, William, and Elizabeth McDonald. Jacob Price, surety—Mar. 14, 1814.

Price, William, and Catherine Long. Mar. by Richard Buckingham—June 12, 1827.

Prillaman, Jacob, and Lucy Snidow. Christian Snidow, surety—Mar. 2, 1803.

Process, Grief, and Margaret Huntsman. Peter Huntsman, surety—Oct. 23, 1821.

Pugh, William, and Susannah Wingate. Mar. by Peter Howard—Mar. 8, 1821.

—Q—

Quesenberry, Frederick, and Molly (Mary in Mar. return) Phillips, dau. Tabias Phillips. Moses Quesenberry, sur. Mar. by Robt. Jones—Dec. 20, 1793.

Quesenberry, George (son o fFrederick) and Sally Cox, dau. Frederick Holliday, surety—Feb. 15, 1820.

—R—

Ragan, Bartholomew, and Sarah Chrisman. Jacob Tearout, surety—May 12, 1825.

Rakes, Leir, and Olive Cochram. Reubem Rakes, surety—Feb. 3, 1826.

Ramsey, George, and Jane Patton. Thomas Patton, surety—Aug. 10, 1801.

Ratcliff, Francis, and Catherine Slushorn. Mar. by Peter Howard—Nov. 11, 1819.

Ratcliff, Jeremiah, and Sally Nester. Frederick Nester, and Nathan Ratcliff, surety—Sept. 6, 1803.

Ratcliff, Nathan ,and Polly Farmer. Min. return — name gone—........., 1781.

Ratcliff, Sumner, and Nancy Arnold. Mar. by J. G. Cecil—Aug. 14, 1827.

Rawton, Joseph, and Molly Payne, dau. Jeremiah Payte. Francis Preston, surety—Aug. 24, 1789.

Ray, Thomas, and Priscilla Gold. Zack Estill, surety —Nov. 13, 1793.

Raeburn (Reyburn, Raburn)

Raeburn, Henry, and Sarah Shanklin, dau. Robt. Shanklin. Sam'l Shanklin, surety—Jan. 24, 1794.

Raeburn, James, and Nancy Watterson. Sam'l Shanklin, surety—Feb. 29, 1792.

Raeburn, James, and Catherine Wysor. Henry Wysor, surety—Oct. 11, 1811.

Raeburn, John, Jr., and Elizabeth Shanklin. Sam'l Shanklin, surety—July 31, 1798.

Raeburn, William W. and ...... Raeburn. Sam'l Shanklin, surety—Nov. 25, 1804.

Raeburn, William W. and Elizabeth Barnett, dau. Jane Barnett. Joseph Barnett, surety — Apr. 28, 1827.

Rector, George, and Anne Atkinson. Milliton Atkinson, surety—Feb. 29, 1792.

Redpath, John, and Polly Cox. Mar. by Jonathan Hall—Mar. 30, 1814.

Reed, Andrew, and Elizabeth Irvine, dau. William Irvine, surety—Dec. 15, 1827.

Reed, Arthur, and Patsy Irvine. John Burgess, surety—Apr. 6, 1809.

Reed, Benjamin, and Sally Green. Mar. by Richard Buckingham—Nov. 20, 1823.

Reed, Emry, and Mariam Dulaney, dau. William uDlaney. Geo. Reed, surety—Jan. 27, 1826.

Reed, Elijah, and Bitey Altizer, dau. Emery Altizer—Nov. 25, 1829.

Reed, Ezra, and Lydia Light, dau. Henry Light, dec. Sam'l Light, sur.—Oct. 22, 1825.

Reed, George, and Nancy McGeorge. Ambrose Cox, surety—July 13, 1786.

Reed, George, and Sally Grimes. Robert Grimes, surety—Feb. 5, 1811.

Reed, George A., and Ann Altizer, dau. Emry Altizer—Dec. 31, 1829.

Reed, George, Jr., and Nancy Skaggs. Joseph Scaggs, surety—Nov. 6, 1821.

Reed, Griffith, (son of Peter), and Olive Reed, dau. George Reed, sur.—June 2, 1818.

Reed, Hiram, and Lucy Reed, dau. Humphrey Reed, Sr., surety—Jan. 18, 1815.

Reed, Humphrey, and Sally Reed, dau. Humphrey Reed, Sr., surety—Jan. 18, 1815.

Reed, Humphrey, and Nancy Reed, dau. George Reed, surety—Nov. 25, 1825.

Reed, James, and Susannah Smith. Bird Smith, surety—Nov. 28, 1803.

Reed, James, and Peggy Price ("Spinster"). Augustine Price, surety—Feb. 15, 1819.

Reed, John, and Rebeckah Conner. Andrew Conner, surety—Dec. 18, 1799.

Reed, Michael, and Delila Reed. Mar. by Peter Howard—Jan. 27, 1825.

Reed, Peter, (son of Spencer), and Nancy Duncan, dau. Blanch Duncan, sur.—Apr. 30, 1827.

Reed, Robert, and Darcus Patrick, dau. Hugh Patrick. Geo. Waggoner, surety. Mar. by Edw. Morgan—Nov. 14, 1787.

Reed, Samuel, and Hannah Long, dau. John Long, surety—Apr. 2, 1812.

Reed, Spencer, and Margaret Reed. Mar. by Peter Howrad—Feb. 1, 1825.

Reed, Stephen, and Margaret Long. John Long, and Cornelius Reed, surety—Feb. 24, 1806.

Reed, William, and Susannah Dickerson. Jacob Powers, surety—Aug. 26, 1818.

Reed, William, and Sally Dulaney, dau. William Dulaney. Griffith Reed ,sur. Mar. by Peter Howard—Nov. 6, 1821.

Reeder, Conrad, an dElizabeth Pry (Fry?). Daniel Etter, surety—July 3, 1788.

Reese, George, and Phebe Smithey. Robert Smithey, surety—Nov. 3, 1808.

Reynolds, John, and Susannah Taylor. William Pain, surety—July 7, 1801.

Reynolds, Pleasant C. and Elizabeth Piper. Henry Stobough, sur. Mar. by Edw. Morgan—May 3, 1797.

Ribble, Christopher, and Mary Keagley. Mar. by Edw. Morgan—Feb .., 1794.

Ribble, David, and Mary Surfus, dau. Martin and Catherine Surfus. Christopher Ribble, sur.—Jan. 2, 1811.

Ribble, George, and Sally Surfus, dau. Martin and Catherine Surfus. Christopher Ribble, sur.—Mar. 16, 1818.

Ribble, Jonas, (son of Christopher), and Mary Croy. Jacob and Adam Croy, surety—Aug. 30, 1806.

Ribble, Philip, and Susan Surface. Christopher Ribble, and Catherine Surface, usrety — Nov. 8, 1822.

Rice, John, and Molly Williams. Jeremiah Williams, surety—July 31, 1799.

Richards, Jeremiah, and Athra Childres. Jeremiah Childres, surety—Aug. 14, 1795.

Richards, Simon, and Rosanna Erwin. John Popijoy, sur. Mar. by R. Whitt—Nov. 17, 1792.

Richards, William and Susannah Lester. Christian Richards, and John Lester, surety—Mar. 4, 1806.

Richardson, Jonathan, and Mary Nester. Frederick Nestor, surety—Aug. 24, 1789.

Richardson, Risden, and Sally Jewell. Thomas Jewell, surety—Nov. 25, 1818.

Richardson, Thomas, and Nancy Quesenbury. George Quesenbury, surety. Mar. by Robt. Jones —June 25, 1790.

Ricker, Peter, and Susannah McGuire. Mathias Senter, surety—May 12, 1788.

Ridenger, George, and Catherine Sowers. Henry Sowers, surety. Mar. by Peter Howard—Mar. 8, 1820.

Riffe, John, and Elizabeth Clay. William Clay, surety—Nov. 20, 1820.

Riffe, Peter, and Mary Bingamon. John Bingamon, and Gabriel Rife, surety—July 10, 1784.

Rightmour (see Ritenour)

Rightmour, Joseph, and Mary Sharp. Mar. by Alex. Ross—June, 1797.

Reigor, Richard, and Jean Harper, (List of Min. returns)—.........., 1794.

Ring, Joseph, and Catherine Lewis, dau. Col. Andrew Lewis. Thomas Lewis, surety—Feb. 20, 1807.

Ritenour (also Ridenour), Henry, and Susannah Webb. John Ritenour, surety—Nov. 11, 1788.

Ritenour, John, and Mary Harless. Peter Harmon, surety—Aug. 11, 1791.

Ritenour, Joseph, and Mary Sharp. Geo. Sharp, and Peter Harmon, surety (see Rightmour)—June 29, 1797.

Roberts, Alexander, and Mary Philips. Henry Lester, surety—Oct. 14, 1828.

Roberts, Hiram, and Elizabeth Roberts, dau. Richardson Roberts. James Roberts, surety—Sept. 7, 1801.

Roberts, John and Jane Wert (West?). John Ogle, surety—May 1, 1798.

Roberts, Philip, and Elinore Silvers, dau. Aaron Silvers, surety—Nov. 26, 1822.

Roberts, Wright ,and Elizabeth Wright, dau. John Wright. G. Price, surety—Feb. 21, 1792.

Robertson, Alexander, (son of Catherine), and Patsey Woods, dau. James Woods. Robt. Woods, surety—Dec. 18, 1806.

Robertson, Archibald, and Jane K. Vanleer, dau. John Vanleer. John Robertson, surety—Aug. 10, 1814.

Robertson, David, and Nancy Mitchell. Archibald Mitchell, surety—June 10, 1800.

Robertson, John, and Milly Stratton, dau. John Stratton. Lindsey Crow, surety—Oct. 29, 1814.

Robins, James, and Hannah Jerrett. David Iddings, surety—Aug. 3, 1790.

Robinet, Daniel, and Mary McGarland. David Finney, surety—Jan. 24, 1786.

Robinet, Michael, and Mary Justine. Daniel Justine, surety—Aug. 22, 1786.

Robinson, Cyrus V. L., and Lucinda Charlton, dau.

James Charlton, sur. Mar. by Peter Howard—Oct. 17, 1815.

Robinson, James, and Margaret Aul, dau. William Aul, sruety. Mar. by Isaac Rentfro—Oct. 7, 1775.

Robinson, Peter, and Peggy Walker. Charles Walker, surety—Nov. 13, 1802.

Robinson, Samuel, and Betsy Surface, dau. Martin Surface, surety—May 9, 1814.

Robinson, William, and Nancy Chrisman. John Robinson, surety—Oct. 1, 1822.

Roble, Christopher (see Ribble) and Mary Keagly ("of age"). Paul Elling, surety—Feb. 14, 1794.

Roche, James, and Francis Collier. Wm. Garrison, surety—July 18, 1793.

Roach, James, and Fanny Coalter. Mar. by Robt. Jones (same as above?)........ .., 1794.

Rogers, Bowley, and Neomi Burk. Moses Winston, surety—Feb. 8, 1798.

Romine, Samuel, and Juda Pate. Zacheriah Pate, surety—Dec. 30, 1788.

Rominos, Zacheriah, and Margaret Stephens. Mar. by Richard Whitt—Feb. 9, 1807.

Ronald, William, and Mary Crow. Patrick Glyn, surety—Sept. 19, 1807.

Rose, David, (son of Gabriel), and Patsy Smith, dau. Peter Smith, sur.—Jan. 18, 1812.

Rose, David, and Sally Delong. Gabriel Rose, surety—Nov. 8, 1814.

Rose, Gabriel and Ariny Consoluant. Mar. by McEllany—Nov. 9, 1830.

Rose, Israel, and Elizabeth Stephens. Mar. by Richard Whitt—Feb. 9, 1785.

Rose, John, and Margaret Stephens. James Wilson, surety—July 11, 1790.

Rose, Joseph, and Katerene Bowsman. John Miveley, surety—Mar. 20, 1790.

Rose, Joseph, and Kurene Terry. Mar. by Peter Howard—Dec. 21, 1813.

Rose, Zacheriah, and Peggy Stephens. Richard Stephens, surety—Feb. 7, 1797.

Ross, Alexander, and Jane Drake, widow. Joseph Ross, surety—Sept. 7, 1803.

Ross, George, and Mary Black. John Black, surety—Aug. 3, 1813.

Ross, James, and Jeany Black. John Black, surety—Sept. 16, 1806.

Ross, Reuben, and Kitty Lawrence, dau. Thomas Lawrence, surety—Apr. 1, 1806.

Ross, Thomas, and Sarah Murray, dau. Archibald Murray. Hamilton Waddle, surety—Nov. 3, 1818.

Ross, William E. and Peggy Shanklin. Samuel Shanklin, surety—Sept. 9, 1827.

Rountree, Henry, and Wealthy Richardson, dau. Barnett Richardson. Richard Neighbors, sur. — Dec. 30, 1812.

Routrough, Henry, and Elizabeth Farris. John B. Farris, surety—Feb. 9, 1821.

Routroff, William and Betsy Sowers, dau. George Sowers. John Routroff, surety—Dec. 7, 1812.

Ruddle, John, and Neomi Pepper. William Pepper, surety—Oct. 25, 1819.

Rugar, Richard, and Jane Harper. Robt. Curris, Surety—Nov. 2, 1793.

Rumberg, Eli, and Polly Hall. Jesse Hall, surety—Mar. 2, 1815.

Runnion, Isaac, and Mary Smith. James Smith, surety—Oct. 10, 1797.

Runnion, James, and Sally Sheppard, dau. Frederick Sheppard, sur.—May 22, 1819.

Runnion, Richard, and Hannah Canaen. Isaac Runnion, surety—Apr. 7, 1798.

Runnion, Stephen, and Nancy Farmer, dau. Barnett Farmer, surety—Mar. 6, 1810.

Runyan, Joseph, and Nancy Jacobs, dau. Roley Jacobs. Richard Runyan, surety—July 24, 1809.

Runyan, Joseph, and Martha G. Redpath. James Redpath, surety—Mar. 8, 1824.

Rupe (Roupe, Roop)

Rupe, Henry, and Polly Thompson. Henry Roupe, and Elswick Thompson, surety—June 7, 1823.

Rupe, James, and Elizabeth Earl. Mar. by Richard Buckingham—July 23, 1830.

Rupe, Jacob, and Susannah Alley. Thomas Alley, sur. Mar. by Richard Buckingham—Apr. 15, 1815.

Roupe, John, and Betsy Thompson. Mar. by Jonathan Hall—Jan. 15, 1813.

Roupe, Thomas, and Betsy Thompson. Henry Roupe, and Elswick Thompson, surety—Jan. 8, 1813.

Rupe, William, (son of Henry), and Esther Akers, dau. Blackburn Akers—June 7, 1823.

Rutherford, John, and Sarah Moss, dau. Gideon Moss. Adam Hance, surety. Mar. by Richard Whitt—Apr. 1, 1794.

Rutledge, George, and Margaret Murray, dau. Archibald Murray. Capt. Holliday, surety—Jan. 16, 1821.

Rutledge, James and Martha Finley.

Rutter, George, and Peggy Carper. John Carper, surety—July 18, 1818.

Ryan, John, and Catherine Fizer, dau. John Fizer, surety—Nov. 23, 1819.

Ryley, John, and Nancy Evans. Richard Becknell, surety—Jan. 25, 1800.

—S—

Sabins, Thomas, and Priscilla Evans. Thomas Evans, surety—Sept. 5, 1808.

Saffell, Joshua, and Hannah Baker. Henry Patton, surety—Dec. 6, 1793.

Safon, John, and Polly Bowen. Hezekiah Akers, surety—July 18, 1797.

Sailor, Phillippe, and Margaret Hartless. Old. mar. list—May 10, 1797.

Sallust, James, and Margaret Shell. Adam Wall, surety—Nov. 4, 1780.

Sallust, James, Jr., and Sarah Heavin, dau. William Heavin, surety—June 1, 1824.

Sansum, John, and Elizabeth Davidson. Mar. by Isaac Rentfro—Apr. 24, 1797.

Sarles, Jacob, and Lydia Lorton. Old mar. list — Apr. 9, 1814.

Sarles, William, and Nancy Bell. John Bell, surety—Apr. 23, 1796.

Sarver, Henry, and Agnes Champ, dau. John Champ, surety—June 8, 1801.

Sarver, John, and Polly Harless. David Price, surety—Nov. 7, 1815.

Sarver, John, and Frances Overhelzer. Christian Overhelzer, sur.—July 31, 1821.

Sarver, Jasper, and Mary Wysong, dau. Joseph Wysong. James Dowdy, sur. Mar. by George Adams—July 30, 1829.

Sassane, Stephen, and Jane Jordon. Richard McDonald, surety—Mar. by J. G. Ceₙil—Deₙ. 15, 1820.

Saunders, Francis, and Elizabeth Thompson, dau. John Thompson, sur.—Mar. 20, 1820.

Saunders, John Thompson, and Susannah Crockett. Jas. Buchannon, sur.—Aug. 11, 1784.

Saunders, Micajah, and Rebeckah Thompson, dau. John Thompson, sur.—Sept. 18, 1824.

Saunders, oRbert, Jr., and Betsy Lorton, dau. Thomas Lorton, surety—Dec. 17, 1822.

Saunders, Samuel Major, and Mary Ingles, dau. John Ingles, surety—Sept. 14, 1814.

Saunders, Stephen, and Isabella Campbell. Robt. Saunders, surety. Mar. by Chas. Cummings — Feb. 4, 1782.

Saunders, William, (son of "Col. Stephen Saunders, of Wythe Co.") and Juliet Charlton, dau. James Charlton. Wm. B. Charlton, sur.—Oct. 13, 1820.

Savels, Jacob, and Lida Lorton. Mar. by Jonathan Hall—Mar. 30, 1814.

Saven (Saver?), William, and Rhoda Reed. Mar. by Peter Howard—Sept. 6, 1821.

Sawyers, James, and Polly Grayson, dau. Rachel Grayson, surety—June 27, 1814.

Saxton, Alidg, and Sara Mills. Mar. by Jeremiah Mastin—Apr. 26, 1791.

Sayers, William, and Sarah Smith, dau. Frederick Smith, Sayres Smith, surety—Sept. 23, 1796.

Scaggs, Isaac, and Nancy Goodwin. John Wylie sur. Mar. by R. Whitt—Oct. 30, 1787.

Scaggs, Jeremiah, and Hannah Lester. Zacheriah Scaggs, surety—Nov. 1, 1788.

Scaggs, Peter, and Marthy Clothon. Wm. Keister, sur. Mar. by R. Whitt—June 24, 1788.

Scaggs, William, and Maram Reed. Peter Reed, sur. Mar. by P. Howard—Feb. 4, 1825.

Scantland, Gideon, and Elizabeth Dougherty. William Dougherty, sur.—Sept. 30, 1800.

Scantland, Samuel, and Catherine Worley. James Worley, surety—Jan. 17, 1827.

Schripole, John, and Catherine Kinser, dau. Michael Kinser, surety—Aug. 1, 1817.

Schroyer, Christian, and Margaret Price. John Price, surety—Nov. 29, 1802.

Schurton, Isiah, and Jane Barnett. John Barnett, surety—May 2, 1797.

Scott, Jesse, and Dianna Taylor, dau. Catherine Kirby. Jas. Charlton, surety. Mar. by Jonathan Hall—Mar. 30, 1812.

Scott, John, and Mary Sykes. Richard Guthrie, sur. Mar. by Edw. Morgan—Aug. 23, 1796.

Scott, John, and Patsey Templeton. James Templeton, surety—Oct. 23, 1815.

Scott, John, and Catherine Heavener. Alex Waddle, sur.—Mar. 4, 1820.

Scott, Thomas, and Sally Shelor. Daniel Shelor, surety—Mar. 7, 1809.

Scruggs, James, and Mary Moss. Mar. by Richard Whitt—Feb. 26, 1794.

Scruggs, Thomas, and Polly Moss. Mar. by Richard Whitt—. . . . ., 1794.

Seaton, Moses, and Rosanna Martin, dau. George Martin. Wm. Calfee, sur.—Aug. 27, 1787.

Server, George, and Susannah Overholtz. Mar. by Richard Buckingham—May 27, 1823.

Servers, William, and Catherine Peck. Jacob Peck, surety—Oct. 14, 1793.

Sesener, Archibald, and Nancy McMullin. Mar. by George Adams—Aug. 22, 1826.

Sevine, Henry, and Catherine Thomas. Mar. by Richard Buckingham—Mar. 2, 1826.

Shanks, John, and Nancy Doosing, dau. F. Doosing. John Doosing, surety—Apr. 1, 1811.

Shanklin, Samuel, and Jane L. Reyburn. John Reyburn, surety—Dec. 21, 1807.

Shannon, John, (son of Thomas), and Jane Hudson, dau. Isaac Hudson. Thomas D. Hudson, surety—May 10, 1816.

Shannon, Jonathan, and Margaret Mares. Hugh Mares, surety—Sept. 23, 1779.

Shannon, Samuel, and Elizabeth Brown. James Mustard, surety—Nov. 3, 1801.

Shaupe, John, and Winnie Kirk. William Kirk, surety—Aug. 24, 1798.

Shaupe, William, and Elizabeth Williams. Edward William, surety—Nov. 29, 1798.

Shealor, John, and Nancy Howell. Daniel Howell, surety—Feb. 16, 1818.

Shearman, Jacob, and Catherine Anderson. Jacob Anderson, surety—July 30, 1804.

Shell, Christian, and Sarah Heavins. Howard Heavins, surety—Oct. 22, 1785.

Shell, Jacob, and Mary Birk, dau. Joseph Birk. Abram Trigg, surety—Dec. 28, 1787.

Shell, Jacob, Jr., and Catherine Price. Henry D. Price, surety—Sept. 9, 1811.

Shell, James, and Tabitha Lowthain. John Lowthain, surety—Oct. 16, 1810.

Shell, John, and Margaret Heavins. Jacob Shell, surety—Jan. 4, 1786.

Shell, John, and Hannah Lincass, dau. Henry Lincass, Sr., surety—Mar. 24, 1817.

Shell, John, and Elizabeth Shufflebarger. John Shufflebarger, sur.—Oct. 21, 1811.

Shell, William, and Sally Sallust. James Sallust, surety—Apr. 20, 1818.

Shefner, Charles, and Nancy Armbrister. George Armbrister, surety—Dec. 28, 1786.

Shelor, Daniel, Jr., and Joannah Goodson. Philip Williams, surety—Nov. 30, 1803.

Shelor, George, and Ruth Banks. Silas Graham, surety—Jan. 27, 1804.

Shelor, William, and Margaret Goodson. Thomas Goodson, surety—Sept. 6, 1803.

Shepherd, Abraham, and Barberry Mowry. Robert Craig, surety—Jan. 1, 1821.

Shepherd, Abram, and Peggy Ritter. John Ritter, surety—May 18, 1801.

Shepherd, Thomas, and Elizabeth Harless. Thomas Hall, surety—Oct. 3, 1797.

Shepperd, Thomas, and Susannah Ritter. John Ritter, surety—June 27, 1801.

Shepherd, William, and Nancy Anderson, dau. Jacob Anderson. Abram Shepherd, surety—Mar. 6, 1821.

Shields, Samuel, and Elizabeth Wade, dau. David Wade. Jos. King, surety—Feb. 2, 1811.

Shilling, Beuford, and Eliza Edwards. George Shilling, surety—Aug. 2, 1825.

Shilling, Jacob, and Elizabeth King, dau. John King, surety—June 3, 1817.

Shipman, John, and Sarah Smtih. John Peatrop, surety—Oct. 7, 1795.

Shively, Daniel, and Catherine Richards, dau. John Richards. Christian Richards, sur. Mar. by P. Howard—Jan. 13, 1818.

Shockley, Henry, and Mary Wiley. Alexander Wiley, surety—Mar. 5, 1816.

Shofflebarger, Abram, (son of John), and Polly Anderson. Jacob Anderson, surety—Feb. 14, 1808.

Shofflebarger, David, and Mary Carper, dau. John Carper. Jas. Wysor, surety—Jan. 23, 1826.

Shofflebarger, Elias, and Mary Wizer. Jacob Wizer, sur. Mar. by Edw. Morgan—Sept. 3, 1791.

Shofflebarger, Elias, and Nancy Carper, dau. John Carper. J. Anderson, surety—Dec. 4, 1824.

Shofflebarger, Isaac, (son of John), and Elizabeth Burton. Benjamin Burton, surety—Apr. 9, 1808.

Shufflebarger, Jacob, and Phebe Trollinger, dau. John Trollinger. Henry Trollinger, surety — Dec. 4, 1824.

Shofflebarger, Jacob, and Christina Beanard. Frederick Beanard, sur.—Mar. 19, 1816.

Shofflebarger, John, and Mary White. Jacob Sherman, surety—Nov. 4, 1817.

Shop, John, and Barcus Shiflets. Henry Lincust, surety—July 28, 1794.

Sifford, Henry, and Linna McCoy, dau. William McCoy. Nathan McCoy, sur.—Oct. 6, 1828.

Silvers, Isaac, and Nancy Wilson. Abram Silvers, and John Wilson, surety. Mar. by Richard Buckingham—Sept. 18, 1829.

Simmons, Cary, and Catey Slusher. Christopher Slusher, surety. Mar. by Peter Howard—Apr. 11, 1815.

Simmons, Thomas, and Delila Booth, dau. Abijah Booth. Chas. Simmons, surety—Dec. 30, 1817.

Simmons, William, and Rhoda Lester, dau. John Lester. Charles Simmons, surety—May 5, 1812.

Simpkins, Absolom, and Fanny Smith. Thomas Turpins, surety—Dec. 21, 1824.

Simpkins, Henry, (son of Robert), and Elizabeth Dunacn, dau. John Duncan, Jr. Mar. by Jacob Weddle—Oct. 2, 1827.

Simpkins, James, and Patience Butterfield. Asiel Snow, surety—Jan. 20, 1823.

Simpkins, John Thomas and Delilah Akers, dau. Austen Akers, surety—June 16, 1815.

Simpkins, John, (son of William), and Peggy Vickers. Elias Vickers, surety—Dec. 31, 1811.

Simpkins, John, and Polly Gibson. Levi Flannagan, surety—Oct. 15, 1810.

Smipkins, John, and Rebecca Elswick. Jonathan Elswick, surety—Feb. 3, 1800.

Simpkins, Lawrence, and Sally Watkins. James Simpkins, surety—Oct. 28, 1815.

Simpkins, Robert, and Elizabeth Dunkan. John Dunkan, and Robt. Simpkins, Sr., surety—Feb. 3, 1807.

Simpkins, Robert, Jr., and Sally Simpknis, widow of Lawrence Simpkins. Robt. Simpkins, Sr., surety—Apr. 17, 1829.

Simpkins, Solomon, and Patience Howard. William Howard, surety. Mar. by Peter Howard—Apr. 23, 1818.

Simpkins, William, and Catey Cooper. John Cooper, surety—June 22, 1815.

Simpson, George, and Nancy Trigg. Robert King, Jr., surety—May 5, 1806.

Simpson, James, and Jane Wallace, dau. William Wallace, surety—Oct. 4, 1830.

Simpson, John, and Elinor Jones. Wm. Heckman, surety—Mar. 4, 1800.

Simpson, John, and Nancy Blair. James Light, surety—Jan. 15, 1824.

Simpson, Randolph, and Margaret Peck. Henry Wysor, surety—May 4, 1826.

Simpson, William, and Nancy Hornbarger, dau. Peter Hornbarger. Allen Simpson, surety—May 12, 1808.

Skiles, Joseph, and Mary Anderson, widow of Geo. Anderson. Jacob Anderson, surety—Dec. 27, 1818.

Sloan, David, and Sarah Gibb. Robert Grimes, surety—Apr. 4, 1787.

Slusher, Jacob, and Tabitha Helton. Archelius Helton, surety—Nov. 3, 1818.

Slusher, Jacob, (son of John), and Mary Covey, dau. Sam'l Covey. John Glenn, surety—Oct. 27, 1829.

Slusher, Jacob, and Polly Boster. John Slusher, and Philip Boster, surety—Dec. 29, 1824.

Slusher, John, and Polly Oatwalt. George Oatwalt, surety—Oct. 11, 1815.

Slusher, John, and Elizabeth Smith. Jacob Hale, surety. Mar. by Richard Buckingham—Oct. 24, 1818.

Slusher, Peter, and Xelia White. Richard White, surety—Nov. 2, 1812.

Slusher, Solomon, and Milly Reed. William Reed, surety—June 2, 1816.

Slusher, Stephen and Charlotte Hylton, dau. Archelius Hylton, surety—Dec. 21, 1824.

Smallwood, Jeremiah, and Martha Warden, dau. Thomas Warden. R. Whitt, surety—Oct. 23, 1810.

Smith, Absolom, (son of Obediah), and Ann Lockhart. Wm. Currin, surety—Apr. 12, 1809.

Smith, Alexander, and Polly Gulliams. William Gulliams, and William Smith, surety—Nov. 18, 1815.

Smith, Byrd, and Rhoda Ingles. Wm. Strode, surety—Nov. 10, 1781.

Smith, Christopher, and Wilmounth W. Watkins, dau. Ebeneazer Watkins, surety—June 16, 1829.

Smith, David, and Freelove Pierce, dau. Richard Pierce. Matthew Smith, surety—Jan. 4, 1804.

Smith, Ezekiel, and Susan Dingus. Peter Dingus, surety—Feb. 2, 1821.

Smith, Francis, and Betsy Thompson. James Thompson, and Thomas Smith, surety—Aug. 26, 1808.

Smith, Harry, and Mary McTaylor. John McTaylor, surety—Aug. 15, 1804.

Smith, Henry, and Pheriby Wright. John Wright, surety—June 2, 1804.

Smith, Henry, and Catherine Harman ,dau. Jacob Harmon, surety—Apr. 1, 1817.

Smith, Henry, and Elizabeth Scott. James Sallis, surety—Feb. 14, 1789.

Smith, Henry, and Rebeca Picklesimer . . . . Picklesimer, surety—Mar. 3, 1825.

Smith, Hiram, and Polly Redpath. Mar. by Jonathan Hall—May 7, 1812.

Smith, James, and Asinatha Craig. Mar. by Jonathan Hall—June 25, 1812.

Smith, James, and Rhoda Bosters. Philip Bosters, surety—July 13, 1824.

Smith, James, and Matilda Akers, dau. Jonathan Akers, surety—Mar. 11, 1817.

Smith, James, (son of Matthew), and Mary Britt. Geo. Walters, surety—Nov. 3, 1794.

Smith, Jacob, and Mary Shokey. James Craig, surety—July 15, 1796.

Smith, Jacob, and Milly Watkins. Old Mar. list—Jan. 27, 1796.

Smith, Jacob, and Elizabeth Harless. Philip Harless, surety—Aug. 10, 1802.

Smith, Jacob, and Evey Shilling. George Shilling, surety—Jan. 11, 1815.

Smith, Jazeb H., and Elizabeth Light, dau. James Light. Humphrey Smith, surety—Oct. 5, 1819.

Smith, John, and Willmuth Hardin. James Craig, surety—Aug. 27, 1786.

Smith, John, and Christina Elkins. Archibald Elkins, surety—Feb. 19, 1788.

Smith, John, and Catherine Farmer. William Farmer, surety—Aug. 13, 1817.

Smith, John, and Hannah Mynatt, dau. Richard Mynatt. Eli Peterson, sur. Mar. by Richard Whitt —June 6, 1785.

Smith, John, and Polly Shilling. Mar. by Peter Howard—July 11, 1824.

Smith, John, and Nancy Lykins, dau. Jonas Lykins. Sam'l Lyikns, sur.—Dec. 5, 1825.

Smith, Joseph, and Elizabeth McCoy. Abram Trigg, surety. Mar. by Isaac Rentfro—Nov. 1, 1796.

Smith, Joseph, and Lydia Scott. Mar. by Richard Buckingham—Oct. 22, 1829.

Smith, Mahaton, and Mary Graham. Jonathan Graham, surety—Sept. 14, 1825.

Smith, Michael, and Beasy Hornbayer. Old Mar. list—Mar. 20, 1797.

Smith, Nimrod, and Sally Walker, dau. Charles Walker, surety. Mar. by Alex .Ross—Jan. 6, 1795.

Smith, Parrot, and Hannah Halfpane. Zecheriah Scott, surety—Sept. 3, 1804.

Smith, Parrot, and Rebecca Worley, dau. Thomas Worley. Nathan Worley, surety—Mar. 23, 1825.

Smith, Peter, and Elizabeth Manning. Wm. Durman, surety—Nov. 26, 1819.

Smith, Peter, (son of Peter), and Ruth Conner. William Conner, surety—Oct. 3, 1822.

Smith, Philip, and Mary Bones, dau. William and Mary Bones. John Peterson, surety—Apr. 7, 1798.

Smith, Richard, and Betsy Howry, dau. Jacob Howry. Abram Baler, sur.—Aug. 1, 1813.

Smith, Robert S., and Sarah T. O'Brian. Mar. by J. Jones—Feb. 3, 1831.

Smith, Samuel, and Elizabeth Broce, dau. John Broce. Jacob Smith, sur.—July 22, 1824.

Smith, Savine, and Sarah Scott. Mar. by Richard Buckingham—Mar. .., 1820.

Smith, Thomas, and Mary Peterson, dau. Matthias Peterson, surety—Feb. 25, 1794.

Smith, Thomas, and Elizabeth Peterson. Mar. by Richard Whitt—.......... .., 1794.

Smith, Thomas, and Lucy Litteral, dau. Thomas Litteral. Jas. Litteral, surety—Feb. 20, 1815.

Smith, Wells, and Jane Brose. Mar. by Richard Buckingham—Oct. 16, 1828.

Smith, William, and Elizabeth Neil, widow of Chas. Neil. J. Dilly, sur.—May 18, 1805.

Smith, William J., and Betsy Ditty. John Ditty, surety—Feb. 7, 1805.

Smith, William, and Franky Guilliams. William Guilliams, surety—Nov. 10, 1815.

Smith, William ,and Elizabeth Croy. David Smith, surety—Sept. 5, 1820.

Smith, William, (son of Henry), and Permelia Gunter, dau. John Gunter, surety. Mar. by J. G. Cecil—Mar. 2, 1824.

Smither, Jesse, and Jean Richards. William Hutson, surety—Sept. 25, 1790.

Snavely, John, and Betsy Zedocker, widow. Jacob Snavely, surety—Sept. 7, 1819.

Snavely, John, Jr., and Elizabeth Martin. John Snavely, Sr., surety—Dec. 28, 1816.

Snavely, Joseph, and Catey Carper. John Snavely, and John Carper, surety—June 16, 1815.

Snider, George, and Elizabeth Surface. Martin Surface, surety—May 9, 1814.

Snider, Michael, and Ann Davis. Mar. by John Burgess—June 1, 1811.

Snidow, Christian and Mary Burk. John Preston, surety—Aug. 24, 1784.

Snidow, Christine, and Celestine Goodrich, dau. J. B. Goodrich. Christian L. Snidow, surety—Feb. 14, 1828.

Snidow, Cornelius, and Sarah Smith, dau. John Smith. David Snidow, surety. Mar. by John Bell —May 28, 1818.

Snidow, Henry ,and Catey Litterall, dau. Thomas Litterall, surety—May 5, 1807.

Snidow, Jacob, and Clary Burk, dau. Thomas Burk. Wh. Burk, surety—Jan. 30, 1790

Snidow, Jacob, and Maria Hankey .Mar. by Alex. Ross—Feb. 13, 1798.

Snidow, Jacob, and Sally Picklesimer. Chas. Taylor, surety—Mar. 6, 1793.

Snidow, John, and Rachel Chapman. Christian Snidow, surety—May 27, 1805.

Snodgrass, Isaac, and Jane Thompson. George Thompson, Sr., Surety—June 10, 1807.

Snodgrass, James, and Rachel Cox, dau. John Cox, dec. David Cox, surety—Oct. 22, 1808.

Snodgrass, Robert, and Nancy Adams. Isaac Snodgrass, surety—Feb. 17, 1789.

Snow, Samuel, and Mary Smith. Russell A. Smith, surety. Mar. by Richard Buckingham—Jan. 1, 1828.

Snuffer, George, and Amy Margrave. Daivd Willis, surety—Jan. 5, 1793.

Snuffer, George, and Else Huff. Philip Huff, surety —July 3, 1798.

Songer, Christian, and Catherine Huckman. Garland Bruce, surety—Nov. 8, 1803.

Songer, Christian, (son of Jacob), and Mary Ann Hess, dau. Benjamin Hess, surety—June 1, 1829.

Songer, George, and Jenny Morgan. John Morgan, surety. Mar. by R. Whitt—Aug. 30, 1815.

Songer, Jacob, and Eve Anderson. Jacob Anderson, surety—Mar. 22, 1808.

Songer, Jacob, and Elizabeth Wilson. Jas. Kirby, surety—Dec. 5, 1815.

Souder (Sowder)

Souder, Daniel, and Martha Sumpter, dau. Edmund Sumpter, surety—Apr. 4, 1823.

Souder, Jacob, and Nancy Shoopman. Harold Silver, surety—Jan. 16, 1798.

Souder, John, and Elizabeth Cecil. Mar. by Edw. Morgan—Oct. 20, 1795.

Sowder, John, and Cynthia Craig, dau. George Craig, surety—Sept. 4, 1830.

Souder, Michael, and Elizabeth Beath. Jacob Souder, surety—July 2, 1802.

Souder, Michael, and Elizabeth McNeely. Wm. Trigg, sur.—Mar. 6, 1805.

Sowers, Anthony, and Caty Smiffer. John Smiffer, surety—Apr. 9, 1816.

Sowers, George, and Mary Spangler. Daniel Spangler, surety—Oct. 22, 1811.

Sowers, Jacob, and Nancy Price. Parker Sowers, surety—Sept. 6, 1803.

Sowers, Jacob, (son of George), and Polly Epperley, dau. Jacob Epperley. Solomon Epperley, sur. Mar. by P. Howard—Apr. 10, 1820.

Sowers, John, (son of George), and Sally Phares. Amariah Phares, sur.—Oct. 25, 1811.

Sowers, John, and Frances Overhelze. Mar. by R. Buckingham—Aug. 2, 1821.

Sowers, John, and Catherine Lester, dau. John Lester. Mar. by P. Howard—Apr. 10, 1824.

Sowers, Peter, and Elizabeth Artrup. Mar. by Isaac Rentfro—Dec. 7, 1795.

Sowers, William, and Rhoda Reed. Peter Reed, surety—Sept. 3, 1821.

Sovern, Moses ,and Maria Lunday. James Lunday, sruety—Feb. 5, 1822.

Spangler, Dan'l, and Betsy Sowers. Henry Sowers, and Daniel Spangler, Sr., surety—June 4, 1805.

Spangler, David, and Margaret Sowers. Henry Sowers, surety—Mar. by Peter Howard—Jan. 19, 1825.

Spangler, George, and Elizabeth Epperley. Daniel Spangler, and Jacob Epperley, surety—Apr. 1, 1806.

Spangler, John Jacob, and Margaret Groseclose. Mar. by J. G. Shrider—.......... .., 1782.

Spangler, Samuel, (son of Daniel), and Catherine

Helton, dau. Jesse Helton. A. Weddle, sur. Mar. by E. Morgan—June 2, 1798.

Spangler, William, and Mary Irvin, dau. William Irvin. A. Reed, surety—Sept. 8, 1828.

Spears, Samuel, and Phebe Skyles. R. Guthrie, sur. Mar. by E. Morgan—June 2, 1798.

Spencer, Nathaniel, and Anne Durgan. Barnabas Durgan, surety—May 28, 1804.

Sperry, Abijah, and Anne Hooger, dau. Randolph Hooger. Benjamin Sperry, surety—Dec. 24, 1792.

Sperry, Benjamin, and Winny Sperry, dau. Sam'l and Abigail Sperry—...... 5, 1773.

Sperry, Benjamin, and Winney Artrip, dau. Susannah Artrip. Jonas Powers, sur. Mar. by Isaac Rentfro—Feb. 6, 1793.

Sperry, Samuel, and Mary Burk. Benjamin Sperry, surety—Sept. 24, 1793.

Sperry, Thomas, Jr., and Sally Roberts. Thomas Sperry, Sr., surety—July 23, 1800.

Spraull, Heazlet, and Elizabeth Fergus. Francis Fergus, surety—Dec. 26, 1824.

Spurlock, Drury, and Olice Clur (Clor?). Old Mar. list—........, 1787-88.

Spurlock, George, and Elizabeth Clore. Mar. by Robt. Jones—June 7, 1791.

Stafford, Edmund, and Keziah Mitchell. James Stafford, and Sam'l Mitchell, surety—Jan. 25, 1811.

Stafford, George, and Catherine Fair. John Stafford, and Stephen Fair, surety—Oct. 6, 1797.

Stafford, James, and Bicey Cecil. Mar. by Landon Duncan—May 24, 1817.

Stafford, James, (son of Edward), and Betsy Cecil, dau. John Cecil. Ralph Stafford, surety—Mar. 29, 1817.

Stafford, James, and Sarah Hoge. John Hoge, surety—Dec. 19, 1803.

Stafford, Joseph, and Polly Taylor. Jaocb Taylor, surety—Aug. 26, 1799.

Stafford, Ralph, and Catey Taylor. Jacob Taylor, surety—Aug. 11, 1800.

Stafford, Thomas, and Catherine Williams. George Williams, sur.—Mar. 18, 1805.

Staffy, Michael, and C...... Snidow. William Snidow, surety—Aug. 22, 1789.

Stapleton, George, and Nancy Newton, dau. Richard Newton, sur.—Nov. 7, 1804.

Stapleton, Robert, and Anne Picklehimer. Jacob Picklehimer, sur.—May 21, 1803.

Stapleton, William, and Mary Brown. Sylvanus Brown, surety—Dec. 6, 1803.

Star, Lewis, and Catey Slusher. Christopher Slusher, surety—Feb. 7, 1821.

Stauger, Jacob, and Elizabeth Lincus. Henry Lincus, surety—Mar. 28, 1808.

Steagall, Maisten, and Fanny Dickenson. Dancy Steagall, surety—Sept. 3, 1793.

Stegleman, John (son of Philip), and Frankv Wade, dau. John Wade. Jas. Craig, surety – Dec. 14, 1811.

Stepe, Jacob, nad Rachel Martin. Thomas Martin, surety—Sept. 8, 1804.

Step, John, and Martha Evans, dau. Robert Evans. James Step, sur.—Aug. 3, 1789.

Stephens, David, and Elizabeth Watterson. Mar. by Isaac Rentfro—Jan. 17, 1793.

Stephens, Henry, and Mary Charlton. John R. Charlton, surety—Dec. 7, 1824.

Stephens, Isiah, and Anne Howard. Batian Howard, surety—Mar. 14, 1791.

Stephens, Isaac, and Anne Davisson. Wm. Britt, surety—Jan. 12, 1803.

Stephens, James, and Elizabeth Lawrence. John Lawrence, surety—Apr. 11, 1804.

Stephens, Jonathan, and Susannah Thompson. Ezekiel Boucher, surety—Dec. 3, 1793.

Stephen, Thomas B., and Mary Hendertiter. Michael Henderliter, sur.—Aug. 11, 1818.

Stevson, Jacob, and Rachel Mony. Mar. by Alexander Ross—Sept. 20, 1801.

Steurd, Daniel, and Jezebel Foster. Mor. by J. G. Shrider—........., 1782.

Stuart, Absolum, and Tabitha Clay. Mar. by publication—May 26, 1798.

Stewart, Absolum, and Susannah Smith. Isaac Smith, surety—July 20, 1793.

Stewart, James, and Nancy Burgess. Mar. by publication—June 7, 1798.

Stewart, James, and Catherine Surface. John Surface, surety—Aug. 18, 1828.

Stewart, Robert, and Mary Clay. Wm. Tracy, surety—June 25, 1788.

Stewart, Ralph, and Mary Clay. Mar. by Edw. Morgan. (same as above?)—June .., 1788.

Stewart, William, and Catey Harless. Philip Harless, usrety—Oct. 15, 1804.

Stinnett, Ralph and Mary Clay. Mar. register—June 15, 1788.

Stinson, Jacob, and Rachel Munsey, widow of Thomas Munsey. Richard Guthrie, surety—Aug. 12, 1801.

Stinson, Robert, Jr., and Catherine Wylie. Robt. Henson, surety—Dec. 25, 1789.

Stobough, Adam, and Peggy Trinkle, dau. Chrisotpher Trinkle—Mar. 12, 1806.

Stobough, Henry, and Rebecca Berry. Isaac Berry, surety—Apr. 24, 1799.

Stobough, Jacob, and Ursula Emmons. John Emmons, surety—Nov. 25, 1818.

Stobough, John, and Leah Carder. Dan'l Waggoner, sur. Mar. by Richard Whitt—Nov. 3, 1787.

Stone, David, and Sarah Gibb. Mar. by Dan'l Lockett ...., 1787.

Stover, John, and Jula Ann Stratton, dau. John H. Stratton. John R. Stratton, surety—Dec. 29, 1829.

Stowers, Travis, (son of Wm.), and Elizabeth Blankenship, dau. Peter—Feb. 29, 1799.

Strailey, Andrew, and Sophia Parson, widow. John Kirk, surety—July .., 1796.

Strailey, Andrew, and Sarah Watkins. William Caldwell, surety—Oct. 2, 1789.

Strailey, Jacob, and Martha French. Henry Sisler, surety—June 16, 1785.

Strailey, Jacob, and Sally Casey. Mar. by R. Buckingham—Oct. 5, 1826.

Straley, Joseph C., and Jane Brown, dau. Michael Brown, surety—Feb. 4, 1832.

Stramler, George, and Catherine Marrs, dau. Hugh Marrs. Sam'l Marrs, sur. Mar. by Richard Whitt —Dec. 9, 1793.

Strope, Peter, and Magdalin Venerick. Nicholas Looser, surety—Mar. 5, 1788.

Stukesberry, Robert, (son of Jacob), and Hannah Horton. Isaac Horton, surety—Dec. 23, 1806.

Stump, Michael, and Sarah Dials (?). George Hensley, surety—Aug. 20, 1788.

Sullins, James, (on of Richard), and Nancy Crow. Lindset Crow, sur.—Nov. 9, 1810.

Summers, David, and Nancy Hoge. James Hoge, surety—Sept. 5, 1797.

Summers, Christly, and Margaret Cruger. Michael Cruger, surety—May 23, 1786.

Summers, George, and Betsy Crum. Matthew Crum, surety—Feb. 26, 1788.

Summers, John, and Elizabeth Farmer. Thompson Farmer, surety—June 27, 1808.
Summers, Owen, and Sally Newton. Mar. by Peter Howard—Nov. 23, 1813.
Sumner, Isaiah, and Nancy Hungate. Mar. by Peter Howard—uJne 7, 1821.
Sumpter, John, and Elizabeth Turman, dau. Chas. Turman, sur. Mar. by Peter Howard—Nov. 4, 1818.
Surface, (Surfus, Surfuss)
Surface, Adam, and Aggy Price. Michael Price, surety—Aug. 27, 1811.
Surface, Andrew, and Elizabeth Harles. David Harles, and John Surfus, surety—Dec. 6, 1803.
Surface, George, Jr., and Catherine Haymaker. Philip Haymaker, sur.—July 22, 1828.
Surface, Jacob, and Catherine Gowens, dau. David Gowens, surety—Dec. 21, 1825.
Surface, Jacob, and Rebecca Haymaker. Philip Haymaker, surety—Aug. 29, 1827.
Surface, John, and Mary Garlic. John Garlic, surety—July 2, 1805.
Surface, John, and Eve Helms. John D. Helms, surety—Dec. 7, 1819.
Surface, John, and Elizabeth Bane. Mar. register—Apr. 21, 1828.
Surface, Michael, and Catherine Nozler. Philip Barringer, surety—July 20, 1792.
Surface, Michael, and Margaret Harless. George Surface, surety—Sept. 17, 1828.
Surface, Michael, and Hasnah Martin. James Martin, surety—Sept. 10, 1823.
Sutphin, Christopher, and Susannah Harman. Jacob Harman, surety—Feb. 10, 1823.
Sutphin, Christopher, and Susannah Harman. Jacob Harman, surety—Feb. 2, 1819.
Swan, Peter, and Sally Surface. Mar. by Rev. L. Harrison—Oct. 11, 1823.

—T—

Tabor, Archibald, and Nacny Shell. William Tabor, surety—Jan. 2, 1792.
Tabor, Jacob, and Elizabeth Shell. Wm. Pepper, and Archibald Tabor, surety—Apr. 2, 1816.
Tabor, Stephen, and Anna Bekelhymer, dau. Abraham and Mary Bekelhymer. John Tabor, surety—Aug. 12, 1811.
Tabor, William, and Sarah Harless. Jacob Tabor and John Price, sur.—Mar. 23, 1830.
Taylor, Adam, and Mary Claxton. Geo. Taylor, sur. Mar. by Alex. Ross—Apr. 5, 1791.
Taylor, Allen, and Rhoda Beal. Chas. Taylor, sur. Mar. by J. Bell—Jan. 28, 1818.
Taylor, Charles, and Polly Trigg. Joseph King, sur. Mar. by J. Hall—Aug. 2, 1798.
Taylor, Creed, and Mary Craig, dau. James Craig. Wm. Wade, surety—June 16, 1824.
Taylor, George, and Polly Sower. Henry Cartey, surety—Aug. 19, 1807.
Taylor, George, and Nancy Hornbarger. Jacob Hornbarger, surety—Oct. 19, 1803.
Taylor, George, and Jane Chrisman. Henry Kirkner, surety—June 7, 1818.
Taylor, Isaac, and Betsy Watterson, dau. Thomas Watterson, surety—Feb. 4, 1822.
Taylor, Jacob, and Nancy Webb, dau. William Webb, surety—Feb. 20, 1786.
Taylor, James, and Nancy Hewitt, dau. Patrick Hewitt, surety—Sept. 8, 1801.
Taylor, James, and Rachel Raeburn. John Raeburn, and Thomas Taylor, surety—Aug. 5, 1800.
Taylor, John, and Catherina Wilson. Mar. by Richard Whitt—........ .., 1791.
Taylor, John, and Betsy Chrisman, dau. Jonathan Chrisman. George Taylor, sur. Mar. by John Bell —Jan. 29, 1818.
Taylor, John, and Lucy Shanklin, dau. Samuel Shanklin, surety—Feb. 7, 1825.
Taylor, Philip, and Margaret Harless. David Harless, surety—May 9, 1796.
Tayqlor, Robert P., and Margaret P. Parker, dau. Robert L. Parker, sur.—Mar. 2, 1830.
Taylor, William, and Mary Watterson, dau. Henry (sur.) and Agnes Watterson—Sept. 5, 1790.
Tatum, Bartlett, and Susannah Becknel. Michael Fisher, surety—May 31, 1826.
Tawney, Daniel, and Elizabeth Price. David Price, surety—Dec. 6, 1796.
Tawney, George, and Elizabeth Godbey, widow. Jacob Olinger, surety—Dec. 19, 1806.
Tawney, John, and Polly Price. James Steward, surety—May 7, 1799.
Tawnskley, Joseph, and Lydia Bartlett, dau. Gardner and Elinor Bartlett. John Wood, surety—Apr. 5, 1807.
Teaney, Samuel, and Joanna Dobbins. John Dobbins, surety—Apr. 16, 1823.
Tearout, Charles, Jr., and Mary Todd (from Henrico Co.), Andrew Todd, guardian of Mary, surety—July 18, 1825.
Templeton, Thomas, and Elizabeth Scott. Thomas Scott, surety—Mar. 5, 1816.
Terry, Aaron (mother, Mary), and Elizabeth Winter. John Winter, sur.—Nov. 21, 1804.
Terry, Elijah, and Mary Right. Jonathan Graham, sur. Mar. by Randolph Hall—Oct. 9, 1795.
Terry, Jasper, and Sally Fuller. Matthew Fuller, surety—Aug. .., 1797.
Terry, John, and Clarissa Gray, dau. Joseph Gray, Jr., surety—June 6, 1826.
Terry, Josiah (son of Josiah and Mary), and Ann Sowdre, dau. Jacob and Anny Sowder—Dec. 10, 1814.
Terry, Silas, and Catey Rutrouth. John McHenry, surety—Apr. 2, 1801.
Terry, William, and Jane Winters. Josper Terry, and John Winters, sur.—Nov. 26, 1804.
Thomas, Charles, and Elizabeth Barnett, dau. David Barnett, surety—Jan. 25, 1813.
Thomas, Jonathan, and Patritia Brown, dau. William Brown. James Newell, surety—Feb. 6, 1787.
Thomas, John, and Phebe Blankenship. Clabourne Blankenship, sur.—Feb. 7, 1791.
Thomas, John, and Susan Croy. Adam Croy, surety —Sept. 25, 1821.
Thomas, William, and Rachel M. Hoage, dau. John Hoge, sur. Mar. by S. H. McNutt—July 6, 1819.
Thomas, William, and Lucretia Howe. William Howe, surety—Dec. 7, 1829.
Thompson, Andrew, and Rebecca McCorkle, dau. Martha McCorkle. Wm. Adams, surety—May 11, 1801.
Thompson, Andrew, and Henrietta Simpkins, dau. James Simpkins, surety—Nov. 22, 1824.
Thompson, Archibald, and Nancy Langdon. Sam Langdon, surety—Sept. 22, 1795.
Thompson, Archbiald, adn Rachel Reed. Mar. by Peter Howard—Mar. 16, 1825.
Thompson, Clairborne, (son of Elswick), and Amy Willson, dau. Benjamin Willson. Mar. by Peter Howard—Mar. 16, 1818.
Thompson, David, and Nancy Coadie, dau. William Coadie, surety—Aug. 17, 1785.
Thompson, Elisha, and Mary Dickerson, dau. Leonard Dickerson, surety—Dec. 12, 1815.

Thompson, Elisha, and Nancy Helton, dau. Samuel Helton, surety–July 10, 1820.

Thompson, Elswick, and Patsey Acers, dau. Blackburn Acers, surety–Sept. 28, 1788.

Thompson, George, Jr., and Elizabeth Willso. George Thompson, Sr., sur.–Mar. 19, 1799.

Thompson, Henry, and Peggy Duncan. Mar. by Randolph Hall–May 12, 1813.

Thompson, Israel, and Mary Vanull, dau. John Vanull. Archibald Thompson, surety – Jan. 15, 1795.

Thompson, James, and Nancy Dickerson, dau. Elijah Dickerson. James Thompson, Sr., surety – Feb. 7, 1797.

Thompson, James, and Phebe Pierce. Richard Pierce, surety–Dec. 21, 1810.

Thompson, James, and Mary Low. John Cloyd, surety–July 23, 1786.

Thompson, John, and Jane Shelladay, dau. George Shelladay, surety–Nov. 19, 1779.

Thompson, John, and Esther Langdon. David Stephens, sur. Mar. by R. Whitt–Jan. 7, 1791.

Thompson, John, and Rebecca Foster. Geo. Chapman, surety–Sept. 25, 1786.

Thompson, John, and Catherine Peters, dau. John Peters, surety–Dec. 29, 1792.

Thompson, John, (son of James), and Nancy Buchannon, dau. Jeremiah Buchannon, surety–Jan. 2, 1804.

Thompson, Joshua, and Elizabeth Carty, dau. H. Carty. Andrew Thompson, surety–Mar. 6, 1827.

Thompson, Joshua (son of Elswick), and Elizabeth Duncan, dau. Thomas Duncan, surety–Mar. 6, 1827.

Thompson, Larkin, and Elizabeth Crow. Geo. Thompson, and Lindsey Crow, sur.–Nov. 9, 1803.

Thompson, Meriday, and Elizabeth Landon, dau. Sam'l Landon. George Thompson, surety–Jan. 16, 1794.

Thompson, Patton, and Judy Farley. William Hickman, surety. Mar. by Edw. Morgan–Feb. 20, 1797.

Thompson, Randolph, and Catherine C. Carty. Sam'l Lucas, surety–June 7, 1825.

Thompson, Sam'l, and Susan Grayson, dau. John Grayson, sur.–Jan. 3, 1775.

Thompson, Samuel, and Nancy Lucas. John Lucas, surety. Mar. by Edw. Morgan–Aug. 27, 1797.

Thompson, William, and Martha Milam. Thomas Parson, surety–Apr. 27, 1793.

Thompson, William, and Nancy Grimes, dau. Robert Grimes, surety. Mar. by Peter Howard–Dec. 27, 1823.

Thompson, William, and Polly Shelor. Jacob Shelor, surety–May 22, 1819.

Thockey, John, and Betsy Simson. Allen Simson, surety–Apr. 28, 1802.

Thorn, Loraine, and Jane Davis. William Davis, surety–Aug. 20, 1821.

Thorn, William B., and Eliza Patton, dau. Henry Patton, surety–Sept. 14, 1830.

Thornhill, William, and Catherine Reader. Thomas Scott, surety–Aug. 1, 1822.

Thrash, John, and Liddy Cole. Old Marriage list– . . . . 1786-1790.

Thrash, William, and Betsy Barnett. Geo. Brown, Jr., surety–Jan. 25, 1802.

Thrash, William, and Catey Lester. Stephen Lester, surety. Mar. by Peter Howard–Jan. 21, 1815.

Tice, Abraham, and Polly Sumpter, dau. George Sumpter, dec. Abraham Sumpter, surety–June 28, 1808.

Tice, John, and Betsy Sowers. Jacob Sowers, surety–Oct. 10, 1808.

Tice, Manassa, and Cynthia Dodd, dau. Benjamin Dodd, surety–Nov. 24, 1828.

Tiffney, James, and Patsey Hance, dau. Adam Hance, sur. Mar. by Edw. Morgan–Feb. 28, 1818.

Tillet, James, and Susan Buck. Martin Buck, surety. Mar. by Sam'l Kennerly–Aug. 28, 1822.

Tillet, Michael, and Catherine Overhalser, dau. Christian Overhalser, surety–Oct. 18, 1827.

Todd, Andrew, and Mary Pepper. John Pepper, surety–Nov. 29, 1824.

Toney, Adam, and Eliza Hoge. Mar. by E. Morgan–Oct. 29, 1824.

Toney, Poindexter, and Jane Lilly. Robt. Lilly, surety–Nov. 1, 1797.

Trigg, Daniel, and Lucy B. Clarke. Adam Trigg, surety–Dec. 14, 1796.

Trigg, John T. and Elissa King. Robert King, surety–May 20, 1805.

Trigg, Thomas C., and Catherine Craig, dau. Thomas Craig. Wm. Anderson, surety. Mar. by J. Harrison–June 21, 1825.

Tripp, Henry, and Sally Boothe, dau. Abijah Boothe, surety–Nov. 5, 1822.

Trollinger, Henry, and Attelia Cecil. James Wall, surety–June 5, 1826.

Trollinger, John, Jr., (son of John), and Charlotte W .Hoge, dau. Wm. Hoge, surety–Aug. 23, 1830.

Trollinger, John, and Elizabeth Burris. William Burris, surety–Dac. 30, 1792.

Trout, Henry, and Nancy Taylor. Jacob Taylor, surety–Nov. 7, 1797.

Trovillo, James, and Nancy Coddell. John Coddell and Dandredge Trigg, surety–Sept. 9, 1826.

Trump, William, and Malinda Hawkins. Mar. by Richard Buckingham–Aug. 4, 1825.

Turman, Elijah, and Barbra Slusher. Christopher Slusher, surety–Aug. 4, 1812.

Turman, George, and Sarah Sumpter, dau. Edw. Sumpter, surety. Mar. by Peter Howard–July 7, 1818.

Turman, John, and Rachel Jones, dau. Robert Jones. Jesse Jones, sur.–Sept. 7, 1791.

Turman, Matthew, and Sarah Cox. Carter Cox, surety–Apr. 1, 1820.

Turner, Thomas, and Ann Carty, dau. Henry Carty, surety–Nov. 11, 1828.

–U–

Underwood, Joshua, and Delila West. Abner Lester, surety–Nov. 3, 1818.

Ustick, William K., and Lydia Lloyd. Moses Lloyd, surety–Aug. 31, 1829.

–V–

Vanlear, William, (son of John), and Elsey Hudson, dau. Isaac Hudson. Isaac Hudson, Jr., surety–Jan. 3, 1823.

Van Over, Henry, and Kezia McDaniel. Mar. by Hall. John King, sur.–Sept. 15, 1827.

Vancell, John, Jr., and Eva Weddle, dau. Benjamin Weddle. John Vancell, Sr., surety–Nov. 5, 1795.

Vancell, Pleasant, and Mary Cantly. Mar. by J. G. Cecil–July 16, 1828.

Vanhooser, Isaac, and Margaret Hoffman. Barnett Hoffman, surety–Dec. 7, 1786.

Vanover, Enocr (son of Henry), and Amy Hall, dau. Asa Hall, Sr., surety–Aug. 20, 1803.

Van Over, Thomas and Nancy Hall, dau. Leonard Hall. Geo. Adams, sur.–April 30, 1829.

Vanlear, William and Elsey Hudson, dau. Isaac.– Jan. 3, 1823.

Vanlear, John, and Sarah Davis. Robt. Guthrie, sur. Mar. by John Bull–June 16, 1817.

Vaughn, Jesse, (son of Wm. and Mary), and Elizabeth Byrd. Wm. Vaughn, sur.–Dec. 5, 1787.

Venable, Joseph, and Matilda Merritt. Major Merritt, surety–May 19, 1809.

Vermillion, Levi, and Elizabeth Miller. James Miller, Jr., surety–Dec. 13, 1808.

Vickers, Alexander, and Rebecca Dobbins. Anderson Dobbins, surety–Nov. 26, 1827.

Vickers, Thomas, and Lucy Beck. Joseph Beck, surety–Dec. 16, 1815.

Vickers, William, nad Peggy Hornbarger: Elias Vickers, and Peter Hornbarger, surety–Oct. 24, 1806.

Vines, William, and Catherine Walker. Mar. by Alex. Ross–............, 1792.

Vineyard, Campbell, and Nancy Pate. Mar. by J. G. Cecil–Nov. 21, 1830.

Vineyard, John, and Malinda Whitt. Mar. by J. G. Cecil–Feb. 6, 1827.

–W–

Waddle, Alby, and Jane Scott. Richard Guthrie, surety–Sept. 2, 1818.

Waddle, Alexander, and Mary Ann Scott. Richard Guthrie, surety–Jan. 3, 1815.

Waddle, Benjamin, and Margaretta Morgal. William Morgal, surety–Dec. 17, 1795.

Waddle, James, and Ann Robinet. David Fanning, surety–Jan. 26, 1786.

Wade, Alexander, and Elizabeth Cox, dau. Carter Cox. David Thompson, surety–Nov. 28, 1808.

Wade, Hamilton, and Mary Anderson. Thomas C. Trigg, surety–Nov. 13, 1821.

Wade, Henry, and Elizabteh Cox. Blanch Duncan, surety–Feb. 22, 1826.

Wade, James, and Eliza Anderson. Rice D. Montague, surety–Oct. 7, 1824.

Wade, John, and Susannah Trigg, dau. Daniel Trigg. John Chapman, surety–Jan. 11, 1819.

Wade, Joseph, (son of Zephinia), and Peggy Dorman, of Rockbridge Co., Va. Joshua Holms, sur. Mar. by B. E. Morgan–Nov. 4, 1817.

Wade, William, and Emily Crow. John R. Charlton, surety–July 7, 1819.

Waggoner, Daniel, and Lucy Day, dau. Lucy Day, widow. Isaac Glass, sur.–Sept. 5, 1785.

Waggoner, John, and Polly Lockhart. David Waggoner, surety–June 30, 1815.

Wagoner, Thomas, and Mayse Ronnton. Mar. by Edw. Morgan–uJly 1, 1789.

Walker, George, and Mary Adams, dau. John Adams. Isaac Snodgrass, sur.–Feb. 17, 1789.

Walker, James, and Nancy Kent. Mar. by Sam'l Mitchell–July 20, 1815.

Walker, John W. (son of Joseph Walker of Rockbridge Co., Va.), and Peggy Woody, dau. James Woody. James Cloyd, surety–May 5, 1800.

Walker, William, and Susannah Graham. Robert Graham, surety–June 4, 1787.

Walker, William, nad Mary Stewart, dau. Ralph Stewart. Alex Ross, sur.–Nov. 15, 1791.

Walker, William and Mary Stroud. Mar. register same as above?)–Nov. .., 1791.

Walker, William, and Margaretta Snodgrass. Robt. Snodgrass, surety–Oct. 28, 1803.

Walker, William, and Anna Scott. Matthew Scott, surety–Apr. 2, 1811.

Wall, Adam, and Betsy Lower, dau. Henry Lower, surety–June 28, 1813.

Wall, Christian, and Hannah Mars, dau. Alexander Mars. Jas. Sallust, surety–May 11, 1812.

Wall, James, and Sarah Ann Dobbins. Thomas Dobbins, surety–June 5, 1826.

Walls, James, and Catherine Shelton, dau. John Shelton, sur.–May 1, 1789.

Wall, John, and Betsy Ott. Henry Ott, surety–June 8, 1816.

Wall, Samuel, and Polly Ott, dau. John Ott. Henry Ott, surety–Aug. 21, 1811.

Wall, William, and Margaret Johnston. Ephriam Johnston, surety–Mar. 9, 1818.

Wallace, David, and Mary Cartmill, dau. James Cartmill. John Cartmill, surety–Oct. 12, 1785.

Wallace, David, and Sally Myers. Peter Myers, sur. Mar. by Richard Buckingham–Dec. 2, 1821.

Wallace, James, and Elizabeth Myers. Peter Myers, surety–Oct. 20, 1813.

Waller, George, and Nancy Hank. Mar. by Alexander Ross–Nov. 8, 1791.

Wallravin William, and Elizabeth Cox. Henry Hance, surety–June 6, 1821.

Walters, George, and Mary Kirby. David Harrison, surety–aJn. 23, 1792.

Walters, George, and Ann Hankla, (widow). Peter Rife, and Alex Ross, sur.–Oct. 26, 1791.

Walters, George, and Peggy Evans. William Walters, surety–Oct. 3, 1826.

Walters, Henry, and Jane Craig, dau. David Craig, surety–Dec. 19, 1829.

Walters, Jacob, and Hannah Iddings. Wm. Walters, and Henry Iddings, surety. Mar. by Peter Howard–July 19, 1822.

Walters, Jacob, and Rachel Redpath, dau. James Redpath. John Walters, surety–Oct. 23, 1826.

Walters, James, and Nancy Pearce, dau. Samuel Pearce. George Walters, surety–July 19, 1824.

Walters, John, and Nancy Bishop. Jacob Bishop, surety–Apr. 10, 1823.

Walters, and Nancy Kirby (Mary Kirby in Mar. register). Archibald Tabour, surety–Mar. 9, 1792.

Walters, William, and Polly Martin. Philip Martin, surety–Mar. by Isaac Rentfro–Sept. 5, 1797.

Walters, William, and Viney Caldwell, dau. Stephen Caldwell, surety–Jan. 15, 1816.

Walters, William, and Mary H. Wright, dau. John Wright, surety–Jan. 7, 1827.

Walters, William, (son of William, Sr.), and Ann Beckett, dau. John Beckett. John Beckett, Jr., sur. –Dec. 7, 1830.

Wampler, George, (son of John), and Elizabeth Sheffy, dau. Peter Sheffy. Wm. Hay, surety–June 2, 1789.

Warden, John, and Nancy Bell. John Bell, surety–Feb. 14, 1822.

Warden, Joseph, and Jemima Farmer. Mar. by Jacob Weddle–Mar. 27, 1825.

Warmon, John, and Mary Boothe. Mar. by J. G. Cecil–Feb. 22, 1827.

Warner, William, Jr., and Nancy Emmons, dau. John Emmons, Wm. Warner, surety–Feb. 20, 1826.

Warrick, John, and Mary Smith. Peter Hornbarger, surety–July 2, 1804.

Wateman, John, and Elizabeth Martin. Philip Martin, surety–Feb. 17, 1810.

Watkins, Archabod, and Dianna Simpkins. James Simpkins, surety—Dec. 10, 1818.

Watkins, George, and Levina Simpkins. James Simpkins, surety—Apr. 9, 1805.

Watkins, Thomas, Jr., and Betsy Wiseheart, dau. John Wiseheart. Thomas Watkins, surety—Jan. 5, 1807.

Watkins, Topal, and Nancy Baylor, dau. Abram Baylor, surety—July 13, 1830.

Watterson, Thomas, and Mary Stephens. David Stephens, surety. Mar. by Sam'l Gray. (Spelled "Stevens" in mar. return)—Feb. 4, 1795.

Wax (Wak?), Peter and Sally Surface. George Surface, surety—Oct. 16, 1823.

Weaver, George, and Polly Sowers, dau. Jacob Sowers, surety. Mar. by Peter Howard—Mar. 15, 1817.

Weaver, Lewis, and Theodocia Lucas, dau. Capt. John Lucas, surety—Nov. 22, 1830.

Webb, George, and Jane Willson. Joseph Anderson, surety—Oct. 11, 1803.

Webb, John, and Sally Eley, dau. "The window Eley." William Webb, sur. Mar. by Alexander Ross—July 24, 1793.

Webb, John, and Joan Porterfield, dau. Josiah Porterfield, sur.—Apr. 2, 1818.

Webb, Samuel, and Mary Barringer, dau. John Barringer, surety—Feb. 24, 1824.

Webb, Stephen, and Rosannah Marrs. Old Mar. list —Sept. 7, 1790.

Webb, Thomas, and Rebecca Bane, dau. John Bane, surety—Mar. 8, 1793.

Webb, William, and Sarah Treadway. Anthony Kirk, surety—Mar. 26, 1806.

Webb, William, and Betty Moore, widow. Eli Peterson, Sr., surety—Dec. 8, 1819.

Weddle, Andrew, and Elizabeth Boon. John Boon, surety—Oct. 21, 1811.

Weddle, Archeleus, and Matilda Lester ,dau. John Lester—Sept. 23, 1825.

Weddle, Benjamin, and Nancy Stickleman. John Weddle, surety—Nov. 3, 1827.

Weddle, David, and Margie Marricle. Mar. by Robert Jones—Nov. .., 1796.

Weddle, David, and Catherine Stygleman. Jacob Clore, surety—Nov. 22, 1825.

Weddle, Dennis, and Elizabeth Harmon, dau. Jacob Harmon, surety—Nov. 1, 1825.

Weddle, Jacob, and Sarah Rutrough, dau. John Rutrough, surety—Oct. 26, 1816.

Weddle, Jonas, (son of John), and Polly Roughtrof. John Roughtrof, surety—Jan. 25, 1806.

Weddle, Samuel, and Elizabeth Howell. David Howell, surety—Oct. 23, 1821.

Weddle, Valentine, and Sophia Webb. Henry Dunkin, surety—Jan. 22, 1823.

Wells, Abram, and Nacy Oats, dau. Rodger Oats, surety—Apr. 4, 1787.

Wells, James, and Barbara Kimbo. Jos. Reyburn, sur. Mar. by Isaac Rentfro—Mar. 16, 1795.

Wells, Job, an dSarah Howard, dau. Peter Howard. Joseph Howard, and Richrad Wells, surety—Oct. 1, 1822.

Wells, John, and Mary Strouse. Mar. by Richard Buckingham—Sept. 24, 1829.

Wells, William, and Margaret Bennett, dau. Sam'l Bennett, surety—Aug. 5, 1827.

West, Humphrey, and Elizabeth Watkins. Ebenezer Watkins, surety—Nov. 20, 1821.

West, Isaac, and Mary Lester, dau. John Lester, James Lester, surety—Nov. 4, 1806.

West, William, and Sarah Thrash, dau. John Thrash, surety—Aug. 17, 1822.

Whaling, Allen, and Nancy Holley. Patrick Whaling and Peter Holley, surety—Feb. 12, 1806.

White, Abijah ,and Elizabeth Elswick. Mar. by Richard Whitt—.........., 1792.

White, John, Jr., and Frances Mills. Thos. Copley, sur. Bar. by Alexander Ross—Aug. 19, 1792.

White, John, and Nancy Copely, dau. Thomas Copely, sur. Mar. by Alex. Ross—Jan. 8, 1793.

White, John, and Susannah Moss. Mar. by Alex. Ross—.........., 1796.

White, John, and Susannah Marcum. Major Marcum, surety—July 29, 1796.

White, John, and Magdalene Plymell, dau. Anthony Plymell. Joshua Copley, surety—Feb. 25, 1827.

White, Richard, and Betsy Baxter. Henry Carty, surety—Oct. 4, 1797.

White, Robert, and Mary Webb. William Webb, sur. Mar. by Isaac Rentfro—May 23, 1795.

Whitlock, Henry, (mother Sarah), and Elizabeth Graham. Jacob Graham, surety—June 18, 1827.

Whitley, William, and Elizabeth Strutton, dau. Solomon Strutton. Wm. Love, surety—Mar. 29, 1786.

Whitmon, Michael, and Christina Epperley. Anthony Hillendolph, (an uncle of Christina), surety — ...., 1786.

Whitt, Abijah, and Elizabeth Elswick, dau. John Elswick. Richard Whitt, surety—Oct. 22, 1792.

Whitt, Abijah, and Nancy Comptno. Joseph Compton, surety—Sept. 18, 1820.

Whitt, Abijah John and Hannah Sarles. William Sarles, surety—Feb. 11, 1815.

Whitt, Archibald, and Hannah Low. Richard Whitt, surety—Apr. 15, 1786.

Whitt, Archibald, and Polly Lorton, dau. Sally Lorton. Philip Hogan, surety—Sept. 20, 1813.

Whitt, Hezekiah, (son of Archibald), and Sally Howerton, dau. John Howerton, surety—Jan. 21, 1815.

Whitt, James, and Susannah Alley, dau. Carey Alley, surety—May 16, 1817.

Whitt, Jesse, and Ruth Whitt, dau. Richard Whitt. Archibald Whitt, surety—Oct. 10, 1787.

Whitt, Jonas, and Susannah Whitt, dau. Archibald Whitt, surety—Oct. 1, 1816.

Whitt, Robert, and Peggy White, dau. John White, Richard Whitt, sur.—Oct. 22, 1792.

Whitt, William, and Mary Meachem. Mar. by Richard Buckingham—Dec. 29, 1825.

Whitten, William. and Lettice Laird, dau. Lettice, wife of Sam'l Marrs, surety—Feb. 7, 1790.

Whipple, David, and Anne Miller. William Reyburn, surety—Oct. 11, 1805.

Wickham, Joshua B., and Jane Young, dau. Joshua Young. John Gudson, surety—Dec. 22, 1824.

Wickham, Robert, and Susannah Reed. Andrew Reed, surety—Mar. 27, 1822.

Wiley, James, and Sally Smith .Elijah Smith, surety —Oct. 25, 1809.

Wiley, Robert, (son of Alexander), and Mary Long, dau. John Long, sur.—Feb. 5, 1820.

Wilkinson, Thomas, and Betsy Akers. Richard W. Crump, surety—Oct. 14, 1816.

Willcox, Abraham F., and Margaret Vineyard, dau. George Vineyard, sur.—Apr. 2, 1820.

Williams, David, and Sarah Stapleton. Richard Wells, surety—Oct. 5, 1791.

Williams, Frederick, (son of George), and Jane Stafford, dau. of James Stafford, sur.—Feb. 8, 1806.

Williams, George, and Nancy Burke. Thomas Burke, sur. Mar. by Edw. Morgan—May 1, 1797.

Williams, Henry, and Susannah Champ. John Champ, surety—June 10, 1805.

Williams, James, and Sarah Fizer, dau. John Fizer. Peter Fizer, sur.—Sept .28, 1829.

Williams, Jacob and Catey Williams, dau. Michael Williams. John Mann, surety—Feb. 2, 1805.

Williams, John, and Elizabeth Tawney, dau. George Tawney, sur. Mar. by Alex. Ross—Sept. 7, 1793.

Williams, Joseph, and Mary Nichols. Mar. by Richard Whitt—. . . . ., 1785.

Williams, Michael, and Margaret Stafford, dau. James Stafford. George Williams, surety—Apr. 8, 1801.

Williamson, Jonathan, and Nancy Jackson. Andrew Lewis, surety—Nov. 7, 1797.

Willion, Jonathan, and Rhoda Taylor, dau. Wm. Taylor. Geo. Taylor, sur.—Feb. 18, 1807.

Willis, Charles, and Juliett Walters, dau. George Walters, surety—Nov. 29, 1830.

Willis, Christopher, and Zilpha Dobbins, dau. Thomas Dobbins, surety—July 2, 1827.

Willis, David, and Sarah Stapleton. Mar. by Isaac Rentfro—Apr. 7, 1791.

Willis, Isiah, and Mary Vest, dau. Hannah Shelor. Wm. Goodson, surety—Feb. 10, 1830.

Willis, James, and Betsy Hall, dau. Leonard Hall. Chas. H. Willis, sur.—July 14, 1823.

Willis, John, and Esther Brown, dau. Jetham Brown. Isaac Rentfro, sur.—Jan. 1, 1793.

Willis, Joseph, and Susannah Beckett. David Wllis, surety—Dec. 1, 1807.

Wills, James, and Barbara Kimball (?). Mar. by Isaac Rentfro—Mar. 18, 1795.

Wilson, Benjamin, (son of Joshua and Catherine), and Sarah Nuton, dau. Richard Nuton. Richard Whitt, surety—Nov. 13, 1787.

Wilson, Daniel, and Margaret Gearheart. Hiram Gearheart, surety—Apr. 6, 1821.

Wilson, Elijah, and Hannah Light, dau. James Light, surety—Sept. 1, 1825.

Wilson, Hiram, and Mary Morgan, dau. John Morgan, surety—Sept. 10, 1813.

Wilson, Isiah, and Polly Taylor, dau. Woldrick Taylor. Geo. Taylor, sur.—Jan. 8, 1802.

Wilson, James, and Catherine Rose, dau. Edward Rose. Israel Rose, sur.—Sept. 29, 1789.

Wilson, James, and Elizabeth Dormond. Mar. by Richard Whitt—May 8, 1793.

Wilson, Jacob, and Eve Helm, dau. George Helm, surety—June 10, 1794.

Wilson, Jonathan, and Elizabeth Reed, dau. Cornelius Reed. William Wilson, surety—Ma y4, 1807.

Wilson, John, and Betsy Cummings. Joshua Willson, surety—Aug. 28, 1797.

Wilson, John, and Mary Thompson Pedan, dau. John Pedañ, surety—Jan. 19, 1793.

Wilson, John, and Rebecca Morgan, dau. Edward Morgan, surety—Sept. 25, 1827.

Wilson, John, and Catherine Martin, dau. Catherine Martin. Peter Hornbarger, surety—May 4, 1829.

Wilson, John, and Catherine Wilson. Mar. by George Adams—July 24, 1829.

Wilson, Jonah, and Elizabeth Durman. Joshua Wilson, surety—Oct. 4, 1791.

Wilson, Joseph, and Mary Langdon. Jashua Willson ,surety—Oct. 4, 1791.

Wilson, Joseph, and Mary Nickols. Mar. register—Feb. 9, 1785.

Wilson, Joshua, and Sarah Lykins, dau. Mark Lykins. John Hough, sur.—Dec. 2, 1792.

Wilson, Joshua, and Christinah Conner. Jonathan Conner, surety—Jan. 5, 1819.

Wilson, Joshua, and Delila Steagall, dau. Mastin Steagall. Fred H. Holliday, sur.—Mar. 7, 1820.

Wilson, Joshua, and Christina Haff. William Haff, surety—Dec. 21, 1826.

Wilson, Peter, and Rhoda Hathaway, dau. Leonard and Susy Hathaway. James Light, sur. Mar. by Isaac Rentfro—Dec. 2, 1795.

Wilson, Samuel, and Mamala Lykins. Jonas Lykins, and Josiah Wilson, sruety—May 31, 1819.

Wilson, Samuel K., and Catherine Peterman, dau. Michael Peterman, sur.—Aug. 20, 1813.

Wilson, Stephen, and Susannah Marcum, dau. John Marcum. Robt. Christian, surety—Oct. 5, 1793.

Wilson, Thomas, and Martha Likens, dau. William Likens, surety—Nov. 4, 1794.

Wimmer, James, and Nancy Agnes Litterall, dau. Thomas Litterall. Jas. Litterall, surety—Jan. 29, 1821.

Wimmer, Samuel, (son of Jacob), and Masa King, dau. John King, surety—Jan. 24, 1827.

Wimmer, William, and Sally Templeton. James Templeton, surety—Sept. 21, 1815.

Windle, George, and Susannah Lefler. David Lefler, surety—Oct. 13, 1823.

Winfro, Joseph, and Margaret Carty, dau. Henry Carty. Thos. Winfro, sur.—. . . . ., 1793.

Winfree, Stephen, and Elizabeth Childress, dau. Boling Childress, sur.—Apr. 4, 1826.

Winters, Spragg, and Permeley Lester. Mar. register—Dec. 12, 1816.

Winter, Thomas, and Nancy Winter. John Winter, and Curtis Elliot, sur.—Jan. 5, 1816.

Winter, Trigg, and Elinor Glen, dau. John Glen. John Winter, sur.—Dec. 14, 1816.

Winters, William, and Lurinia Stephens. Thomas Lawrence, surety—Jan. 20, 1787.

Wirt, Andrew, and Anna Consolver. Mar. by George Adams—Feb. 7, 1829.

Wirt, Humphrey ,and Elizabeth Watkins. Mar. by Peter Howard—Nov. 22, 1821.

Wirt, William, and Mary Meacham, dau. Elijah Meacham, surety—Dec. 29, 1825.

Wisely, Jonas, and Margaret Whitzel. Mar. by J. G. Shrider—. . . . ., 1782.

Wisehart, Benjamin, and Sally Lothrain. John Lothrain and John Wisehart, surety—Apr. 4, 1804.

Wiseheart, James, and Sarah Simpkins. Robert Simpkins, surety—June 12, 1820.

Wiseheart, Thomas, and Mary Addair. John Addair, surety—July 27, 1805.

Wishong, Jacob, and Jane Vozler, dau. Boston Vozler. Edw. Bane, sur.—Mar. 12, 1829.

Wishong, Joseph, and Margaret Bowen. Mar. by Geo. Adams—July 16, 1829.

Wood, Henry, and Nancy Bryan Ambrose Bryan, sur. Mar. by S. Hubbard—Aug. 6, 1821.

Wood, John, and Lydia Bryant, dau. Ambrsoe Bryant, surety—Nov. 3, 1829.

Woolf, Frederick, and Nancy Love. Henry Love, surety—Nov. 3, 1818.

Woolwine, Jacob, and Catherine Keffer. Mar. by George Adams—Aug. 8, 1829.

Woolwine, John A., and Catherine Collins, dau. Hezekiah Collins—Sept. 29, 1828.

Woolwine, Philip, (mother Betsy), and Mary Reyburn. Wm. W. Reyburn, surety—Aug. 7, 1827.

Woolwine, William, and Polly Robertson. John Woolwine, surety—Jan. 27, 1807.

Woolrick, Peter, Jr., and Martha Mattox, dau. Sarah Mattox. Peter Woolrick, Sr., surety—July 2, 1804.

Workman, Abraham, and Margaret Lightner, dau. Mathias Lightner. Gabriel Rife, sur.—Sept. 24, 1785.

Worley, James, (son of Nathan), and Sarah Wilson, dau. Asa Wilson. John Hanees, surety—Oct. 22, 1830.

Worley, Nathan, and Betsy Putol (?). Sam'l Hanes, sur. (Signed in German)—Dec. 31, 1805.

Worley, Nathan, Jr., and Magdalene Smith, dau. Henry Smith. John Brunk, surety—Aug. 12, 1820.

Wright, Berien, and Mary Horton. Isaac Horton, surety—Jan. 11, 1805.

Wright, Dow, and Margaret Brookman. Mar. by J. G. Cecil—Dec. 4, 1824.

Wright, James G., and Ann King, dau. Anthony King, surety—Jan. 9, 1827.

Wright, Robert, and Rachel Sensentaffy. John Sensentaffy and Charles Wright, surety — Mar. 12, 1821.

Wright, Smith, and Rebecca Barnett. Mar. by Jonathan Hall—May 16, 1812.

Writtennan, John, and Mary Harles. Mar. by Richard Whitt—........ .., 1792.

Wygal, Wygle.

Wygal, Boston, and Elinor Collins. John Wiley, surety—Feb. 14, 1785.

Wygal, James, and Mary Cecil. Sabastian Wygle, and Thos. Cecil, sur.—Jan. 7, 1811.

Wygal, John, Sr., and Catherine Barringer, dau. Adam Barringer. Jacob Barringer, surety—Feb. 1, 1825.

Wygal, William, and Lenny Cecil. Samuel Cecil, surety—Apr. 24, 1826.

Wynn, Josiah, (son of Wm.), and Mary Whitley, dau. Robt. Whitley—Mar. 1, 1786.

Wysor, Henry, and Cynthia Charlton. John Charlton, surety—May 31, 1811.

Wysor, Jacob, and Margaret Miller, dau. James Miller, deceased. Henry Wysor, and Wm. Miller, surety—Jan. 5, 1819.

—Y—

Young, Frederick, and Polly Taylor, dau. George Taylor, sur. Mar. by Peter Howard—Aug. 9, 1820.

Young, Henry, and Betsy Kedey, dau. Kasper Kedey. Geo. Vineyard, sur.—May 16, 1795.

Young, William, and Jane Rutledge. Edward Rutledge, surety—Dec. 7, 1814.

—Z—

Zigler, Michael, and Elizabeth Litterall. James Litterell, surety—Oct. 7, 1823.

Zolls, Jacob, and Elizabeth Sallust. James Sallust, surety—Apr. 9, 1827.

........ing, William, and Phyllis Moss. Mar. by Simon Cickrell—Jan. 1, 1783.

........, Joseph, and Elizabeth Stump. Mar. by Simon Cickrell—Nov. 1, 1782.

Marriages Omitted by Printer First Edition

Day, Thomas, and Pricilla Ervin. Nov. 17, 1792.

Kirk, Thomas (Giles Co.) and Ruth Howe. Jas. Howe, sur.—Dec. 30, 1815.

Lower, John, and Elizabeth Cecil, Oct., 1796.

Miller, Dr. Joseph, and Matilda Charlton, Dec. 8, 1812.

Patton, Thompson, and Judy Farley—Feb. 10, 1798.

Pratt, James, and Sarah Hall—Aug. 25, 1808.

Richardson, Noah, and Jane Jewell, dau. Thomas, Jan. 24, 1839.

Shelor, Thomas and Mary Pearce (dau. Jotham)—Sept. 20, 1830.

Wood, John, and Catherine Huffman, by publ.—June 7, 1797.

Wills and Records of Montgomery and Fincastle Counties, 1773-1831.

—A—

Adam, William, dec. Apr. of estate ordered April 1, 1829.

Addair, James, dec. Apr. of estate ret. March, 1824.

Aldridge, William. Will probated July 1818. Names —Wife,......; two sons, Ezekiel and Leonard; four daughters, (names not given); and a son-in-law, Andrew Conner.

Akers, Clabourne, dec. Apr. of estate returned Feb., 1815.

Allee, Nicholas. Will probated July, 1808. Names— wife, Mary; and children, Anne, Nicholas, Merry, Betsy, Joseph, Isaac, Hannah, (by present wife, Mary); and Sarah Stephens, Jeremiah, Keziah Collins, David, John, and William by a first wife. The wife, Mary, a daughter of Joseph Dennis.

Allen, Peter, dec. Apr. of estate returned March, 1773.

Allison, John, Sr. (of Botetourt Co.). Will probated June, 1792. Names—wife, Lucy; children, iWlliam, Andrew, John, Sarah Vanlear; and a son-in-law, John Rutledge.

Altizer Emry. Will probated Oct. 1819. Names— wife, Mary; and children, John, Elias, Emry, William, David, Jonas, Betsy, Read, and Nancy Akers.

Anderson, George, dec. Apr. of estate ordered Dec., 1819.

Anderson, James, dec. Apr. of estate returned .... 14, 1815.

Anderson, James, dec. Apr. of estate returned June 16, 1836.

Anderson, James, dec. Apr. of estate returned Dec., 1841.

Anderson, John, dec. Apr. of estate returned Sept. 1838.

Anderson, Lydia. Will probated Jna., 1809. Names —children, Livice, Lewis, James, Frances and Charles.

Argubright, George, dec. Apr. of estate returned April, 1843.

Argabright, Joseph, dec. Apr. of estate returned Jan., 1833.

—B—

Bailor, Daniel. Will probated May, 1801. Names— wife, Catherine; and children, Adam, Isaac, and Jacob; and daughters, names or number not given.

Bain, Alexander, (of Botetourt Co.). Will probated March, 1807. Frees all his slaves, and leaves rest of property to Col. William Bain, "son of Rev. James Bain, of Scotland."

Bain (See Bane).

Baker, Joseph, dec. Inv. of estate returned Aug. 19, 1786.

Baker, Josiah. Will probated Nov. 15, 1815. Names— wife, Mary; and children, Thomas, Josiah, Rhoda, Mary, Peggy, and Betsy.

Bane, Edward. Will probated March, 1840. Names wife, Susannah; and children, Elizabeth Surface, Rebecca, Kinser, Margaret Kinser, Sarah Hall and George B.

Bane, James. Will probated Feb. 1790. Names— wife, ...; and children, Catherine Keen, James, Neomi, Godby, Sarah Smith, Mary McDonald and Edward.

Bane, James, dec. Apr. of estate returned Feb., 1838.

Barger, John. Will probated March 21, 1821. Names —wife, Jenny; and William by name. Mentions only John and William by name.

Barger, Peter, dec. Dower assigned his wife, Barbara, Sept., 1803.

Barnett, David. Will probated April, 1845. Names— wife, Mary Wallace; and children, James, Elizabeth, Thomas, Jane Davis, Mary Wallace, Samuel, and William.

Barnett, Elizabeth. Will probated Oct., 1833. Names children, Mary Ann, Mahala, Nancy, John, Delila, Sally; and her friend, James Smith.

Barnett, James. Will probated Oct. 4, 1791. Names —wife, ...; and children, James, John, William, David, and Rebecca.

Barnett, James. Will probated Dec., 1808. Names— children, William, Sykles, David, James and John dec.). Grandchildren, Elizabeth, Rachel, Sally (daus. of dec. son, John), and James (son of his son, David). Also names a son-in-law, James Barnett.

Barnett, James. Will probated Dec., 1821. Names— wife, Hannah; and children, Thomas, Sally, Johnson, Robert, John, and Capt. Joseph.

Barnett, James. Dill probated March, 1834. Names —wife, Mary; and children, Charles L., David, James, George and Sally.

Barnett, Jane, dec. Bill of sale recorded Jan., 1840.

Barringer, Adam. Will probated March, 1835. Names—wife, Hannah; and children, John, Jacob, Rosanna (wife of Joseph Covey); and grandchildren, the children of his deceased son, Daniel.

Bariger, Philip, dec. Apr. of estate returned Oct., 1802.

Bartlett, Gardner. Will probated Nov., 1811. Names —wife, ...; and children, William, Reuben, John, Thomas, Lydia Townsley, and three others, unnamed.

Baylor, Daniel. Will probated May, 1799. Names— wife, Kathren; and children. Abraham, Isaac, Jacob, and daughters, name or number not given.

Beard, William, dec. Adm. of estate appointed Mar. 7, 1775.

Beckett, Richard. Will probated Feb., 1804. Names —wife, Susannah; and children, William Thomas, Jonah, John, James, Richard, Ann, Rebecca, Mary, Ruth, Susannah and Martha.

Bell, Jeremiah, dec. Settlement of estate June, 1833. Wife's name, Elizabeth.

Bell, John. Will probated May, 1833. Names—wife, Sarah; and children, Elizabeth Ridenhouse, Lanslot, Rebecca, Hayden, John, Stephen, Benjamin and Jane.

Billups, Edward. Will probated June, 1822. Names children, John, Edward, Thomas, Richard, William, Elizabeth, Lucy, Margaret (dec.), and Sally (dec.).

Bishop, Samuel. Will probated July, 1802. Names— wife, Elizabeth.

Black, Samuel (of Kentucky). Will probated Oct., 1821. Name wife, Polly.

Blair, James, dec. Apr. of estate Dec., 1807.

Bones, Joseph, dec. Apr. of estate returned Mar., 1841. Dower wife, Nancy, Oct., 1842.

Bones, William. Will probated Oct., 1810. Names— children, Anny, Polly, Rosanna, Hannah, William, James and Joseph.

Boon, John. Will probated March, 1825. Names —wife, Elizabeth; and children, Mary, Elizabeth (wife of Andrew Weddle), Catherine Zemmerson (?), Abraham, Sariah Harter, Nancy Flegar and Jacob.

Boothe, James. Will probated Aug., 1807. Names— wife, Frances; and son, William.

Bowles, William. Will probated Dec., 1798. Names— wife,........; and children, Abigail Charlton, and Molly Lynch. Grandchildren, Iannah and William Lynch, William Charlton, and Izalia Davis.

Bowen, William. Will probated May, 1823. Names —wife, Margaret; and children, William, Johnson, and daughters, number or names not given.

Bowman, Peter. Will probated May, 1796. Names —wife, Sarah; and children, Elisha, Jesse, William, Emmy, and Phebe.

Bowman, Philip, dec. Estate sold, Jan. 16, 1807.

Bowman, Samuel, dec. Apr. of estate ret. Oct. 1793.

Bowyer, Henry, dec. Inv. of estate returned Aug., 1782.

Bowyer, Thomas, dec. Sale bill ret. Apr., 1841.

Bratton, James. Will probated Feb., 1814. Names— wife, Doratha; and children, Nancy, Cary and Malvina.

Brillheart, Daniel. Will probated Sept., 1844. Names —wife, Catherine; and children, Samuel, Abraham, Daniel, Adam, Jacob, and Henry.

Broce, John. Will probated Aug., 1844. Names— wife,........; and children, Frederick, Elizabeth, dec. (was wife of Sam'l Smith), Jacob, Peter, George, Catherine Kinser, Jane Smith, Polly Harless, Ann Kinser, and Margaret Hambrick.

Brookman, Samuel, dec. Apr. of estate rec. May, 1838.

Brown, Abraham. Will probated Dec., 1784. Names —wife, Margaret; and children, Abraham, Jr., Robert, Peter, Cornelius, Henry, Michael, Elizabeth and Sarah.

Brown, Abraham. Will probated May, 1789. Names his mother, Margaret; and bro., Robert, Peter, James, Henry, Cornelius. States his father, Abraham, dead.

Brown, John. Will probated March, 1830. Names— children, Sarah Dolittle, Mary Conrod, Margaret (wife of Thomas Brown), John, James, (of Augusta Co.), William, Thomas, and Elizabeth Hite, dec.

Brown, Margaret. Will probated Feb., 1803. Names children, Michael, Robert, Peter, Cornelius, Henry, James, Sarah Peekings, Margaret Tollet, and Elizabeth Barringer.

Brunk, Magdalene, dec. Apr. of estate returned Mar. 15, 1841.

Bryant, Elizabeth. Will probated Oct., 1842. Names —daughter, Mary Morton, and Mary's children, Martha Ann, Rhoda, Jane and Robert Craig Morton. States she is window of James Bryant.

Bryan, James. Will probated Aug., 1839. Names— wife, Elizabeth; and children, Mary (wife of Sam'l Wilson), Elizabeth Jane, John, and a grandson, James Wilson.

Bryans, Thomas O. Will probated Aug., 1821. Leaves entire estate to his step-daughter, Margaret, wife of Moses Beavers.

Buchannon, John. Col. dec. Executors release of land Jan. 5, 1773.

Burk, Thomas. Will probated Feb., 1798. Names— four brothers, Josiah, Samuel, John, and Benjamin; and two sisters, Hannah Peterson, and Betsy Burk.

Burk, Joseph, dec. Apr. of estate returned Nov. 25, 1786.

Burks, Samuel. Will probated Dec., 1815. Name wife, Nancy.

Burton, Benjamin, dec. Apr. of estate recorded Mar. 22, 1838.

—C—

Caddall, Sam'l, dec. Apr. of estate ret. Nov., 1832.

Campbell, Henry. Will probated Oct. 7, 1839. Names —wife, Sarah; and grandson, William StClair.

Carlton, Mary. Will probated Sept., 1819. Names sister, Susannah Carlton, brother, Joseph, and brother-in-law, Samuel Edings.

Carper, William, dec. Apr. of estate returned June, 1834.

Carty, Henry. Will probated June, 1809. Names— wife, Frances; and children, Peggy (wife of Joseph Rentfro), Million Jacobs, (wife of Roland Jacobs), Sarah, (wife of John Harrison), Elizabeth, (wife of William Gibson), Nancy, (wife of John Charlton), and his "only living son", Henry; grandson, William Carty, son of his deceased son, William.

Carty, Henry, dec. Apr. of estate ret. Mar., 1821.

Castle, Benjamin, dec. Adm. of estate granted Aug. 6, 1779.

Cassaday, Andrew, dec. Dower assigned widow, Leah, April, 1798.

Cassaday, John. Will probated May, 1835. Names— wife, Ann; and children, William, Thomas, James, Kennerley, Alexander, Elizabeth, Margaret, Martha, Nancy, Leah and Polly.

Casey, William, dec. Apr. of estate made Nov. 2, 1806.

Cecil, John. Will probated Sept., 1830. Names— wife, Keziah; and children, Philip, Keziah Eato,n Nancy Crandall, Rebeckah Clay, Jenny Grennup, Bicey Stafford, and Betsy Louther, deceased.

Cecil, Keziah, dec. Apr. of estate June, 1836.

Cecil, Samuel, dec. Adm. of estate granted his wife, Rebecca, March 28, 1786.

Charlton, Elizabeth, dec. Inv. of estate Feb. 20, 1808.

Charlton, Hannah. Will probated May, 1827. Names —children, Charles, Wellington, Elizabeth and Ann.

Charlton, John. Will probated June, 1790. Names— wife, Elizabeth; and children. Francis, James, John, Susannah, Jane, Mary Taylor (wife of

Geo.) and Elizabeth Davidson, (wife of William).

Childress, Stephen. Will probated Nov., 1815. Names—wi,fe Elizabeth; and children, Jenny Nancy, William, and others, number or names nto given.

Chrisman, Abraham. Will probated Oct., 1798. Names—wife, Kezia; and children, Jonathna, Joseph, Isaac, Elizabeth, Rebeckah, Phebe, Mary, and Anna.

Chrisman, Jonathan. Will probated June, 1818. Names—wife, Jane (his second wife); and children, Abram, Elizabeth, Nancy, and Sally.

Chrisman, Kezia. Will probated June, 1814. Names —David Stephens, sole heri.

Christian, Israel. Will probated Nov., 1784. Names —wife, Elizabeth; and children, William, Rosanna, Sarah Winston, Priscilla, Ann Fleming, (wife of William Fleming); grandchildren, Stephen Fleming and Polly Trigg.

Christian, Nathanial. Adm. of estate grnated his widow, Jane, Mar. 2, 1779.

Christian, William, (of Ross Co., Ky.). Will probated Feb., 1834. Names—wife, Mary; and children, Allen, John, Thomas, Susannah, Margaret, Mary (wife of M. Hester), and Martha, widow of George Jones; states that Martha is his eldest daughter.

Chumley, Lucy, dec. Apr. of estate ret. June, 1821.

Clary, David, dec. Inv. of estate ret. Nov. 7, 1792.

Clay, Meredith, dec. Apr. of esatte ret. Oct., 1806.

Cloyd, Gordon. Will probated Apr., 1833. Names— brothers, Thomas, David, James R.; Mary Kent, wife of James Kent; and Levi Vermillion's six sons, Gordon, Joseph, James, Uriah, David and John.

Cloyd, Joseph. Will probated Nov., 1833. Names— children, Gordon (wlil made before Gordon's death), Thomas, David; and grandchildren, Polly Kent, and Cynthia, Mary, Nancy, Lucinda, Peggy, Gordon and Joseph Cloyd.

Cochran, William, dec. Apr. of estate ret. Oct., 1773.

Cofer, John. Will probated April, 1840. Names— wife, Nancy; and children, John, Joseph, William, Polly, Catherine Hawley, and Nancy Cardin.

Cofer (See Copher).

Collins, Davis, dec. Apr. of estate Dec., 1819.

Collinsworth, Joseph, dec. Inv. of estate returned May 3, 1744.

Campton, Joseph, dec. Apr. of estate March 18, 1842.

Conner, Daniel. Will probated Jan., 1815. Names— children, Andrew, Jonathan, William, Daniel, Jacob, Zadok, Barbra Sheilor, Mary Hill, Rebecca Read, Sarah Conner, and Christina Conner. His wife, dec., was named Mary.

Connelly, Thomas, dec. Apr. of estate ret. Dec. 8, 1792.

Cooper, Nathaniel, dec. Apr. of estate ret. Feb., 1805.

Copher, Joseph. Will probated March, 1804. Names —wife, Mary; and children, Catrout Harmon, Christina Stobough, Joseph and John.

Cornutt, William, dec. Settlement of est. Mar. 7, 1826. Names—children, William, Bird, John, Jane, Polly Farmer, and Sarah Elkins.

Cragi, Ann. Will probated Dec., 1841. Names—her husband, James; and children, John, and Polly (wife of Creed Taylor); and the four children of her deceased daughter, Catherine Trigg— names not given.

Craig, Benjamin. Will probated June, 1824. Names —his children ,George, David, Thomas, and Polly Curby; and Polly Townsley, and her children; John, Jane, Martha, Kathren, William, Solomon, and Polly. Relationship of Polly Townsley not given.

Craig, James. Will probated March, 1834. Names— wife, Anne; and children, John, Robert, Elmira, Clementina, and Susannah; grandchildren, James, William, Ann, and Margaret, children of his deceased daughter, Celina, and her husband, William Kyle.

Crawford, John. Will probated April 7, 1779. Names friends. No relatives.

Crawford, Thomas, dec. Apr. of estate made Dec., 1797.

Cravens, Joseph, dec. Adm. of estate granted his wife, Neomi, Feb. 7, 1775.

Crockett, Hugh. Will probated May, 1817. Names— wife, Rebecca; and children, Walter, Hugh, Robert, Lyda, Polly, Rebecca, Samuel, Agnes and Jain.

Crockett, Rebecca, dce. Apr. of estate March 30, 1838.

Crockett, Samuel, (of Fincastle Co.). Will probated March 3, 1773. Names—wife, Jean; and children, Jean, Susannah, Joseph, and Robert.

Cromer, William, dec. Apr. of estate made May 9, 1810.

Crouch, David, dec. Inv. of estate returned Aug., 1799.

Crow, John. Will probated May, 1830. Names— wife, Hannah; and his sisters, Sarah Kerr, Agnes Shannon (wife of Thomas Shannon), Margaret Kerr, and Anne, (wife of Thomas Evans).

Cubbage, George. Will probated July, 1800. Names —wife, Kerzia; and children, Jonathan, Joseph, Isaac, Elizabeth, Rebeckah, Phebe, Mary and Anna.

Currin, Robert. Will probated Jan., 1802. Names— wife, ...; and children, George, James, William, Hugh, Robert, Jonathan, Waddy, Christina, Anne and Mary.

—D—

Davis, John. Will probated Aug., 1799. Names— wife, Anna; and children, Joshua, Catey, Anna, Charles, Dolly Britt, Deborah Carter, and three more in Penn., unnamed.

Davis, Mary. Will probated Jan., 1810. Names— her sisters, Elizabeth and Janny.

Davis, Thomas. Will probated Mar. 26, 1789. Names —wife, ...; and children, Robert, Sarah, and others, number or names not given.

Davidson, Walter, dec. Apr. of estate ret. Aug. 12, 1785.

Davers, Richard, dec. Adm. of estate appt. Nov. 3, 1778.

Dean, Adam. Will probated June 12, 1787. Names —wife, Elizabeth; and children, Robert, Ally, Elizabeth, James, Joseph, Mary, and Ann.

Deaver, John, dec. Sale bill ret. Oct., 1833.

Deweese, Paul (Botetourt Co.). Will probated March, 1797. Names—wife, Hannah; and children, number or names not given.

Deweese, William. Will probated Oct., 1807. Names —wife, ...; and children, William, Mary, Samuel, David, Jesse and Elinor.

Oct., 1807. Names—wife, ...; and children, William, Mary, Samuel, David, Jesse and Elinor.

Deyerle, Abram, dec. Apr. of estate ret. Aug,, 1831.

Deyerle, Charles, dec. Apr. of estate Sept., 1838.

—47—

Deyerle, Crockett, dec Apr. of estate ret. Jan., 1837.
Deyerle, Jane, dec. Apr. of estate ret. July, 1842. (Widow of John).
Deyerle, John, dec. Apr. of estate ret. May 9, 1827.
Deyerle, Peter. Will probated Jan., 1813. Names—wife, Regina; and children, Charles Abram, Anna Mitchell, Sally Gatewood, Rose Smith, and John.
Deyerle, Regina. Will probated May, 1828. Names—grandchildren, Rachel, Nancy, Mary Ann, and Mahala Barnett; Sally, Eliza and Rebecca Crow; and Nancy Chapman.
Dickerson, Griffith, (of Botetourt Co.). Will probated Mar., 1802. Names—wife, ...; and children, Griffith, Jr., Elijah, and others, number or names not given.
Dickerson, Read, dec. Apr. of estate returned March, 1816.
Doak, David. Will probated Oct. 7, 1787. Names——wife, Mary; and children, Henley, Madison, ert, Thomas, David, Samuel, William, James, Nathanial, Mary Margaret, Elizabeth, Sarah and Jean.
Dobbins, Abner. Will probated Nov., 1844. Names—wife, Mary; and children, Henly Madison Elizabeth Howerton ,Rebecca Vickers, Nancy Lincus, Margaret Cofer, and Martin Anderson.
Dobbins, Elizabeth (widow of Abner). Will probated Dec., 1821. Names—children, John, Dicia, Joanna, Abner, Thomas and Daniel.
Dobbins, Thomas, dec. Apr. of estate ret. March, 1839.
Dobbins, William, Dec. Settlement of estate, July 31, 1844.
Doosing, Jacob. Will probated Nov., 1842. Names—children, Jacob, William, John, Elizabeth, and Nancy (wife of John Shanks).
Doover, John. Will probated June 7, 1791. Names friends.
Dougherty, Michael. Will dated Apr. 7, 1787 (probation date missing). Names—wife, ...; and children, Robert, Sarah, and others, number of names not given.
Dougherty, William, dec. Inventory of estate ret- Nov. 2, 1773.
Douglass, John. Will probated Mar. 7, 1775. (Fincastle Co.). Names father and two brothers. Names not given.
Drake, Michael. Will probabed May, 1798. Names—wife, Jane; her children by former marriage (number or names not given); and his son, James.
Dudley, Jesse P. Will probated Aug., 1844. Names—children, John E. Coleman, and others, names or number not given.
Duff, William, dec. Appr. of estate Aug. 1, 1775.
Dulany, Samuel. Will probated July, 1812. Names—children, William, Benjamin, Daniel, Sarah Reide, Rachel Grimes, Mary Davis, and Elijah.

—E—

Earheart, Abram, dec. Settlement of estate Feb., 1834.
Earheart, John. Will probated Apr., 1804. Names—children, John, Henry, Adam, Margaret Davis, Mary Hutsell.
Early, Abner, dec. Apr. of estate ret. Dec. 18, 1839.
Early, Jacobus, dec. Apr. of estate ret. Oct., 1838.
Early, Jeremiah, dec. Apr. of estate ret. Feb., 1836.
Eckils, Michael. Will probated June, 1837. Names

—wife, Catherine; and children, Michael and Henry.
Elkins, Archibald. Will probated Sept. 6, 1791. Names—wife, Margaret; and children, Absolum, Mary, Elizabeth and Lydia.
Elliot, Curtis. Will probated June, 1833. Names—wife, Mary; and children, William, John, Stephen, Elizabeth, Rachel, Mary Jane, Nancy Martin, Peggy, Thomas, Polly Dobbins, Lewis, and Jonathan.
Elliot, Polly. Will probated Oct., 1837. Names—children, Rebecca Covey (child by her first husband, Jeremiah Pate), Rachel and Mary Jane Elliot. A grandson, Jeremiah Covey. (Note: Polly Elliot, widow of Curtis Elliot.)
Elliot, Robert. dec. Apr. of estate ret. Feb. 14, 1838. (His wife named Elizabeth.)
Elliott, Stephen, dec. Apr. of estate ret. June 14, 1840.
Elswick, Jonathan. Will probated March, 1818. Names—children, Nancy (wife of George Godby), Phebe O'Donald, Rebecca Simpson, Lydia Hays, and Polly Liper. Also mentions grand-children, Jackson, Maria, Rachel, and Crockett.
Emmons, John. Will probated Feb. 1, 1841. Names—wife, Polly; and children, Mroton, and Ursula Stabough. Grandchildren, name or number not given, but states they are the children of Gideon Akers and his deceased daughter, Polly.
Evans, James. dec. Apr. of estate ret. Aug., 1839.
Evans, Jane, dec. Guardian appt. for her children, Alexander, John and Mary. States that father also dead.
Ewing, John. Will probated Mar. 5, 1788. Names—children, Elinoe Cocke, Betsy, Alexander, William and Charles.
Ewing, Samuel. Will probated May 23, 1786. Names—wife, Mary; brothers, John and James; sister, Margaret Porter, (wife of Robert Porter); and a nephew, Alexander Ewing.

—F—

Failey, Thomas. Will probated Oct., 1796. Names—wife and sons. No names given.
Farmer, Jeremiah, dec. Apr. of estate ret. Aug. 25, 1792.
Farmer, Thompson. Will probated Oct., 1815. Names—wife, Martha, (a secnod wife); and children, Jemima (by first wife), and children of second wife, number, or names not given.
Ferguson, Andrew. Will probated June 1792. Names—wife, Catherine; and minor children, names or number not given.
Finch, Nathaniel, dec. Inventory of estate ret. Mar. 3, 1774. (Wife, Milly).
Fisher, James, dec. Apr. of estate ret. Feb., 1811.
Fizer, Henry. Will probated Oct., 1815. Names—wife, Margaret; and children, Michael, Adam, Henry, John, Jacob, Peter, George, Peggy Keffer, Polly Jones, Elizabeth Haymaker, and Catherine Overhoser. Leaves son, Michael, twenty-five dollars more than others, "for serving in my stead during Revolutionary war."
Fizer, William. Will probated July 7, 1818. Names—wife, ...;and his daughter Elizabeth, wife of Philip Haymaker.
Fowler, William, dec. Adm. of estate granted Feb. 7, 1775.
Francis, Henry Capt., dec. Apr. of est. ret. Apr., 1781.
Francis, Miles, dec. Apr. of estate, ret. by his guardian ...., 1809.
Fry, George. Will probated Aug., 1793. Names—

wife, ...; and children, George, Mary Adkins, Catey Eley, Barbra Eley, and Susannah Byars.

Gardner, John. Will probated March, 1816. Names—wife, Martha; and children, Jane Smilie, Ann, John, Elizabeth Meadows, Robert, Dianna, Prudence, William, Alexander and James.

Garlick, Gasper. Will probated July, 1805. Names—wife, Christina; and children, Eve, Mary, Catherine, John and George.

Garner, Henry, Dec. Adm. of estate report by his wife, Mary; and son, Henry, Feb. 28, 1786.

Genell, Francis, dec. Apr. of estate July, 1820.

George, Catherine. Dower assigned from est. of husband (name not given), Oct., 1809.

Gibb, James. Will probated July 26, 1785. Names—wife, Sarah; and children, Mary, Elizabeth, and James; and a brother, Michael.

Glen, John. Will probated Oct., 1837 Names—children, Jennet Baylor, Mary Newlea, Sarah Gardner, Martha Latmiore, Catherine Latimore, Robert, Agnes Albert, Eleanor Wineteer, and Elizabeth Webb, dec A sister, Jennet Glen, and a son-in-law, George Bowman.

Godbey, William. Will probated Jan. ,1833. Names—wife, Zanner; and children, Benjamin, Francis, William, Gabriel, Sarah Gunter (dec.), George, Patsy Farmer, Luch Hedge, Susannah Covey (dec.).

Goodson, Thomas. Will probated June, 1815. Names—wife, Sarah; and children, Margaret (wife of William Shelor), Joseph, Thomas, Nancy Eason, John, Sarah (wife of James King), Mary Page, Martha McHenry, Jane Reavely and Rhoda English.

Goodykoontz, George, dec. Apr. of estate ret. June, 1825.

Graham, Jacob. Will probated Nov., 1812. Names—children, Amos, Enoch, Aaron, Olive Johnson, Matthew Hancock, Aditha, Jacob, Jonathan, Sileus.

Grayham, Jonathan. Will probated March, 1827. Names—wife, Mary; and son, Jacob; other children, but number or names not given.

Grayson, John. Will probated Oct., 1802. Names—children, Betty, Lucy, John, William, Mary and Nancy. Also a partner, Wm. Hall, of Wythe Co.

Grayson, William. Will probated Aug., 1801. Names—wife, ...; and children, Billey, Reuben, Ambrose, John, Betsy, Sally and Polly.

Greyson, Robert, dec. Dower assigned Catherine Greyson, his wife, Oct. 3, 1797.

Greenway, Elijah. Will probated June, 1828. Names his mother, ...; and brothers, and sisters, Joseph, George, Richard, Sarah, and Nancy Abbot.

Greenway, Thomas, dec. Set. of estate Sept., 1838.

Gullion, Hugh, dec. (Fincastle Co.). Apr. of estate ret. May 2, 1775.

—H—

Hale, Agnes. Will probated Sept. 6, 1841 (widow Thomas Hale). Names—children, William, Jacob, Job, Elizabeth Lucas, Hannah Lucas, Mary Lucas, Margaret All, and Nancy Bowles.

Hale, Peter, dec. Apr. of estate ordered May, 1824.

Hale, Thomas. Will probated July, 1802. Died far away from home, stated to friend that he want-

ed his three little sons to have his land after the daeth of his wife, Agnes; wanted her "to do justice to all my children."

Hall, Asa, dec .Apr. of estate ret. Mar. 6, 1841. Wife named Mary.

Hance, Adam. Will probated March, 1823. Names—wife, Hannah; and children, Peter, Henry, James, John, Patsey (wife of John Tiffany), Ann (wife of Wm. Harrison), and Prissa, (wife of Daniel Harman).

Hancock, George Col. dec. Apr. of estate ret. April, 1822.

Harless, David. Will probated Feb., 1817. Names—children, Jacob (wife named Elizabeth), Philip, Rebecca (wife of Philip Layton), Elizabeth (wife Andrew Surface), Hannah (wife Abraham Cromer), Mary, and Catherine.

Harless, Emanuel. (Fluvanna Co.). Will probated Mar., 1797. Names—wife, Elizabeth; and children, Philip, Elizabeth, and Eve.

Harless, Henry, of Anderson Co., Tenn., gives power of atty., 1810.

Harless, Philip. Will probated Mar. 1823. Names—wife, Hannah; and children, Samuel, Philip, Daniel, and daughters, number or names not given.

Harless, Samuel, dec. Sale bill ret. May, 1841.

Harris, Nicholas, dec. Inv. of estate ret. May 27, 1784.

Harrison, Amos. Will probated March, 1794. Names—wife, Phebe; and children, Moses, Nancey, Richard, Betsy, and one unborn.

Harrison, John, (of Franklin Co., Tenn.). Will probated June, 1828. Names—daughter, Feebe Hankins; and grandsons, Jafaniah and David Harrison.

Harrison, Richard. Will probated Aug. 5, 1783. Names—wife, ...; and children, William, Amos, Stephen, Phebe, Nancy, Susan, Farlana, Elizabeth, John, Louriana, Richard, and Eleanor, by a first wife.

Hart, John, dec. Apr. of estate Dec., 1804.

Hash, John. Will probated May 27, 1784. Names—wife, ...; and children, (by a first wife), John, William and Thomas.

Haven, John. Will probated Aug. 6, 1782. Names—wife, Mary; and children, Richard, James, Rebeckah, Margaret, Ruth, Rhodey, and Elizabeth.

Haymaker, James, dec. Apr. of estate ret. Feb. 19, 1841.

Haymaker, John, dec. Settlement of estate, March, 1844.

Heavin, Howard. Will probated Jan., 1787. Names—wife, Ruth; and children, William, John, Nancy, Elizabeth Bane, Mary Brown, and Sarah.

Heavener, John, dec. Apr. of estate March, 1816.

Heavner, Philip. Will probated May, 1804. Names—wife, Martha; and children, Jacob, Batsy, John, Sally, David and Catey.

Henderson, John. Will probated Sept. 1813. Names—wife, Mary; and children, Joseph, John, Jonas, Robert, Samuel, William, Thomas, Sally Mitchell and Polly Bean.

Henderson, Mary. Will probated June, 1834. Names—children, William, Polly Bane, Jane Johnston, and John.

Henderson, Samuel, dec. Apr. of estate Oct., 1842.

Herbert, William. Will probated Sept. 3, 1776. Names—wife, Sarah; children, William (eldest son), Thomas, Martha (eldest daughter), and Joanna; provided for his mother and father (father named David), both of whom are living.

(Comment: Wm. Herbert's widow, Sarah, married a Francis Day).

Hill, Abagail, dec. Apr. of estate ret. May 15, 1787.

Hogan, Philip. Will probated April, 1825. Names wife, Polly; and their children, Francis, Jackson, Eminah, and Rebecca. Mentions children of a first marriage, but does not give names or number. (Comment: Philip Hogan's first wife was Elizabeth Pate, dau. Jeremiah Pate).

Hoge, James. Will probated May, 1812. Names—wife, Elizabeth; and children, James, Joseph John, Daniel, William, Mary, Sarah (wife James Stafford), Martha Brawley, Elizabeth Foster, Elinor Alford, and Agnes Summers.

Holms, William, dec. Sale bill returned May, 1834.

Hoops, Lewis. Will probated May, 1837. Names—wife, Margaret; and children, names or number not given.

Howard, Ezekiel. Will probated May, 1824. Names — children, Alexander, Anderson, Sophia (wife of John Calfee, of Wythe Co.), Evelina, Margaret, Juliette and Rebecca.

Howard, Hiram. Will probated Oct., 1844. Names—wife, ...; and children, Anderson, Thomas, Joseph, Reuben, and Sarah.

Howard, Peter. Will probated Apr., 1825. Names—wife, Sarah; and children, Joseph, Nancy, Peter, Sarah Wells, Irah, Elizabeth, and Major.

Howe, Daniel. Will probated Feb. 3, 1838. Names—children, Joseph Howard, John, Dunbar, William Henry, Luenna P., Lucretia H., Thomas, Susannah J., Elizabeth Pearis, Elinor Hoge (wife of James), Judy Cuill, Ruth Kirk, and Nancy Deskins.

Howe, Joseph. Will probated Sept. 7, 1790. Names —wife, Elinor; and children, David, John, Daniel, and twosons-in-law, Robert Pearis and James Hogge.

Howerton, Thomas, dec. Apr. of estate, Feb. 11, 1802.

Howell, Benjamin. Will probated August, 1799. Names—children, David, Benjamin, and Mary; also a brother, Joshua.

Howry, Michael, dec. Apr. of estate returned Aug., 1819.

Hudson, Isaac. Will probated March, 1820. Names —wife, Sarah; and children, Isaac, Thomas, Sarah, Alice, Mary, Jane Shannon, and George, the eldest son.

Huff, Absolum. Will probated May, 1817. Leaves his estate to his father, Philip, his mother, and his brother, James.

Huff, Elizabeth, of Cocke Co., Tenn. Says she is widow of Leonard Huff, and gives power of atty. to her son John Huff, August, 1800.

Huff, Philip. Will probated Feb., 1823. Names—wife, Rachel; an dchildren, Daniel, William, Sarah Walker, Philip, Nancy Miller, Elcey Snuffer, John, Henry and James.

Huff, Samuel. Will probated Feb., 1826. Names—wife, Catherine; and children, Samuel, John, Lewis, Francis, William, Christina, Elizabeth, Lidda, Sally, and Peggy; grandchildren, Patience and Elizabeth Cooper, daugters of Washington Cooper.

Hughs, Thomas, dec. Apr. of estate June, 1799.

Huston, David, dec. Apr. of estate ret. April, 1838

Hylton, Gordon. Inv. of estate returned Mar., 1826.

—I—

Ingles, John. Will probated Mar. 8, 1836. Names—wife, Elizabeth; and children, William, Crockett, John, Thomas, Mary Saunders, Malinda Charlton, Lockey Hale, and Peggy Hyde (wife of Cyrus Hyde).

Ingles, William. Will probated Nov. 5, 1782. Names —wife, Mary; and children, John, Mary, Susannah (wife of Abram Trigg), Rhoda (wife of Byrd Smith), and Thomas. Mentions land he obtained through military warrant.

Ingram, Samuel. Will probated July, 1801. Names— wife, ...; and children, William, Aaron, Samuel, Rachel, and three other sons, and two daughters, names not given.

Irvin, John, dec. Adm. of estate granted wife, Jane, Apr. 6, 1779.

—J—

Jackson, Thomas, dec. Adm. granted his wife, Margaret, Sept. 7, 1773.

John, Griffith. Will probated Nov., 1833. Leaves estate to his nephews, James, and Eleazer, and niece, Leah, children of his brother, John John.

Johnston, David. Will probated .... Will dated July 25, 1786. Names—wife, ...; and children, David, Andrew, and James. Also a brother, John Chapman. (Comment: Possibly a half brother, or brother-in-law).

—K—

Keister, Peter. Will probated Nov., 1835. Names—children, Polly, Betzey, John, George and Susannah.

Keister, Peter. Will probated Feb. 3, 1840. Names—wife, Elizabeth, (who was dead at making of will, June, 1839), and children, Henry, Peter, Susannah and Catherine.

Kent, David, dec. Inv. of estate ret. Aug., 1844.

Kent, Jacob. Will probated March, 1812. Names—his mother, Mary Kent; his sister, Jane Beuford; and the following nephews: Jacob Kent, of Wythe Co.), Robert Kent (son of his brother, John), and Robert and Joseph McGavock, sons of his sister, Nancy.

Kent, Robert, dec. Inv. of estate returned March 26, 1796.

Kester, Phliip. Will probated Nov., 1814. Names—children, Philip, John, Polly Bumgardner, and Rebeckah Dedrecks and Peter.

Key, Jesse W., dec. Apr. of estate ret. Sept. 26, 1841.

King, Joseph, dec. Apr. of estate July, 1839.

King, Robert. (of Washington Co.). Will probated Sept., 1828. Names—children, Robert, Joseph, Margaret, Elizabeth and Agnes.

Kinser, Michael. Will probated Nov., 1835. Names —children, John, Katherine, Philip, Michael, Susanna, Elizabeth, George, Christian and Jacob and wfie, Hester.

Kirby, William. Will probated Nov., 1810. Names—children, Mary (wife of Seth Duncan), Martha Morgan, Ann Cassada; grandsons, Joseph and Harvey Morgan.

Kipps, Michael. Will probated July 1835. Names—wife, Catherine; and children, John, Hannah, (wife of Christian Price), Margaret Cook, Catherine, (wife of Philip Beavers), Mary, (wife of John Hinsgardner); and heirs of his dec. daughter, Sarah, and her husband, Peter Kenopp.

Kyle, William (a merchant). Will probated Apr. 29, 1833. Names—children, Elizabeth, James, William, Ann, Margaret, Ellen, David, and John.

Lackland, George. Will probated Dec. 5, 1820. Names–wife, Elizabeth; and daughter, Polly.

Latshaw, Isaac. Will probated June, 1822. Names– wife, Catherine; daughters, Elizabeth, and Leah; and the children of his deceased daughter, Susannah, and Isaac Himes, names not given.

Lawrence, John. Will probated Oct., 1801. Names wife, Levinah; and three sons, John, William and Thomas, and daus. Patience, Macey, Mary, Elizabeth and Zelphia.

Lawrence, Thomas, dec. Apr. of estate ret. July, 1837.

Lewis, Thomas. Will probated June, 1803. Names –children, Thomas, (son by his first wife, Mary), Edward, Elizabeth, Sally, David, and James. Also a son-in-law, James Boucher.

Light, Henry, dec. Apr. of estate Aug., 1823.

Linkous, Henry. Will probated Sept., 1822. Names– wife, Elizabeth; and children, John, George, Jacob, Henry, Adam, Thomas, Alexander, Hannah Schell, and Elizabeth Stonger.

Littlepage, Elizabeth. Will probated Dec., 1832. Names–grandchildren, George, Octavia, and Elizabeth Todd; and Mary Yearout.

Long, John, dec. Apr. of est. returned March, 1832.

Lore, Henry, dec. Apr. of estate April, 1822.

Lore, Samuel, dec. Apr. of estate August, 1823.

Lorton, Israel, dec. Inv. of estate made Feb. 1, 1808.

Love, Samuel. Will probated March 4, 1781. Names –children, Robert, James, Thomas, William Sarah and Mary.

Lumsdale, James. Will probated Nov. 7, 1781. Entire estate to "my shipmate, Martin Knowland."

Lybrook, Palser. Will probated March, 1804. Names –wife, Catherine; and children, Philip, John, Henry, Catherine Philips, and others, nunamed.

Lykins, Marcus. Will probated Jan., 1814. Names– wife, ...; and children, William, Isaac, Peter, Polly, Jean, Sally, Hannah, and Nancy. Names son-in-law, Joshua Wilson.

Lyons, William. Will probated July, 1808. Names– wife, Betsy; and children, Polly, Jenny, and Betsy.

Maddox, Samuel, dec. Sale bill June, 1841.

Madison, Eliz. Will probated March, 1837. Leaves property to "my widowed, and only child, Agatha S. Peyton," and Agatha's children, William Madison, Benjamin Howard, John R., and James M. Peyton.

Martin, Christian. Will probated March, 1809. Names–wife, ...; and children, Nancy, Mary, Sally, Jacob, Andrew, John, Hannah, James, David, Peggy, and Evelina.

Martin, Hugh. Will pro. Nov., 1815. (Clarke Co., Ga.). A statement of clerk of court says will contains bequest of slaves to his daughter, Nancy, wife of Thos. McHenry, of Montgomery.

Martin, Philip. Will probated June, 1821. Names– wife, Catherine; and children, George, Philip, Catherine, Malinda, Polly (wife of William Walters) Peggy, (wife of George Howry), Betsy, (wife of John Waitman), and Nancy, (wife of David Martin).

Maxwell, John ,dec. Adm. of estate granted his widow, Rebecca, March 2, 1779.

McAdams, Samuel, (of Fincastle Co.). Will pro-

bated Aug. 1, 1775. Leaves estate to his brothers, John, and James, and sister, Susannah.

McCorkle, James. Will probated May, 1794. Names –niece, Margaret, wife of William Adams.

McCoy, Richard. Will probated July, 1793. Names –wife, Susannah; and children, William, George, and daughters, name and number not given.

McDonald, Bryan, dec. Appraisement of estate May, 1802.

McDonald, George. Will probated March, 1815. Names–wife, Ruth; and children, George, Edward, Susannah, Ann, and Mary.

McDonald, Joseph. Will probated May, 1809. Names–children, Bryan, Joseph, Richard, Alexander, William, Jonas, James, and Elizabeth Ingram.

McDonald, Susannah, (of Botetourt Co.). Will probated March, 1801. Names–children, William, George, Susannah Walker, Edward, Mary Ross, and Jane.

McElheney, James, dec. Adm. of estate granted Nov. 7, 1775.

McHenry, John, dec. Apr. of estate June, 1819.

McHenry, William, dec. Apr. of estate returned Oct., 1808.

McMullin, James, dec. Apr. of estate April, 1837.

McNeeley, William. Will probated Sept., 1810. Names–wife, Rebecca; and children, William, Matey Munsey, Rebecca Johnson (deceased, leaves property to her three children, unnamed).

Meurhead, Andrew, Sr., dec. Apr. of estate returned June, 1837.

Meurhead, Enoch. Will probated Feb., 1805. Names –wife, ...; and children, Ruth, George, Mary and Eli.

Meurhead, George, dec. Apr. of estate returned June 6, 1818.

Miller, James, dec. Apr. of estate ret. Feb., 1816 (Same as below?)

Miller, James, dec. Account rendered Oct. 8, 1830.

Minnick, Jacob. Will probated Jan., 1821. Names– wife, Mary; and children, Mikle, Samuel Barnes, Terry, and daughters, number or name not given.

Mitchell, John H. Will probated July, 1821. Leaves estate to brothers and sisters, number or names not given.

Mitchell, John. Will probated Aug., 1838. Names– wife, Obedience, (late Bemer"); sons, John, Jr., Fabius, James V., and leaves property to the following, but relationship not given: Elizabeth Mitchell ("late Deaton"); Nancy H. Mitchell, ("late Foster"); Martha Mitchell, ("late Goodwin") Sarah Mitchell, ("late Deaton"); Thomas Mitchell; Ellen Mitchell, ("late Robinson").

Mitchell, Mary Ann. Will probated Oct., 1835. Names–children, Sarah Crow, Rachel Barnett, George W., Mary Ann, Betsy Barnett (dec.), and others, number, or names not given.

Mitchell, Thomas. Will probated Feb., 1820. Names –wife, Mary Ann; and children, Thomas, George W., Mary Ann, Reuben, William, Archelius, and Susannah Donaho; grandchildren, Thomas, Harvy, Stephen, Mary Jane, Robert, Frederick, Martha, (children of William and Luisa Mitchell); Thomas, Hervey, Mary, Charles, Chrsitopher and Monroe, (Susannah and Henry Donaho's children); and children of his son, Archelius, "names unknown" to him.

Moffett, William, dec. Adm. of estate granted his wife, Mary, Aug. 1, 1775.

Moore, James, Captain, dec. Apr. of estate returned Nov. 28, 1786.

Morricle. Will probated May, 1820. Names—children, William, Jacob, and John.

Munsey, Luke. Will probated Sept., 1831. Names—wife, Mary; and children, Jane, Polly, Luke, Elijah, James, Levi, Betsy, Nathaniel, and John.

—N—

Napper, Thomas, dec. Apr. of estate June, 1799.

Nester, Jacob. Will probated Oct., 1823. Names—wife, Catherine; and children, John, Nancy Ratliff, Frederick, William, Polly Dueling, Joshua, Abraham, Andrew, Sally, Daniel, Elizabeth, James and Jonathan.

Newbury, Samuel. Will probated Jan. 28, 1787. Names—wife, Bethian; and children, Elizabeth, Samuel, James, Robert, David, Joseph, and one unborn.

Newell, James. Will probated Dec. 11, 1784. Names—wife, ...; and children, John, James, William, Elizabeth, Mary, Nancy, and Grizly.

—O—

Ollinger, Philip, dec. Apr. of estate returned Sept. 1832.

Owen, David. Will probated June, 1798. Names—wife, ...; and children, Barnett, Arthur, Daniel, Thomas, Robinson, William, Sally Smith, Caroline Robinson, and Mary Shoopman.

—P—

Page, Alexander. Will probated Aug., 1823. Leaves estate to wife, Malinda, for her life, and then to the "Methodist Society."

Page, John. Will probated Feb., 1833. Names — children, Polly Pearce, Robert, Samuel, David, and Elizabeth Gardner.

Page, Robert, dec. Adm. of estate appointed June, 1836.

Payte, Anthony. dec. Inv. of estate returned Dec., 6, 1782.

Pate, Christina (widow of Jeremiah, Sr.). Will probated June 18, 1815. Names—children, Jeremiah, Jacob, Catey Richards, Lover Canaday, Daniel and Elizabeth Hogart (wife of Philip Hogan), Adam and Sarah Cook.

Pate, Jeremiah, Sr., dec. Inv. of estate returned July, 1812. (wife, Christina).

Pate, Jeremiah, dec. Apr. of estate ret. Apr. 5, 1819. (Son of Jacob, grandson of the Jeremiah above. Wife was Polly Howerton).

Pate, Jeremiah, dec. Guardian appt. for infant children; Christian, Lockey, Fanny, Nancy and Sarah.

Pate, Matthew, dec. Apr. of estate returned Feb. 12, 1798.

Patterson, Catherine. Will probated Oct., 1819. Names—children, John, Elizabeth, Mary, Leah, Margaret; grandchildren, Margaret and Elizabeth Safly.

Patterson, George, dec. Apr. of estate ordered Nov. . . ., 1803.

Patterson, William, dec. Apr. of estate returned Sept. 13, 1788.

Patterson, William, dec. Apr. of estate returned May 12, 1837.

Patton, James, dec. Release of land by adms. May 2, 1775.

Pearce, Richard. Will probated Jan. ,1822. Names—wife, Peggy; and children, Samuel, Thomas, Jothain, William, Richard, Sally Garlick, Phebe Thompson, and Abagail.

Pearce (See Pierce).

Peatross, Matthias, dec. Apr. of estate Feb. 12, 1798.

Peckens, William. Will probated Nov. 19, 1783. Names—wife, Ann; and son, Thomas.

Peery, Miles H., dec. Apr. of estate June, 1835.

Pepper, James, dec. Apr. of estate Feb., 1811.

Pepper, Joseph, dec. Apr. of estate Oct., 1801.

Pepper, Samuel. Will probated Apr., 1805. Names—wife, Neomi; and children, Polly Heavin, William, James, Sally, John, Jesse, and James, dec.

Pepper, William. Will probated Feb., 1835. Names—wife, Jane; and children, Samuel, John, George Pearis, William, Polly Todd, Jane, Sally, Malinda; and grandchildren, Catherine, William, Stephen, and Jane Ruddle.

Pepper, William. Will probated June, 1836. Names—wife, Sally; and children, Elizabeth, Mary, Joel W., Neomi and Sally.

Peters, Jacob, dec. Apr. of estate ret. July, 1803. (States date of death, May 22, 1801.)

Peterson, John. Will probated Mar. 2, 1819. Names—brothers, Eli Isaac, William, Morton; and sisters, Christina, Lydia Anderson, Polly Smith (wife of Thomas Smith), and Hannah Emmons.

Peterson, Matthias. Will probated Jan., 1802. Names—wife, Mary; and children, Isaac, Christina Lydia Anderson, Eli, William, Polly Smith, Morton, Hannah, Jehu; son-in-laws, John Emmons and John Peterson; grandchildren, Polly, Betsy, and Hannah, Seegar ,ch. of Christina.

Phlegar, Eli., dec. Settlement of estate May, 1842.

Pierce, Thomas, dec. Inv. of estate ret. Nov., 1782. Mentions certificate for military service.

Pittman, Joshua. Will probated Jan., 1790. Names—wife, Mary; and step-son, John Page.

Poff, Peter. Will probated Nov., 1830. Names—wife, ...; and children, Henry, Anthony, Michael, Charles, Peter, John, Samuel Christinah, Ann, and three other daughters, names not given.

Porter, Robert, dec. Inv. of estate returned Feb. 5, 1782.

Perston, James, dec. Apr. of estate ret. Aug., 1843.

Preston, Susannah. Will probated Nov., 1823. Names—children, James, Letitia, Floyd, Elizabeth Madison, Sarah, Mary, Peggy; daughter-in-law, Ann T. Preston; granddaughters, Aggy and Susannah Preston; children of James. States that she has five daughter-in-laws.

Preston, William. Will probated Aug. 5, 1783. Names—wife, Susannah, and children, Elizabeth Madison, John, Anne, Francis, Sarah, William, Susannah, James, Patton, Mary and one unborn. Says he has no brother.

Preston, William ,(of Jefferson Co., Ky.). Will probated Feb. 9, 1821. Names—wife, Caroline (nee Hancock); and children, Hancock, William C., Henrietta Maria, Caroline, Josephine, Susanna; and his brother, Francis.

Price, George. Will probated June, 1799. Names—wife, Rachel; and children, John, Nancy, Elizabeth, Hannah, and Mary.

Price, Henry, (of Rocknigham Co.). Will probated Mar., 1797. Names—wife, Mary; and children, Henry ("the first born"), David and Adam.

Price, Henry D. Will probated Mar., 1834. Names—

wife, Mary; and children, John, David, Henry, Christian, Sally, Adam, Elizabeth Harless, Kathren (wife of Jacob Shell), Peggy Surface; grandchildren, Sally Harless and James and Nancy Server, children of his dec. daughter, Nnacy Server.

Price, Michael. Will probated Oct., 1802. Names—wife, Margaret; and children, David, Michael, Jacob, Christian, Henry, George, Alexander, and grandson, Lewis, the son of Michael.

Price, Michael. Will probated Aug. 5, 1839. Names—wife, Esther; and children, Lewis, Alexander, Elizabeth Biggs, Margaret Helvey, and Agnes Surface.

—R—

Ratliff, Nathan. Will probated Jan., 1835. Names—children, Jeremiah, William, John, Thompson, Sally (wife of Jonas Altizer), Rebecca (wife of John Akers), Mary and Martha.

Ratliff, Squiar. Will probated April 1, 1777. Leaves everything he has to Lauh Ratliff. Made just before starting upon a long journey (1773), from which he never returned.

Read, George, Sr. Will probated Oct., 1807. Names—wife, ...; and children, Humphrey, William, and others, names or numbers not given.

Reyburn, Henry, dec. Apr. of estate returned June 29, 1792.

Reyburn, James. Will probated Sept., 1814. Names—wife, Nancy; and children, William W., James, Jenny Burk, Margaret Crockett, Polly Brown, Patsey Campbell, Rebecca Johnson, Robert, and others unnamed; and one, unborn.

Reyburn, Jane. Will probated Jan., 1828. Names—granddaughter, Jane Reyburn, daughter of son, William; and seven children, unnamed.

Reyburn, James M. Will probated May 24, 1836. Names—sister, Mary Elizabeth Reyburn; and half brothers and sisters unnamed. Says they are children of Robert Blackwell.

Reyburn, John. Will probated Mar., 1808. Names—wife, Jenny; and children, Peggy, Henry, Mary Shanklin, Jenny Pepper, John, Rachel Taylor, and Rebecca Williams; grandson, Hiran, son of Henry.

Reyburn, Joseph. Will probated July, 1800. Names—wife, Margaret; and children, Thomas, Joseph, and others, number or name not given.

Reyburn, William W., dec. Apr. of estate ret. July, 1835.

Rhotroff, John. Will probated Feb., 1825. Names—wife, Mary; and children, Henry, William, and daughters, number or names not given.

Ribble, Christopher. Will probated June, 1836. Names—wife, Mary; and children, Catherine Garst, Magdalene Mayers, Hannah Epling, Barbary Kegley, Elizabeth Combs, Susan Kegley, Mary Markley, Jonas, David, Christopher, George, Philip, John, James, Henry, Sarah, and Leah.

Roberts, John, dec. Apr. of estate returned Mar. 7, 1775.

Roberts, Reuben, dec. Inv. of estate returned Mar., 1825.

Robertson, Alexander Hart. Will probated June 1823. Names—wife, Martha; and children, James Woods, Robert Rayburn, Joseph Walker, and Alexander.

Robinson, David, dec. Apr. of estate returned Mar. 1816.

Robinson, Gertrude. Will probated Feb., 1816. Names—children, William, Letitia Preston, Cynthia, Cyrus, Tamer (a girl), James, David; grandchildren, Gertrude Preston, Bird S. Grills, Gertrude Abney, and Gertrude Robinson.

Robinson, James, dec. Adm. allowed his wife, Elizabeth, of estate, Sept., 1825.

Robinson, John. Will probated May, 1801. Names—wife, Gerty; and children, William (land in Ky.), James, David, Cyrus, Letitia, Cynthia and Hannah; grandchildren, Bird, and John Grills, ch. of dec. daughter, Margaret, and her husband, John Grills.

Rogers, Boling. Will probated Dec. 6, 1841. Names—children, Thomas, Joseph, James, William, Elizabeth and Rebecca.

Rose, Gabriel. Will probated June, 1833. Names—wife, Elizabeth; and son, Gabriel.

Ross, Edward. Will probated March, 1824. Brothers, Thomas, Robert; and sisters, Grizzy and Mary.

Ross, John, dec. Settlement of estate July, 1830.

Ross, John, dec. Apr. of estate returned Aug., 1844.

Ruddle, John, dec. Apr. of estate returned March, 1824.

Rutledge, Edward, dec. Apr. of estate Dec., 1837.

Rutledge George. (son of Thomas). Will probated June, 1821. Names—children, William, Edward, Eliza A. Hoge, Jane R. Hoge, Elizabeth B. Gibson, Mary Evans, Lucinda Hatton, and Nancy Rutledge; grandchildren, Harriet Hatton and George R. Hatton.

Rutledge, George. Will probated July, 1836. Names—wife, Ann; and children, Thomas E., George, John, Rosy Ann, Jane Young, Mary Thompson, and William E., grandchildren Eliza Ann, William Correll, Margaret Jane, Edward, and Robert—all children of his daughter, Jane Young.

Rutledge, Jane, (widow of James). Will probated Apr., 1834. Names—son, Thomas; and grandchildren, Mary Ann Rose, and Esther Jane McKinnis ;sister-in-laws, Jane Rutledge, and Jane Brook Rutledge.

Rutledge, John. Will probated Mar., 1815. Names—wife, Martha; nephew, John Rutledge; nieces, Martha Allison, and Sally Vanlier; and John Ruddall.

Rutledge, Martha. Will probated Oct., 1825. Names—adopted daughter (a niece) Sally King (wife of John King); nieces, Sally King, Polly Carson, Rosanna Allison, and a nephew, William Vanleer.

Rutledge, Nancy. Will probated Sept., 1822. Names nieces and nephews, number or names not given.

Ryan, William, dec. Dower assigned wife, Frances, July 31, 1838.

—S—

Sallust, James. Will probated Nov. ,1825. Names—wife, Margaret; and children, Elizabeth, Fanny, Sally Shell, Nancy Shell, and James.

Sallust, Margaret. Will. pro. Mar., 1832. Names—daus. Frances Todd, and Eliz. Zoll.

Savain, Lydia, (widow of Abraham). Will probated June, 1828. Names—children, Nancy Burk, and others, names or number not given.

Sayers, William. Will probated Mar. 4, 1781. Names

—wife, Elizabeth; and children, Robert, John Thompson, Alexander, and Samuel. Mentions warrant for 2000 acres of land for military servcie.

Scott, John. Will probated May, 1809. Names—wife, Mary; and children, John, Mary Ann, and Jane.

Scott, Matthew. Will probated Feb., 1815. Names—wife, ...; and children, John, Jehu, Elizabeth, Mary, Delilah, Ann, Dianna, Thomas, and Hercules.

Shanklin, Robert. Will probated Jan., 1808. Names —children, Samuel, Nancy, Reyburn, and others, names or number not given.

Shealer, Lawrence. Will probated Nov., 1817. Names —wife, Mary; and children, Jacob, Mary, Lawrence, Daniel, Jacob, Sophia, Margaret, Catrin and Mary.

Shell, John. Will probated July, 1807. Names—wife, Margaret; and children, John, Christian, James, William, Heavin, Henry, Isaac and Catey.

Shell, Jacob, (spelled Shaul in body of will, and signed in German). Will probated Sept., 1802. Names—wife, Catherine; and children, Jacob, John, Christian, Catherine, Elizabeth, Gertrude Williams, Phanney Wall, Molley Helvey, Peggy Salles, Barbary Heavin, and Nancy Taylor.

Shell, Jacob. Will probated Mar. 12, 1812. Names –his children, Polly, Christian, Jacob, John, Elizabeth, Fanny, Peggy, Margaret, Catey and Hannah; his sister, Elizabeth, and her daughters, Polly, Elizabeth, Fanny, Peggy and Catey; and his brother, Christian Shell.

Shepherd, George. Will probated Sept., 1841. Names—children, Nancy, Elizabeth Long, Allison and David.

Showalter, Daniel, dec. Sale bill, Feb. 17, 1837.

Chufflebarger, Jacob. Will probated Feb., 1802. Names—wife, Margaret. Had no child.

Shufflebarger, John, dec. Apr. of estate ret. Sept. 1832.

Sibole, John. Will probated July, 1831. Names—two children, John and Mary.

Simpkins, James. Will probated Jan., 1834. Names —wife, Patience; and children, James H., Robert, John, Catherine, (wife of William Elliot), Polly Clore, and other daughters, number or names not given.

Simpkins, Lawrence, dec. of estate returned July, 1825.

Simpkins, Robert. Will probated Feb., 1834. Names –children, Sarah, Rebecca Crandall (states that Rebecca has eight children), John, William, Lawrence, Robert and Thomas, (deceased, 1830.).

Simpson, John, dec. Apr. of estate Nov. 28, 1786.

Slusher, John. Will probated June, 1840. Names—children, John, Peter, Jacob, Sally McConley (wife Archibald), and Polly Brookman.

Smiley, James, dec. Apr. of estate returned Oct. 8, 1824.

Smith, Casper. Will probated Sept., 1817. Names—wife, Catherine; and children, Christopher, Henry, Frederick, John, Eve, Elizabeth, and Mary.

Smith, Daniel, dec. Apr. of estate April, 1940.

Smith, Frederick. Will probated Mar., 1806. Names wife, Margaret; and children, Sawyers, Nancy, and others ,name or number not given; granddaughter, Elizabeth McDonald, dau. John McDonald.

Smith, Frederick, dec. Apr. of estate Jan., 1821.

Smith, Horatio. Will probated Jan., 1842. Names—son, Fleming.

Smtih, James, dec. Apr. of estate returned Aug., 1833.

Smith, John, dec. Apr. of estate Apr., 1832.

Smith, John. Will probated July, 1820. Names—children, Samuel, Thomas, William, John, Colman, Henry, Wyatt, Stephen, Lucy Divers, Nancy English, Milly Wilson. Polly Holland, Susannah Naper, Fannay Robinson, and Nancy Stone.

Smith, Margaret. Will probated May, 1811, (widow of Frederick). Names—children, Robert, Sawyers, Cathreine Patterson, Nancy McDonald, and Sarah Sawyers, and granddaughter, Margaret Patterson.

Smith, Samuel, dec. Apr. of estate Oct. 1787. (wife named Sarah).

Smith, Thomas. Will probated Feb., 1820. Names—wife, ...; (second wife) and their children. Number or names not given. Children by his first marriage, Benjamin, Joseph, James, William, Francis, Larkin, Elizabeth and Thomas.

Smith, Thomas. Will probated Mar., 1820. Names—children, William, Hugh, Floyd, Thomas, Russell, John, Hannah, Polly and Eliza.

Snavely, John, Jr. Will probated July, 1833. Names wife, Elizabeth; and children, Nancy, Sarah Elizabeth, Polly Lane, Peggy Burton ,Peny, John and Jacob.

Snider, Abraham. Will probated May, 1848. Names—children, Catherine, Susan Argabright, Polly, John, and Michael.

Snidow, Philip, dec. Adm. account returned (first account) Sept., 1792.

Snodgrass, Rebecca. Will probated June, 1827. Names—children, Mary, Rebecca, John and Sarah.

Snuffer, Jacob, dec. Apr. of estate May, 1814.

Songer, George, dec. Apr. of estate May, 1811.

Sowder, Jacob. Will probated May, 1819. Names—wife, Anna; and children, Adam, Jacob, Christian, Michael, Anthony, Daniel, John, Joseph, Polly Deweese, Barbary Beckett, Betsy Bond, Sally Poff, Anna Teary, Caty Cina and Rebeckah.

Spencer, William, Will probated Sept., 1794. Names —wife, ...; and children, Levi, William, Francis and Dolly French.

Stafford, Ralph. Will pro. Aug., 1794. Names—wife, Jane; and children, John, James, Ralph, and one unborn.

Stapleton, Charles. Will probated Sept., 1799. Names—wife, Sarah; and minor children, names or number not given; also a brother, Wliliam, in Pennsylvania.

Stapleton, Sarah. Will probated July 6, 1819. Names –children, William, Sarah, Barnett, Elizabeth Hornbarger and Sarah Willis.

Stratton, John, dec. Apr. of estate returned July 9, 1838. (Wife named Mary Ann).

Sublett, William, Jr. Will probated Oct., 1844. Names—wife, Mary; and children, number or names not given.

Suiter, Alexander, dec. Apr. of estate returned Nov. 4, 1786.

Sumner, Ezekiah. Will probated Mar., 1823. Names —wife, Mary; and children, Isiah and Charity.

Sumpter, George. Will probated Dec., 1806. Names —wife, Elizabeth; and children, George, Edmund, Richard, and daughters, number or names not given.

Surface, Adam, dec. Apr. of estate returned July, 1823.

–T–

Taylor, Charles. Wil probated Aug., 1843. Names—wife, Polly; niece, Juliet G. Eskridge; and a nephew, J. B. Taylor, son of his brother Allen.

Taylor, George. Will probated Mar., 1801. Names—wife, Mary; and children, James, Joseph, Adam, Jacob, George, Ulrie, John, Elizabeth, Mary, Susannah and Anna. Also his wife's brother, John Charlton. Says his present wife the mother of four of his children.

Taylor, George. Will probated Aug., 1814. Names—wife, Mary; and son, Charles; nephew, George Taylor; and mother-in-law, Catherine Lower.

Taylor, Isaac. Will probated Feb., 1781. Names—children, George, Isaac, Andrew, and Lettice Campbell; grandchildren, Elizabeth Campbell, and Sarah Taylor.

Taylor, Isaac. Will probated June, 1807. Names—his friend, William Taylor.

Taylor, Isaac. Will probated April, 1801. Names—Children, Thomas, Isaac, William, Joseph, Mary Bryan, and Jane Hutson; a cousin, Isaac Taylor; and his wife, Rebecca.

Taylor, John. Will probated Feb., 1814. Names—wife, Elizabeth; and William, John McC., Elizabeth Crockett, Charles, Mary McC., and son-in-law, Henry Smith.

Taylor, John, dec. Apr. of estate June, 1816.

Taylor, Lewis, dec. Apr. of estate Sept., 1826.

Taylor, William. Will probated Oct., 1807. Names—wife, Mary; and children, John, Isaac, Joseph, William, Henry, Jane, Nancy and Priscilla.

Terry, Jasper. Will probated July 6, 1819. Names wife, Margaret; and children, Kezia Graham, Jemima Dewease, Karon Happuck, Rose, William, Jonathan, Elijah; and a step-daughter, Susannah Snidow.

Terry, William. Will probated Feb., 1826. Names—wife, Patience; and nieces, Elizabeth and Patience Cooper, daughters of Washington Cooper.

Thompson, Archibald, dec. Apr. of estate made Nov., 1809.

Thompson, Archibald, dec. Dower assigned wife, Nancy, April, 1842.

Thompson, James. Will probated Dec., 1813. Names—wife, Phebe; one son, unnamed; and an unborn child.

Thompson, John. Will probated May, 1805. Names—wife, Rebecca; and children, Thomas, and others, number or names not given.

Thing, William, dec. Inv. of estate returned Aug., 1792.

Townsley, James. Will probated Nov., 1812. Names—wife, Margaret; and children, Robert, William, Jeany, Betsy, Margaret, John, Joseph, and Mary.

Townsey, Thomas (of Monroe Co., N. Y.). Will probated June, 1841. Names – brother, Joseph, and a school in N. Y. State. –

Trigg, Dandridge. Will pro. July, 1830. Names—John Wade.

Turner, Elizabeth, dec. Apr. of estate returned Mar., 1836.

Turner, Richard. Will probated Feb., 1827. Names—wife, Elizabeth; daughter, Nancy; and son-in-laws, James King and Lewis Harless.

Turpin, Thomas. Will probated Dec., 1832. Names –Levina Smith.

–V–

Vanderpiece, William, dec. Apr. of estate returned Dec., 1842.

Vanleer, John, Sr. Will probated Oct., 1829. Names –wife, Sally; and children, William, John, Sally Liking, and Lucy Logan.

Vanover, Cornelius, dec. Inv. of estate, May 15, 1797.

Vickers, Elias. Will probated Apr., 1822. Names—wife, Phebe; and children. William, Peggy Simpkins, Thomas, John, Alexander, Elizabeth Munsey, Hannah, Sally, Parhenia, Lucinda, Malinda and Elias.

–W–

Wade, David. Will probated Mar., 1801. Names—wife, Rebecca; and children, Elizabeth Hamilton, John, James, William and David.

Wade, Eliza F., dec. Apr. of estate Nov. 5, 1839.

Wade, James, Apr. of estate Aug., 1839.

Waggoner, Adam. Will probated ...., 1785. Names–wife, Jane; and children, George, Daniel, Jacob, David, Rebeckah, Sarah, Christina, Susannah and Anne.

Wallace, James, dec. Adm. appointed Jan., 1829.

Wallace, William. Will probated Apr., 1825. Names –children ,Samuel, James, Robert, Hugh, and David.

Wall, Adam. Will probated July, 1799. Names the children of Mary Trollinger, William, Peggy, and James as his heirs; also names his brothers, John and James.

Wall, Conrod. Will probated Dec., 1830. Names—wife, Elizabeth; and children. Sampson, Joseph; Thomas, Elijah, Christian, Mary Frances, Elizabeth and Sarah Heavins.

Wall, Joseph K., dec. Apr. of estate returned Jan., 1845.

Walling, James. Will probated Mar. 28, 1786. Names–wife, ...; and children, John, James, Marning, Anderson, Betsy, and others, unnamed or number not given.

Waldren.

Walrond, William, (spelled Waldren in text of will). Will probated Sept., 1810. Names–wife, Nancy; and children, Benamin, Sally (wife of Daniel, Motley), Anny, Reuben, John and Jesse.

Walters, James, dec .Inv. return Mar. 28, 1786.

Walters, John. Will probated Apr., 1841. Names—wife, Sarah; and children, John, and others, names or number not given.

Watkins, Mary. Will probated Nov., 1825. Names—children, George, Thomas, Alsbad, Sally Simpkins, and Topal; son-in-law, Philip Johnson.

Watterson, Agnes, dec. Inv. of estate ret. Feb. 4, 1817.

Watterson, Joseph. Will pro. Mar., 1842. Names—wife, Susannah; and children, William and others, number or names not given; are the children of his dec. daughter, Elizabeth, (was wife of John G. Burgess.

Webb, Rachel, dec. Apr. of estate Sept. ,1841.

Webb, Samuel, dec. Adm. appointed Dec., 1832.

Weddle, Benjamin. Will probated Apr., 1807. Names–wife, ...; and children, Andrew Jonas, John, Elizabeth, David, Catey, Susannah, Sarah, Elizabeth, Rebecca, Barbary, and one other, unnamed.

Weddle, Benjamin, dec. Sale bill, Feb., 1834. (Wife Mary).

Welshire, Nathaniel. Will pro. April, 1777. Names —wife, ... ; and children, Elizabeth Buchannon, and Esther Herbert; grandsons, George Sash and George Forbis of North Carolina.

West, Isaac. Will probated Sept., 1814. Names— wife, Rosanna; and children, Jane Roberts, John, Sary Ogle, Isaac, Jacob, Mary, Rachel Luster, Elizabeth Dobbing and Anna.

Whtie, Samuel, dec. Settlement of estate Mar., 1838.

Whitt, Archibald, dec. Sale bill returned Dec., 1831. (wife Frances).

Whitt, Frances, dec. Bill of sale Dec. 7, 1836.

Whitt, Richard. Will probated Jan., 1813. Names— wife, ... ; and children, Archibald, Elizabeth Cassiday, Ruthy and Susannah.

Wiley, Alexander. Will probated Dec., 1822. Names —wife, ... ; and children, James, Robert, Peggy Picken, John, Alexander, Ann Huff, Sally, and Polly Shockey; grandsons, Alexander, and Preston Shockey, and Andrew Wiley.

Williamson, John. A conveyance, made May 15, 1800. State his father Michael Williamson, dec., of Smith Co., Tenn., left his entire estate to him; he conveys land in Smith Co., Tenn., to his brother, Joseph, "the same being right, and just."

Willis, David, dec. Apr. of estate returned March, 1838.

Willis, John, dec. Apr. of estate Oct., 1818.

Willson, Andrew. Will probated Oct., 1805. Names —wife, Jane; and children, Billy, Andrew, John and Elizabeth.

Willson, Matthew. Will probated Dec., 1795. Names —wife, Mary; and children, Thomas, John Steel, Sam'l (land in Ky.), Matthew, Jennett, Beasy, Polly, Sally and Nancy, a friend, James Patton of Rockbridge Co.

Wineteer, John. Will probated Sept., 1831. Names— wife, Peggy; and children, Thomas (of Indiana), Spragg, Hannah, and others, nomes or number not given.

Winteer, Margaret, dec. Sale bill May 14, 1839.

Woods, James. Will probated May, 1817. Names— wife, Polly; and children, Joseph, Robert, James, Andrew, Archibald, Nancy Woods; son-in-laws, John M. Walker and Alexander Robertson.

Woods, Joseph. Will probated Dec., 1793. Names— wife, Margaret; and children, Samuel, Dinah, Enos, Margaret, Jean, Joseph, and Nathan.

Worley, Nathan, dec. Apr. of estate Oct. 6, 1838.

Wygal, Sebastian, dec. Apr. of estate Sept., 1835.

Wysor, Jacob, dec. Apr. of estate June, 1820.

–Y–

Yearout, Charles. Will probated Jan., 1841. Names —wife, Elizabeth; and children, John, Hezekiah, Carolina, Isabella, and Eliza Ann Durman (wife of Thomas).

Yearout, Jacob, dec. Apr. of estate May 11, 1840.

Young, Alexander. Will probated Oct. 6, 1818. Names—wife, Catherine; and brothers-in-law, Lewis Reedy; and Susannah Thornton.

NOTE—In many instances where the will fails to name children, these may be ascertained by a careful search of settlements, deeds, etc. I wish I could have included that search so as to have embodied that information with the wills.

www.ingramcontent.com/pod-product-compliance
Lightning Source LLC
Chambersburg PA
CBHW070519090426
42735CB00012B/2840